# Beginners' Greek

Aristarhos Matsukas

First published in the UK in Great Britain in 2001 by Hodder Headline.
An Hachette UK company.
First published in US in 2001 by The McGraw-Hill Companies, Inc.
*Get Started in Greek* published in 2014 by John Murray Learning.

This edition published by Teach Yourself in 2025
An imprint of John Murray Press



1



Illustrations by Nadene Naude (Beehive Illustration)
Photographs © Shutterstock.com
Editorial support from Haremi Ltd



A CIP catalogue record for this title is available from the British Library

Paperback ISBN 978 1 399 82143 8
ebook ISBN 978 1 399 82144 5

Typeset by Integra Software Services Pvt. Ltd., Pondicherry, India

Printed and bound in Great Britain by Clays Ltd, Elcograf S.p.A.

John Murray Press policy is to use papers that are natural, renewable and recyclable products and made from wood grown in sustainable forests. The logging and manufacturing processes are expected to conform to the environmental regulations of the country of origin.

John Murray Press
Carmelite House
50 Victoria Embankment
London EC4Y 0DZ

123 S. Broad St., Ste 2750
Philadelphia, PA 19109

www.teachyourself.com

The authorised representative in the EEA is Hachette Ireland, 8 Castlecourt Centre, Dublin 15, D15 XTP3, Ireland (email: info@hbgi.ie)

John Murray Press, part of Hodder & Stoughton Limited
An Hachette UK company

# Contents

# Acknowledgements

Several people have contributed directly or indirectly to the writing of this book. Special thanks go to: Sue Hart, Rebecca Green and Ginny Catmur, my editors at Hodder & Stoughton; my colleagues Sonia Krantonelli, Daniel Gorney and Christine Easthope at the British Hellenic College for comments, corrections and encouragement; one of my most unique students Karl Kirchner for questioning and discussing everything with me; my daughter Arianna for giving me inspiration and my wife Joanna for putting this inspiration in perspective. (1st edition, 2001)

I would like to thank my students who over the years have showed me what is important for them to learn and not what is important for me to teach! Through them I have also realized that teaching is part of learning and learning part of teaching. It just needs ... open minds! (3rd edition, 2010)

Many thanks go to Anna Stevenson, my editor for the 4th edition. She has lent her expertise to many tricky issues, especially regarding how to simplify complicated aspects of the Greek language. My students at Berlin Community College continue to inspire me and challenge me daily. They have made me be constantly alert and not take anything for granted. Their direct or indirect contribution towards what teacher and/or author I am today is much appreciated. (4th edition, 2014)

Ten years have already passed since the last edition. This edition brings a lot of new ideas and activities in terms of language developments but also methodological norms and trends. All endeavors though attempt to alleviate the burdens of self-learners who want to learn this historical and unique language. We have found ways to group grammatical points anew, to give simpler explanations and to challenge for every major or minor point the personal involvement of learners. That way, we believe we enhance the learning experience and we better facilitate the long-term learning process and results. The adult students who have challenged me and questioned me over every little thing regarding Greek language and culture have made me aware to write this new edition mirroring their hopes and aspirations. For their direct and indirect contribution to what an author or teacher I am today, I am deeply grateful. (this edition, 2024)

# About the author

I have worked as a professional author and language teacher for over 35 years. I have written language books with a special focus on Greek as a foreign language, including a bilingual English–Greek, Greek–English pocket dictionary. I have lived about two-thirds of my life away from Athens, my birthplace, firstly in the USA for 14 years, where I had studied Teaching English as a Foreign Language (TEFL) and Applied Linguistics, and now in Berlin for over 20 years.

My accumulated teaching experience of Modern Greek comes from teaching adults and college students in New York City, then Athens, and more recently Berlin. My professional experience also includes university teaching in the USA, working as a head of department in a community college in Athens, as a language school director in Ioannina (Greece) and as the translator of three cookery books.

I have attended many teacher training seminars over the years. Three of them were EU funded, two in Athens and one in Barcelona. I have also successfully completed a post graduate certificate in educational management from the University of Leicester (2003) and a one-year online further training seminar in Greek as a foreign language from the University of the Aegean (2022).

When not at my desk, I can usually be found in the kitchen, in a bookshop, or at a language book fair. I love traveling (having visited more than 20 countries), watching TV and learning languages.

**Aristarhos Matsukas**

# About the course

Welcome to *Beginner's Greek!* Modern Greek is a fascinating language, with a history of more than 3,000 years, and the first language which introduced '*vowel*' letters to accommodate and complement better its '*consonant*' counterparts. This course assumes no previous knowledge of Greek. Its emphasis is put first and foremost on language use, but it also aims to give you an idea of how Greek works, so that you can create new examples from learned patterns on your own. Although the course covers all four basic skills, listening and speaking are more emphasized compared to reading and writing. This course also uses many '*tips and tricks*' along the way in order to facilitate you with short-cuts and empower you to keep on learning instead of discouraging you with the false notion that Greek is a difficult language to learn. We wish you *all the best* for your time and effort in this exciting endeavor!

## How to use this book

**A little goes a long way!**

This book consists of an introductory **Pronunciation guide** to familiarize you with the Greek alphabet and the basic sounds of Greek. The core of the book are 10 units which will help you learn basic language function and introduce key topics for everyday communication.

Try to use the book little and often, rather than for long stretches at a time. This will help you to create a study habit, much in the same way you would learn a sport or music. Leave the book somewhere handy so that you can pick it up for just a few minutes to refresh your memory.

**Before you start, make a plan!**

Setting goals affects the programming of your brain, strengthening neural pathways and ultimately making it more likely that you will achieve those goals. Before you begin, think about how much time you want to devote to learning, which skills or areas you want to focus on, and identify specific ideas you want to be able to communicate or activities you want to engage in.

**Track your progress!**

Start a notebook to use for study, where you can create vocabulary lists, a grammar summary, questions you'd like answered, etc. Keep track of your resources--write down the names of films, podcasts, songs or blogs you like, and jot down a few words or expressions you may have recognized or learned. The more you can reflect on your learning process, the deeper your connection with the language will be. If you need more guidance in this process, we recommend Teach Yourself *Fluentish: Language Learning Planner & Journal* by Jo Franco.

Use the tools at the beginning of each unit to help you set goals, plan your time, and keep track of the work you do.

## IN THIS UNIT, YOU WILL LEARN HOW TO

Each unit begins with an overview of the language you will be learning and skills you will be acquiring.

## MY PROGRESS TRACKER

Use the progress tracker to plan your study time and to keep a record of what you've accomplished. The first column tracks time, and the remaining five columns represent the skills you'll be working on: listening, pronunciation, reading, writing, and spoken interaction.

**Personalize the tracker:** Instead of the date or day, you can enter an increment of time (15 minutes, 1 hour...). Add columns for culture, vocabulary, grammar or any other area you wish to focus on. Give yourself a star when you feel you've done particularly well. Make it your own! Review your tracker regularly and see which areas could use more practice.

Use the **Self check** at the end of each unit to evaluate your progress.

**Try to practice each skill every day.**

The icons in the progress tracker are used throughout the book to help you easily identify and locate the skills you want to practice:

 Listening skills

 Speaking – pronunciation skills

 Reading skills

 Writing skills

 Speaking – conversation skills

Remember: there are many ways to build your skills in addition to those provided in this book: use a language-learning app, listen to music or podcasts, watch TV shows or movies, go to a restaurant, follow social media accounts in Greek, read blogs, newspapers or magazines, switch the language settings in your apps, or sign up for a language exchange or a tutor.

## UNITS 1-10

Each unit in the book is centered on a single topic and begins with a **cultural reading** in English to familiarize you with various aspects of life in Greece and enable you to see some new Greek words in a context that is easy to understand.

**Vocabulary builder** presents new words grouped by theme related to the unit topic. There is also a list of new words and expressions which present additional vocabulary introduced in the unit that you will need to understand the conversations in the unit.

**Conversations** follow a story with characters you will meet throughout the course. Don't be afraid to learn the dialogues by heart like a script.

Listen to the conversations several times until you feel confident you understand them well. Don't feel disheartened when, initially, a conversation seems to be just a string of unrecognizable sounds. After listening several times you will begin to hear when one word ends and another begins. After a few more times you will be able to understand everything that is said. And finally, you will feel confident enough to repeat whole sentences.

**Language discovery** previews upcoming information in the unit. You will be asked to note similarities and do other activities that will help you put the language together for yourself.

**Grammar discovery** is a section that explains how the Greek in the material you have just studied is put together. You will find varying types of facts and information related to the unit's grammar, spelling, expressions or cultural information.

**Practice** exercises are included at the end of the section to help you test yourself.

**Test yourself** contains exercises that you may turn into your own flash cards, which in turn can be used to create your own language quiz. Just write the correct answers on the back of the card in pencil (so it's not very visible). Collect the cards and keep them close by you so you can spend five or ten minutes going over the cards every day while waiting for the bus, on the train or at coffee breaks. You can do it any time, anywhere and there's no need to have a textbook with you. Successful learning depends on repetition and revision and the cards are a great help in doing this.

After Units 3, 6 and 10, you will find a **Review test** for checking your understanding of the material, and at the back of the book there is an **Answer key**. Check the **Answer key** when you have completed the exercises to check your progress. You will also find an **English–Greek glossary** and a **Grammar summary** in which all the grammatical and linguistic material discussed in the course is gathered and some additional points explained.

The course is accompanied by audio for the conversations, some exercises and parts of the Practice exercises at the end of each unit.

# Learn to learn

## The Discovery method

There are lots of approaches to language learning, some practical and some quite unconventional. Perhaps you know a few, or even have techniques of your own. In this book we have incorporated the **Discovery method** of learning, a sort of DIY approach to language learning. What this means is that you will be encouraged throughout the course to engage your mind and figure out the language for yourself, through identifying patterns, understanding grammar concepts, noticing words that are similar to English, and more. Simply put, if you **figure something out for yourself**, you're more likely to understand it. And when you use what you've learned, you're more likely to remember it. And because many of the essential but (let's admit it!) daunting details, such as grammar rules, are taught through the **Discovery method**, you'll have more fun while learning. Soon, the language will start to make sense and you'll be relying on your own intuition to construct original sentences **independently**, not just listening and repeating.

Everyone can succeed in learning a language – the key is to know **how to learn it**.

## How to be a successful language learner

There are many strategies that can help you become a successful language learner. Different people have different learning styles and some of these approaches will be more effective for you than others. Use this list as a point of inspiration when you want to find the most effective ways to advance your skills and begin your journey to fluency.

### VOCABULARY

Words are the building blocks of language. The more you use the words you're introduced to, the more quickly they'll lodge into your memory. These study tips will help you remember better:

- Organize your study of vocabulary. Group new words under **generic categories**, e.g. *food, furniture*; **situations** in which they occur, e.g. under *restaurant* you can write *server, table, menu, bill*; and **functions**, e.g. greetings, parting, thanks, apologizing.

- Say the words out loud as you read them.
- Write new words over and over.
- Listen to the audio several times and say the words out loud as you hear or read them.
- Cover up the English translations and try to remember the meanings.
- Associate the words with similar-sounding words in English.
- Create flash cards, drawings and mind maps.
- Write Greek words for objects around your house and stick them to objects.
- Pay attention to patterns in words.
- Experiment with words. Use the words that you learn in new contexts and find out if they are correct.

## GRAMMAR

Grammar gives your language structure. It allows you to experiment with the vocabulary you learn because you'll understand how they work together to create meaning. In other words, you'll begin to develop a feel for the language. Here are some tips to help you study more effectively:

- Check the **Grammar summary** for terms you don't understand.
- Experiment with grammar rules. Sit back and reflect on the rules. Compare the rules for Greek to those of other languages you know. Predict rules, or go looking for them, and be ready to spot exceptions. You'll remember them better and get a feel for the language.
- Write your own glossary. Add information as you go along. Look for examples and keep a 'pattern bank' that organizes examples by the structures you've learned.
- Use vocabulary to practice new structures. When you learn a new verb form, write the conjugation of different verbs that follow the same form.

## PRONUNCIATION

The best way to improve your pronunciation is simply to practice as much as possible. Study individual sounds first, then full words and sentences. Don't forget, it's not just about pronouncing letters and words correctly, but using the right intonation. So, when practicing words and sentences, mimic the rising and falling intonation of Greek speakers.

- Make a list of problem words and practice them.
- Repeat the conversations, line by line. Listen to yourself and try to mimic what you hear. Record yourself if you can.

## LISTENING AND READING

The conversations in this book include questions to guide you in your understanding, but you can go further by following some of these tips.

- **Imagine the situation.** Try to imagine the scenes, and make educated guesses about the topic and vocabulary – a conversation in a café is likely to be about drinks or food.
- **Get the gist.** When watching a film in another language you can usually get the gist of the story from a few scenes. Understanding a conversation or article is similar. Concentrate on the main parts to get the gist and don't worry about individual words.
- **Guess the meaning of words.** Use your own experience or knowledge of the topic to guess the sorts of words in a reading or dialogue, and use context – the sense of nearby words, sentences or paragraphs – to guess the meaning of specific words in the passage.

## WRITING

You'll have plenty of writing practice using this book. Creating vocabulary lists, grammar summaries and taking good notes as you study is another great opportunity to practice writing. If you're keeping your lists or notes on your phone, computer or tablet, remember to switch the keyboard language to be able to include all accents and special characters. Here are some other ways to practice writing:

- Write out the answers to all Practice and Test Yourself questions.
- Create your own vocabulary lists and a grammar summary.
- Look up writing prompts for language learning or try writing a daily gratitude journal in Greek.
- Write out your To Do and shopping lists in Greek.
- Join online forums and discussion groups about or in Greek.

## SPEAKING

Practice makes perfect. Successful language learners learn how to overcome their inhibitions and keep going. Here's how to do it:

- Speak out as you go through the course. Answer questions out loud. Rehearse dialogues out loud, then try to replace sentences with ones that are true for you. Remember to mimic the speakers' pronunciation.

- Translate the world around you. Look at objects and try to name them in Greek. Look at people and try to describe them in detail. After you have conducted a sales transaction in your own language, do it in Greek. That is, buy the gift or order the food in Greek!
- Don't be shy. Seek out Greek speakers and practice! When you cannot understand what they say, simply ask them to slow down and repeat. Or, ask for clarification.
- Don't let errors interfere with getting your message across. Realize that many errors are not serious. Some types of errors do not affect meaning, as in using the wrong ending, wrong gender or wrong adjective ending.

### LEARN TO COPE WITH UNCERTAINTY

- **Don't give up if you don't understand.** When at some point in the course you feel lost, don't panic! Just keep going and try to guess what is being said or, if you cannot, isolate the expression or words you haven't understood and have them explained to you, then go back to the material and try again.
- **Keep talking.** The best way to improve your fluency is to speak. Talk at every opportunity, and keep the conversations flowing. When you get stuck, paraphrase or replace a troublesome word with one you do know, even if you have to simplify what you want to say.
- **Don't over-use your dictionary.** Don't be tempted to immediately look up every new word. Underline new ones, then read the text several times, concentrating on getting the gist. If after the third time there are still words which prevent you from getting the general meaning of the text, look them up in the dictionary.

## The Greek language

Greek is an inflected language. That simply means that grammatical relationships in a sentence are expressed not by the word order of words but changes in the form of words. Different forms are necessary for some word groups including articles, nouns, adjectives, pronouns, and verbs. English does this as well but compared to Greek much less. This book will often make use of two grammatical terms regarding inflection: declination and conjugation. Going through the units, this information will become much clearer.

# Pronunciation guide

## THE GREEK ALPHABET

The Greek alphabet has 24 capital letters and 25 lowercase letters. The letter **Σ** [sígma] becomes **σ** in any position of a word except at the end, where it is **ς**.

**00.01 You are now going to hear the Greek alphabet. First listen a couple of times without looking at the text. Then look at the text as you listen, and repeat each letter after the speaker.**

**Ελληνικά Γράμματα**

| | | | | | |
|---|---|---|---|---|---|
| **Α α** | [álfa] | **Ι ι** | [yióta] | **Ρ ρ** | [ro] |
| **Β β** | [víta] | **Κ κ** | [kápa] | **Σ σ/ς** | [sígma] |
| **Γ γ** | [gáma] | **Λ λ** | [lámTHa] | **Τ τ** | [taf] |
| **Δ δ** | [THélta] | **Μ μ** | [mi] | **Υ υ** | [ípsilon] |
| **Ε ε** | [épsilon] | **Ν ν** | [ni] | **Φ φ** | [fi] |
| **Ζ ζ** | [zíta] | **Ξ ξ** | [ksi] | **Χ χ** | [hi] |
| **Η η** | [íta] | **Ο ο** | [ómikron] | **Ψ ψ** | [psi] |
| **Θ θ** | [thíta] | **Π π** | [pi] | **Ω ω** | [oméga] |

You can find many different presentations of the Greek alphabet on the internet, including a children's chorus, an adults' symphonic orchestra, a university students' group, or even an American gospel group!

One effective way to actually learn the Greek alphabet and be aware how to avoid pitfalls is for you to become familiar with the three following letter groups. Group 1: letters which look alike and sound alike in both languages. Group 2: letters which look alike but they have a different sound (often called 'false friends'). Group 3: unique letters found only in the Greek alphabet with an unfamiliar appearance, although most of them have similar sounds in both languages.

Greek, unlike English, is a phonetic language. This means that you can read or pronounce most words once you know the alphabet, similarly to German, Italian or Spanish.

Distinguish the different sound of [TH] and [th]. The first is used to produce the sound of **Δ δ** as in *this, though* or *then*. The second is used to produce the sound of **Θ θ** as in *thin, thought* or *thug*.

Be careful with two letters that have almost the same name: **Ε ε** [épsilon] and **Υ υ** [ípsilon].

Remember that **Ηη**, **Ιι** and **Υυ** have the same sound (**i** as in *sit*). Also, **Οο** and **Ωω** have the same sound (**o** as in *lot*).

## VOWELS AND CONSONANTS

There are seven vowels and 17 consonants in Greek.

| Vowels | Consonants |
|---|---|
| **α, ε, η, ι, ο, υ, ω** | **β, γ, δ, ζ, θ, κ, λ, μ, ν, ξ, π, ρ, σ/ς, τ, φ, χ, ψ** |
| Two-letter vowels | Two-letter consonants |
| **αι, ει, οι, ου, υι** | **γγ, γκ, γχ, μπ, ντ, τσ, τζ** |
| Vowel combinations | Two same-letter consonants |
| **αυ, ευ** | **ββ, κκ, λλ, μμ, νν, ππ, ρρ, σσ, ττ** |

The sounds of vowels and consonants in each sub-group above are explained in the following section.

## LETTERS AND SOUNDS

In general, remember that all letters have basically one sound, except for **Γ γ** [gáma] and **Σ σ/ς** [sígma]. The vowel or consonant sounds are always pronounced in the same way in Greek, in contrast with English where one letter usually has more than one sound, e.g. a as in *mat*, *mate*, *mayor*, etc.

## VOWEL SOUNDS

**00.02 You are now going to hear the vowel sounds of the Greek alphabet. First listen a couple of times without looking at the text. Then look at the text as you listen and repeat each letter after the speaker.**

| | | |
|---|---|---|
| **Α α** | [álfa] | ***a*** as in *r**a**ft* |
| **Ε ε** | [épsilon] | ***e*** as in *m**e**t* |
| **Η η** | [íta] | ***i*** as in *s**i**t* |
| **Ι ι** | [yióta] | ***i*** as in *s**i**t* |
| **Ο ο** | [ómikron] | ***o*** as in *l**o**t* |
| **Υ υ** | [ípsilon] | ***i*** as in *s**i**t* |
| **Ω ω** | [oméga] | ***o*** as in *l**o**t* |

Greek vowels are generally pronounced short, sometimes a little bit longer, but rarely for very long. The transliteration system used in this course does not show this since in Greek, unlike in English, you will rarely find word pairs such as *fit-feet* or *sit-seat*. Consequently, the Greek word **σπίτι** house is transliterated as [spíti] although the first [í] is pronounced for longer than the second [i].

## CONSONANT SOUNDS

**00.03 You are now going to hear the consonant sounds of the Greek alphabet. First listen a couple of times without looking at the text. Then look at the text as you listen, and repeat each letter after the speaker.**

| | | |
|---|---|---|
| **Β β** | [víta] | ***v*** as in ***v**et* |
| **Γ γ** | [gáma] | 1 ***y*** almost as in ***y**ield* |
| | | 2 ***y*** as in ***y**es* |
| **Δ δ** | [THélta] | ***TH*** as in ***th**is* |
| **Ζ ζ** | [zíta] | ***z*** as in *zip* |
| **Θ θ** | [thíta] | ***th*** as in ***th**in* |
| **Κ κ** | [kápa] | ***k*** as in ***k**it* |
| **Λ λ** | [lámTHa] | ***l*** as in ***l**et* |
| **Μ μ** | [mi] | ***m*** as in ***m**et* |
| **Ν ν** | [ni] | ***n*** as in ***n**et* |
| **Ξ ξ** | [ksi] | 1***ks*** as in *ban**ks*** |
| | | 2 ***x*** as in *si**x*** |
| **Π π** | [pi] | ***p*** as in ***p**et* |
| **Ρ ρ** | [ro] | ***r*** as in ***r**est* |
| **Σ σ/ς** | [sígma] | 1 ***s*** as in ***s**et* |
| | | 2 ***z*** as in ***z**ip* |
| **Τ τ** | [taf] | ***t*** as in ***t**ea* |
| **Φ φ** | [fi] | ***f*** as in ***f**it* |
| **Χ χ** | [hi] | ***h*** as in ***h**it* |
| **Ψ ψ** | [psi] | ***ps*** as in *la**ps*** |

Remember that these are approximate sounds and only real words in context can present precise sounds. The letter **γ** will probably challenge you more than any other Greek letter. Learn its different possible sounds in words found throughout the units and don't worry if no English sounds match the **γ** sounds perfectly.

## TWO-LETTER VOWELS

**00.04 You are now going to hear the two-letter vowels of the Greek alphabet. First listen a couple of times without looking at the text. Then look at the text as you listen, and repeat each letter after the speaker.**

| | | |
|---|---|---|
| **αι** | [álfa-yióta] | ***e*** as in *m**e**t* |
| **ει** | [épsilon-yióta] | ***i*** as in *s**i**t* |
| **οι** | [ómikron-yióta] | ***i*** as in *s**i**t* |
| **ου** | [ómikron-ípsilon] | ***oo*** as in *c**oo**l* |
| **υι** | [ípsilon-yióta] | ***i*** as in *s**i**t* |

You are probably wondering about the sound [i] in Greek. Yes, it has six different spellings producing the same sound! Not an easy task for a spell-checker, is it?

## TWO-LETTER CONSONANTS

**00.05 You are now going to hear the two-letter consonants of the Greek alphabet. First listen a couple of times without looking at the text. Then look at the text as you listen, and repeat each letter after the speaker.**

The following two-letter consonants have only one sound:

| | | |
|---|---|---|
| **γγ** | [gáma-gáma] | ***ng*** as in *E**ng**land* (not as in *e**ng**ine*) |
| **γχ** | [gáma-hi] | ***nh*** as in *i**nh**erent* |
| **τσ** | [taf-sígma] | ***ts*** as in *se**ts*** |
| **τζ** | [taf-zíta] | **dz** as in *a**dz**e* |

The remaining two-letter consonants have two different sounds each:

| | | |
|---|---|---|
| **γκ** | [gáma-kápa] | 1 ***g*** as in ***g**o*<br>2 ***ng*** as in *E**ng**land* |
| **μπ** | [mi-pi] | 1 ***b*** as in ***b**oy*<br>2 ***mb*** as in *ti**mb**er* |
| **ντ** | [ni-taf] | 1 ***d*** as in ***d**ay*<br>2 ***nd*** as in *e**nd*** |

The **g, b** and **d** sounds mostly occur at the beginning of Greek words, whereas the **ng, mb** and **nd** sounds mostly occur within a Greek word.

## VOWEL COMBINATIONS

**00.06 You are now going to hear the vowel combinations of the Greek alphabet. First listen a couple of times without looking at the text. Then look at the text as you listen, and repeat each letter after the speaker.**

| | | |
|---|---|---|
| **αυ** | [alfa-ipsilon] | 1 ***af*** as in ***af**ter*<br>2 ***av*** as in ***av**enue* |
| **ευ** | [epsilon-ipsilon] | 1 ***ef*** as in *l**ef**t*<br>2 ***ev*** as in ***ev**er* |

The difference between the two depends on what letter follows. The phonetic rule is as follows: The sounds [af] and [ef] are when any of the following letters follow: **θ, κ, ξ, π, σ, τ, φ, χ, ψ**. The sounds [av] and [ev] are when any of the following letters follow: **β, γ, δ, ζ, λ, μ, ν, ρ**, or any of the seven vowels.

### TWO SAME-LETTER CONSONANTS

All two same-letter consonants have the same sound as the corresponding one-letter consonant, e.g. **β** [víta] or **ββ** [víta-víta] have the same sound **v** *as in **v**et.*

The transliteration system used in this book employs all the different sounds presented above. Once again, these sounds are a close approximation and cannot replace real Greek speakers.

Attempting to write Greek letters or words is a daunting process for many in these early stages, so please don't worry if you make mistakes.

### THE STRESS MARK IN GREEK

A written accent is used in all words of more than one syllable to show where the stress falls, both in the Greek script and in the transliteration. There are, however, a few exceptions. Some words then have different meanings, e.g. the word **η** (meaning *the*) and the word **ή** (meaning *or*). Changing the stress can alter the meaning entirely. For example, the word **πότε** (meaning *when*) and the word **ποτέ** (meaning *never*). When a whole word or phrase is written in capital letters, no stress marks are used. Compare: **Άννα** and **ANNA** (Anne or Anna).

### PUNCTUATION MARKS

Most punctuation marks are similar in English and Greek. However, pay attention to the semi colon **(;)** which is the question mark in Greek. This sign **(?)** does not exist in Greek.

Here are some exercises regarding the Greek alphabet for you to practice. Each exercise concentrates on a specific feature of the alphabet. You can check your answers in the **Answer key** section at the back of the book.

**1 There are some unique capital letters in the Greek alphabet. Can you fill out the chart with the missing letters below working horizontally?**

| A | B | | | E | Z | H | |
|---|---|---|---|---|---|---|---|
| I | K | | M | N | | O | |
| P | | T | Y | | X | | |

**2 There are also some unique lower-case letters in the Greek alphabet. Can you complete the alphabet?**

| α | | | | ε | ζ | η | |
|---|---|---|---|---|---|---|---|
| ι | | | | ν | | ο | π |
| ρ | | τ | υ | | χ | | |

**3 Some Greek letters look like English but have a different sound. Which option is right?**

| **B**: **/b/** or **/v/** | **Z**: **/s/** or **/z/** | **H**: **/i/** or **/h/** | **P**: **/r/** or **/p/** | **Y**: **/u/** or **/i/** | **X**: **/x/** or **/h/** |
|---|---|---|---|---|---|
| **β**: **/b/** or **/v/** | **η**: **/i/** or **/n/** | **ν**: **/n/** or **/v/** | **ρ**: **/p/** or **/r/** | **υ**: **/i/** or **/u/** | **χ**: **/x/** or **/h/** |

**4 Some Greek capital letters look very different from their lowercase pair letters. Can you complete the grid?**

| **a Γ** | | **b Δ** | | **c H** | | **d K** | |
|---|---|---|---|---|---|---|---|
| **e Λ** | | **f M** | | **g N** | | **h Ξ** | |
| **i Σ** | | **j T** | | **k Y** | | **l Ω** | |

**5 Let's see if you can decipher some international words written in Greek. Match the following words to their Greek equivalent.**

| | |
|---|---|
| pizza | τραμ |
| feta | μετρό |
| jazz | φέτα |
| rock | γκολφ |
| golf | θέατρο |
| basket | πίτσα |
| taxi | σινεμά |
| tram | όπερα |
| cinema | τζαζ |
| opera | ταξί |
| theatre | ροκ |
| metro | μπάσκετ |

**00.07**

Now practice your pronunciation by with some geographical regions in Greece. Although all 13 names of these regions still exist, nowadays there are new geographical merges and divisions resulting in only nine new regions some with the same old name and some with a new one.

**a** [atikí] – [nisiá saronikoó] **ΑΤΤΙΚΗ – ΝΗΣΙΑ ΣΑΡΩΝΙΚΟΥ**

**b** [kikláTHes] **ΚΥΚΛΑΔΕΣ**

**c** [THoTHekánisos] **– ΔΩΔΕΚΑΝΗΣΟΣ**

**d** [vorioanatoliká nisiá eyéoo] **– ΒΟΡΕΙΟΑΝΑΤΟΛΙΚΑ ΝΗΣΙΑ ΑΙΓΑΙΟΥ**

**e** [thráki] – [samothráki] **– ΘΡΑΚΗ – ΣΑΜΟΘΡΑΚΗ**

**f** [makeTHonía] **– ΜΑΚΕΔΟΝΙΑ**

**g** [thesalía] **– ΘΕΣΣΑΛΙΑ**

**h** [ípiros] **– ΗΠΕΙΡΟΣ**

**i** [évia] – [sporáTHes] **– ΕΥΒΟΙΑ – ΣΠΟΡΑΔΕΣ**

**j** [kendrikí eláTHa] **– ΚΕΝΤΡΙΚΗ ΕΛΛΑΔΑ**

**k** [nisiá ioníoo] **– ΝΗΣΙΑ ΙΟΝΙΟΥ**

**l** [pelopónisos] **– ΠΕΛΟΠΟΝΝΗΣΟΣ**

**m** [kríti] **– ΚΡΗΤΗ**

Did you pick up the words for *Greece* [eláTHa] **Ελλάδα** and for *islands* [nisiá] **νησιά**? They will come in handy later on.

## Language discovery

Before moving on to Unit 1, think again about Greek letters and their sounds. All geographical regions in the previous activity were written in capital letters. Try to write three regions in small letters. A full list is provided for you at the end of the book.

A second challenge could be to play the audio again. Look at the name of the region, try your best pronunciation of it and compare it afterwards with the audio.

[kalí epitihía]! **Καλή επιτυχία!** means *good luck!* Now move on to the first unit.

1

**In this unit you will learn how to:**

» say *hello* and *goodbye*.
» exchange greetings.
» ask and say how people are.
» introduce yourself and your family.
» address people when you meet them.

# Γεια σου! Τι κάνεις;

My progress tracker

| DAY / DATE | Listening | Speaking | Reading | Writing | Conversation |
|---|---|---|---|---|---|
| | ○ | ○ | ○ | ○ | ○ |
| | ○ | ○ | ○ | ○ | ○ |
| | ○ | ○ | ○ | ○ | ○ |
| | ○ | ○ | ○ | ○ | ○ |
| | ○ | ○ | ○ | ○ | ○ |

## Greetings, introductions and wishes

Greek speakers always enjoy hearing others using their language, even if you initially make a few mistakes. So let's start with some greetings: [kaliméra] **καλημέρα** *good morning*, [kalispéra] **καλησπέρα** *good evening*, [kaliníchta] **καληνύχτα** *goodnight*, [yia soo] **γεια σου** *hi/see you*, [yia sas] **γεια σας** *hello/goodbye*. Other than [kalispéra] and [kaliníchta] all other phrases can be used both as greetings and farewells.

You can introduce yourself with: [me léne...] **Με λένε ...** *My name's ...* and [íme o/i...] **Είμαι ο/η ...** *I'm ...* Simply follow either phrase with your name! Be careful with the second phrase, where you should say either [íme o ...] if you are male, or [íme i ...] if you are female.

What do you say when introducing people to each other in Greek? [na sas sistíso ...] **Να σας συστήσω ...** *Let me introduce you to ...* is the most common expression, followed by the names of the people being introduced. [yiásas] **Γεια σας** and [héro polí] **Χαίρω πολύ** are more formal replies. [héro polí] means *Very pleased to meet you* (lit. *I am very pleased*).

From the same word root you might hear [hárika] **Χάρηκα** *Nice to have met you* (lit. *I was pleased*) when you say goodbye to someone you have met for the first time and [hérete] **χαίρετε** *hello/goodbye* used in formal situations. The phrase [apó eTHó o/i...] **από εδώ ο/η ...**, or more commonly [apo'THó o/i ...] **από 'δω ο/η ...** in its contracted form, means *this is* or *here is* (lit. *from here the*) and is also used to introduce people.

Finally, two more words are important for you to learn by heart as soon as possible: [efharistó] **ευχαριστώ** *thanks* and [parakaló] **παρακαλώ** *you're welcome*. These words are heard more often in English than in Greek, but you should still learn them and use them as often as possible!

---

**1 What are the Greek words for *hello* and *goodbye*?**

**2 What phrase(s) can you use when you want to introduce yourself?**

---

# Vocabulary builder

**01.01 Listen to the audio as you look at the words and complete the English translations. Then listen again and try to imitate the speakers.**

| ***GREETINGS*** | **ΧΑΙΡΕΤΙΣΜΟΙ** | |
|---|---|---|
| [kaliméra] | καλημέρα | *good morning* |
| [hérete] | χαίρετε | *hello/goodbye* (fml) |
| [yiásoo] | γεια σου | *hi/see you* (infml/sing) |
| [yiásas] | γεια σας | *hello/_______* (fml/pl) |
| [kalispéra] | καλησπέρα | *good evening* |
| [kaliníhta] | καληνύχτα | _______________ |

| ***INTRODUCTIONS*** | **ΣΥΣΤΑΣΕΙΣ** | |
|---|---|---|
| [na sas sistíso...] | Να σας συστήσω ... | *Let me introduce you to ...* (fml/pl) |
| [na soo sistíso...] | Να σου συστήσω ... | *Let me introduce you to ...* (infml/sing) |
| [apo'THó...] | από ΄δω ... | *This is ...* |
| [héro polí] | χαίρω πολύ | *How do you do?/Pleased to meet you.* (lit. *I'm very pleased*) |
| [hárika] | χάρηκα | *Nice to have met (lit. found) you!* |

| ***WISHES*** | **ΕΥΧΕΣ** | |
|---|---|---|
| [kalós orísate]! | Καλώς ορίσατε! | *Welcome!* (fml/pl) |
| [kalós órises]! | Καλώς όρισες! | ______________ (infml/sing) |
| [kalós se/sas vríka]! | Καλώς σε/σας βρήκα! | *Nice to have met* (lit. *found*) *you!* |
| [efharistó] | ευχαριστώ | ___________________(I) |
| [efharistoóme] | ευχαριστούμε | *thank you* (we) |
| [parakaló] | παρακαλώ | *you're welcome* (lit. *please*) |

**LANGUAGE TIP**

[se] is used in informal situations, [sas] in formal situations.
Similar is also true for [soo] and [sas] in [yiásoo] or [yiásas]. The two English pronouns *you* and *your* may pose a small challenge here as there are more forms in Greek. Allow yourself some time to understand this and always pay close attention to how these different forms are used in context.

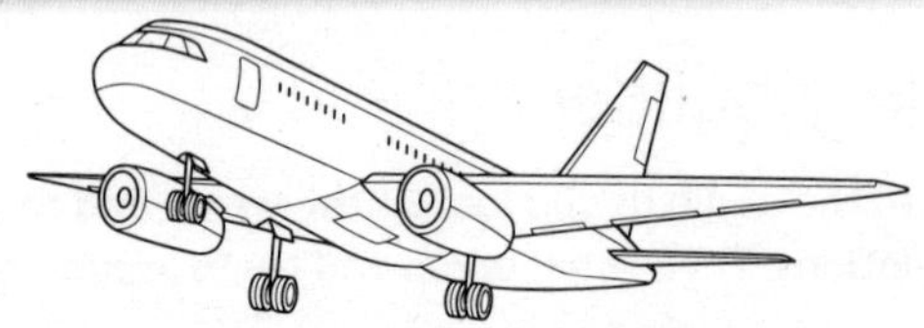

# Conversation 1 At the airport

**01.02 Listen to the words and expressions that are used in the conversation and note their meaning. Then listen again and repeat after the speaker.**

| | | |
|---|---|---|
| [sto aeroTHrómio] | στο αεροδρόμιο | *at the airport* |
| [kaliméra] | καλημέρα | *good morning* |
| [yiásoo] | γεια σου | *hi/hello* |
| [ti kánis]? | Τι κάνεις; | *How are you?* |
| [íme] [kalá] | Είμαι καλά | *I'm fine.* |
| [esí]? | Εσύ; | *You?* |
| [eTHó] | εδώ | *here* |
| [polí kalá] | πολύ καλά | *just fine* (lit. *very well*) |
| [yiatí]? | Γιατί; | *Why?* |
| [íse]? | Είσαι; | *Are you?* |
| [periméno] | περιμένω | *I wait/I am waiting* |
| [THío] [fíloos] | δύο φίλους | *two friends* |
| [apó] [to] [lonTHíno] | από το Λονδίνο | *from London* (lit. *from the London*) |

01.03 [ángelos] **Άγγελος** *Angelos is at Athens airport when he bumps into his friend* [ána] **Άννα** *Anna.*

**1 Listen to the conversation without looking at the text. What phrase does Angelos use to ask Anna how she is?**

| | | |
|---|---|---|
| **Anna** | [kaliméra ángele]! | *Good morning, Angelos!* |
| **Angelos** | [yiásoo ána] [ti kánis]? | *Hello, Anna. How are you?* |
| **Anna** | [íme kalá] [esí]? | *I'm fine* (lit. *well*). *You?* |
| **Angelos** | [kalá], [polí kalá]. | *Fine, just fine.* (lit. *Well, very well.*) |
| **Anna** | [yiatí íse eTHó]? | *Why are you here?* |
| **Angelos** | [periméno] [THío híloos] [apó to lonTHíno]. | *I'm waiting for two friends from London.* |

| | |
|---|---|
| **Άννα** | Καλημέρα, Άγγελε! |
| **Άγγελος** | Γεια σου, Άννα. Τι κάνεις; |
| **Άννα** | Είμαι καλά. Εσύ; |
| **Άγγελος** | Καλά, πολύ καλά. |
| **Άννα** | Γιατί είσαι εδώ; |
| **Άγγελος** | Περιμένω δύο φίλους από το Λονδίνο. |

**2 Now read the conversation and answer the questions.**

**a** How is Angelos?

**b** How is Anna?

**c** Why is Angelos at the airport?

**3 Listen again and pay attention to the words which run together. Practice speaking the part of Angelos and concentrate on getting your pronunciation correct.**

# Language discovery 1

**1 Read the conversation again and find two forms of the verb *to be* and one form of the verb *to wait*. Do you notice anything? Did you only find one word in Greek for each verb?**

**2 The name Angelos appears in two different forms. Can you work out when each form would be used?**

### 1 GREEK VERBS

Verbs are words used to express an action or state of being. [íme] **είμαι** *I am* and [periméno] **περιμένω** *I wait* are both examples of verbs.

## 2 SUBJECT OR PERSONAL PRONOUNS

In English, verbs are usually preceded by words such as *I*, *you*, *they*, etc.; these are called subject or personal pronouns and indicate the subject, that is, who or what is carrying out the action of the verb. These words are generally omitted in Greek because, unlike in English, the ending of the verb changes to indicate the subject, and so there is no need to mention the subject explicitly. The exception to this is if special emphasis is required. Compare, for example, the following two sentences:

| | | |
|---|---|---|
| [íme kalá] | **είμαι καλά** | *I am fine.* (neutral statement; no subject required) |
| [egó íme kalá] | **εγώ είμαι καλά** | *I am fine.* (The emphasis is that *I* am fine and not somebody else.) |

All subject pronouns, including [eghó] **εγώ** *I* and [esí] **εσύ** *you* will be introduced in Unit 2.

**LANGUAGE TIP**

There is no difference in Greek between *I wait* and *I am waiting*. For both you say [periméno] **περιμένω** or [egó periméno] **εγώ περιμένω**.

This is true for all Greek verbs in the present tense. There is only one verb form, *I usually wait for* ... [siníthos periméno ya ...] **Συνήθως περιμένω για** ... or I'm now waiting for ... [tóra periméno ya ...] **Τώρα περιμένω για** ...

## 3 THE VERB *TO BE*

The verb [íme] **είμαι** *to be* is the most commonly used verb in both English and Greek.

| | | |
|---|---|---|
| [íme] | **είμαι** | *I am* |
| [íse] | **είσαι** | *you are* (sing/infml) |
| [íne] | **είναι** | *he/she/it is* |
| [ímaste] | **είμαστε** | *we are* |
| [ísaste]/[íste] (both forms are correct) | **είσαστε/είστε** | *you are* (pl/fml) |
| [íne] | **είναι** | *they are* |

1 [pos íse]? **Πώς είσαι;** or [pos íste]? **Πώς είστε;** can both be used to say *How are you?* The first is used when you know someone well and the second in more formal situations.

2 *he/she/it is* and *they are* are the same in Greek: [íne] **είναι**. This is, however, an exception to the rule as Greek verbs normally have two different forms for the third person singular and third person plural.

### 4 THE VERBS *TO DO* AND *TO WAIT*

In dialogue 1 the question [ti kánis] **Τι κάνεις;** was translated as *How are you?* Literally though, it means *What are you doing?* or asking about the health of somebody *How are you doing?*

Here is the full verb table in the present tense of **κάνω** and **περιμένω**. As a rule of thumb, there are two parts in each verb, the stem and the ending. Note the different endings which show the person involved in an action or in a state.

| | | | |
|---|---|---|---|
| κάν-ω | I do / I am doing | περιμέν-ω | I wait / I am waiting |
| κάν-εις | you do / you are doing | περιμέν-εις | you wait / you are waiting |
| κάν-ει | s/he, it does, -is doing | περιμέν-ει | s/he, it waits, -is waiting |
| κάν-ουμε | we do / we are doing | περιμέν-ουμε | we wait / we are waiting |
| κάν-ετε | you do / you are doing | περιμέν-ετε | you wait / you are waiting |
| κάν-ουν(ε) | they do / they are doing | περιμέν-ουν(ε) | they wait / they are waiting |

In this book verbs are divided into eight major groups, Verb Group 1, 2, 3 etc., according to their different conjugations. Almost two thirds of all Greek verbs belong to the conjugation shown above of **κάνω** and **περιμένω**.

## Conversation 2 Pleased to meet you!

Greek people shake hands only in formal situations. Informally, good friends and relatives – both men and women – kiss each other when they meet or depart. The notion of personal space is different in Greek culture. Greek people usually allow less distance between themselves and the other person when introducing themselves or being introduced, talking to others or standing in a queue. Stepping back in a face-to-face conversation might only invite the other person to move forward and try to get closer to you!

**01.04 Listen to the words and expressions used in the conversation and note their meaning. Then listen again and repeat after the speaker.**

| | | |
|---|---|---|
| [na] [sas] [sistíso] | Να σας συστήσω. | *Let me introduce you.* |
| [ke] | και | *and* |
| [héro] [polí] | Χαίρω πολύ. | *Pleased to meet you.* |

| | | |
|---|---|---|
| [kalós orísate] | καλώς ορίσατε | *welcome* |
| [stin] | στην | *to/in/at* (used with nouns) |
| [eláTHa] | Ελλάδα | *Greece* |
| [efharistoóme] | ευχαριστούμε | *thank you* (lit. *we thank you*) |
| [pos se léne]? | Πώς σε λένε; | *What's your name?* |
| [me léne] | Με λένε ... | *My name is* ... (lit. *they call me*) |

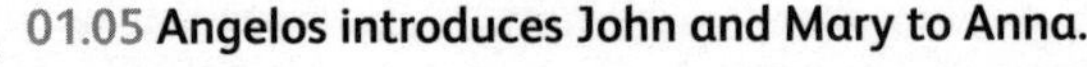

**01.05 Angelos introduces John and Mary to Anna.**

**1 Listen to the conversation a couple of times. Without looking at the text, can you identify which phrase means *Welcome to Greece!*?**

| | | |
|---|---|---|
| **Angelos** | [na sas sistíso]. [apo'THó] [o John] [ke i Mary]. | *Let me introduce you. This is John and Mary.* |
| **Anna** | [yiásas]. [héro polí]. [kalós orísate] [stin eláTHa]. | *Hello. Pleased to meet you. Welcome to Greece!* |
| **John** | [efharistó]. | *Thanks.* |
| **Mary** | [efharistoóme]. [pos se léne]; | *Thank you. What's your name?* |
| **Anna** | [ána]. [me léne ána]. | *Anna. My name is Anna.* |

| | |
|---|---|
| **Άγγελος** | Να σας συστήσω! από ΄δω ο John και η Mary. |
| **Άννα** | Γεια σας. Χαίρω πολύ. Καλώς ορίσατε στην Ελλάδα! |
| **John** | Ευχαριστώ. |
| **Mary** | Ευχαριστούμε! Πώς σε λένε; |
| **Άννα** | Άννα. Με λένε Άννα. |

**LANGUAGE TIP**

Have you noticed the semi-colons used here? This is the sign for a question mark in Greek.

**2 Now read the conversation and answer the questions.**

**a** What is the difference between **Ευχαριστώ** and **Ευχαριστούμε**?

**b** What is the difference between the words **Από** and **Πώς**?

**3 Listen to the conversation again and pay attention to the words which run together. Practice speaking the parts of Anna and Mary or Angelos and John and pay particular attention to your pronunciation.**

# Language discovery 2

**Read the conversation again and find the Greek word for *the* in three different forms preceding the following words. How is it different from English?**

**a** John **b** Mary **c** Greece

## 1 THE GREEK ARTICLE *THE*

Greek has several different forms for the word *the* as it changes according to gender, number (singular or plural) and function in the sentence of the noun it accompanies. In the two conversations in this unit the Greek word for *the* appeared in the following instances:

| | | |
|---|---|---|
| [sto aeroTHrómio] | **στο αεροδρόμιο** | *at the airport* (n) |
| [to lonTHíno] | **το Λονδίνο** | *London* (n) (lit. *the London*) |
| [o John] | **ο John** | *John* (m) (lit. *the John*) |
| [i méri] | **η Mary** | *Mary* (f) (lit. *the Mary*) |
| [stin eláTHa] | **στην Ελλάδα** | *in Greece* (f) (lit. *in the Greece*) |

The words [sto] **στο** and [stin] **στην** are a combination of the preposition [se] **σε** *to/in/at* plus the word for *the*. Notice also that the Greek word for *the* is used before names, i.e. [i méri] **η Mary** *Mary* and not simply [méri] **Mary**. It is also used in front of other proper nouns, e.g. **στην Ελλάδα** (lit. *in the Greece*).

## 2 GREEK NOUNS

Nouns are words that typically refer to a person, thing or abstract concept (such as friend, airport, happiness). In Greek, nouns usually have several forms, depending on their gender, number and function in the sentence. Two examples from this unit are the name **Άγγελ-ος** or **Άγγελ-ε** and the word **φίλ-ος** or **φίλ-ους**.

There are three noun groups, or three genders, namely masculine, feminine and neuter. The ending will usually help you to work out the gender of each noun.

## 3 CONTRACTED FORMS

Angelos introduced John and Mary with the contracted phrase [apo'THó] **από ΄δω** instead of the complete phrase [apó eTHó] **από εδώ**. In Greek, contracted forms are used extensively in everyday informal language, and occur especially when the first word ends in a vowel and the second word starts with a vowel.

### 4 THE QUESTION *WHAT'S YOUR NAME?*

Dialogue 2 included this question: [pos se léne]? **Πώς σε λένε;** *What's your name? (lit. How do they (they = other people) call / name you?)*. The answer [me léne ...] **Με λένε** ... *My name is ... (lit. They (they = other people) call / name me ...)* also requires attention when it comes to Greek male names. Notice the different form (different case) with the following names:

**Άρης: Με λένε Άρη, Νίκος: Με λένε Νίκο, Κώστας: Με λένε Κώστα, Άγγελος: Με λένε Άγγελο, Μάριος: Με λένε Μάριο, Κωνσταντίνος: Με λένε Κωνσταντίνο.** This new form (case) is the accusative. Greek female names, English names, or international names do not have a new form in this case, something similar to vocative case explained above. Some examples include: **Μαρία: Με λένε Μαρία, Ελένη: Με λένε Ελένη, Ηρώ: Με λένε Ηρώ, Με λένε Τομ / Τζον / 'Εμμα / Αν.**

# Practice

**1 Which greeting would you use at these times of day?**

**a** 10:00 **b** 18:00 **c** 23:00

**2 Match the words to form pairs.**

| | |
|---|---|
| **a** [yiásoo] | **1** [hárika] |
| **b** [kalispéra] | **2** [parakaló] |
| **c** [héro polí] | **3** [yia] |
| **d** [efharistó] | **4** [kalós sas vríka] |
| **e** [kalós orísate] | **5** [kaliníhta] |

**3 Match each question to its corresponding answer.**

| | |
|---|---|
| **a** [yiatí íse eTHó]? | **1** [periméno fíloos] |
| **b** [ti kánis]? | **2** [eléni] |
| **c** [pos se léne]? | **3** [kalá] |
| **d** [pos íste]? | **4** [ímaste polí kalá] |

**4 You have learned that the definite article (*the*) has many forms in Greek. Choose the correct one in the following examples.**

| | | | |
|---|---|---|---|
| **a** [méno] _____ [lonTHíno] | **1** [sto] | **2** [stin] | **3** [to] |
| **b** [íme apó] _____ [lonTHíno] | **1** [sto] | **2** [stin] | **3** [to] |
| **c** [íme apó] _____ [eláTHa] | **1** [tin] | **2** [stin] | **3** [i] |
| **d** [méno] _____ [athína] | **1** [tin] | **2** [stin] | **3** [i] |

**5 Someone introduces you to several Greek friends of theirs. Choose the correct form, [o] or [i], in each case.**

**a** [apo'THó] _____ [ioána]
**b** [apo'THó] _____ [vasílis]
**c** [apo'THó] _____ [yiánis]
**d** [apo'THó] _____ [ángelos]
**e** [apo'THó] _____ [ána]
**f** [apo'THó] _____ [eléni]

**6** 01.06 **Listen again to Conversation 2 and fill in the blanks with words from the box. Alternatively, complete the dialogue first and then listen to the conversation to check your answers.**

| [o] [i] [sas] [stin] [polí] [se] [me] |
|---|

| | |
|---|---|
| **Angelos** | [na] **a** _____ [sistíso]. [apóTHo] **b** _____ [John] [ke] **c** _____ [Mary]. |
| **Anna** | [yiásas]. [héro] **d** _____. [kalós orísate] **e** _____ [eláTHa]. |
| **John** | [efharistó]. |
| **Mary** | [efharistoóme]. [pos] **f** _____ [léne]? |
| **Anna** | [ána]. **g** _____ [léne ána]. |

**7 How many Greek words can you find in this word search? There are nine to be found! The words read across, down, up, backwards and diagonally. Capital letters have deliberately not been used here.**

| | | | | | | | |
|---|---|---|---|---|---|---|---|
| k | a | l | i | m | e | r | a |
| a | p | o | p | s | t | i | n |
| l | o | o | o | t | h | i | o |
| a | y | i | a | s | o | o | t |
| p | e | r | i | m | e | n | o |

**8 Now go back to the previous exercise and rewrite the words you found in the word search using the Greek alphabet.**

**a** ____________________
**b** ____________________
**c** ____________________
**d** ____________________
**e** ____________________
**f** ____________________
**g** ____________________
**h** ____________________
**i** ____________________

**9 Greek pronunciation. Read the advertisement and answer the question:**

**a** Is the pronunciation of the letters **ω** and **ο** different in the first?

**10 Now write the text in lowercase Greek letters.**

______________________________________________

______________________________________________

## Test yourself

**1** What would you say in the following situations?

**a** You meet your friend Anna. Say hello to her.
**b** Ask her how she is.
**c** Ask her why she is at the airport.
**d** Say *thank you* to a friend.
**e** Say *goodbye* to your teacher.
**f** How would you say *good morning* and *goodnight*?
**g** Say *Pleased to meet you* when you are introduced to Mr X.

**2** Rearrange these lines to make a dialogue. Then choose one line and write it in Greek script.

**a** [kalá, kalá] [yiatí íse eTHó]?
**b** [yiásoo yiáni]! [ti kánis]?
**c** [periméno THío fíloos]
**d** [kalá efharistó]. [esí ti kánis]?

**3** How many words can you translate into English from the word search in exercise 8 of the Practice section?

### SELF CHECK

| | **I CAN. . .** |
|---|---|
| • | . . . say *hello* and *goodbye*. |
| • | . . . exchange greetings. |
| • | . . . ask and say how people are. |
| • | . . . introduce myself and my family. |
| • | . . . address people when I meet them. |

# 2

In this unit you will learn how to:

» ask and say where someone comes from and where they live now.
» ask which languages someone speaks.
» say the names of some cities and countries.

# Μιλάτε Ελληνικά;

My progress tracker

| DAY / DATE | | | | | |
|---|---|---|---|---|---|
| | ○ | ○ | ○ | ○ | ○ |
| | ○ | ○ | ○ | ○ | ○ |
| | ○ | ○ | ○ | ○ | ○ |
| | ○ | ○ | ○ | ○ | ○ |
| | ○ | ○ | ○ | ○ | ○ |

## Greece

[eláTHa] **Ελλάδα** *Greece* occupies an area of 132,000 km$^2$, approximately 4 % of the EU. The country is around 800 km from north to south and 1,000 km from east to west. Around 81 % of the country is on the European mainland with the remaining 19 % made up of islands. [athína] **Αθήνα** *Athens* is the capital and largest city, with more than 4 million inhabitants, and [thesaloníki] **Θεσσαλονίκη** *Thessaloniki* the second largest, with roughly 1,200,000. The total population is around 10 million, with another 4 million Greeks living abroad. Mount [ólimbos] **Όλυμπος** *Olympus* is the highest mountain (2,920 m). [kríti] **Κρήτη** *Crete* is the biggest island with an area of 8,380 km$^2$. Other major islands include [evia] **Εύβοια** *Euboea* (or *Evvoia*), [lezvos] **Λέσβος** *Lesbos* (or *Lesvos*) and [roTHos] **Ρόδος**. Greece is divided into nine large geographical areas: [stereá eláTHa] **Στερεά Ελλάδα** *Sterea* (population 4.5 million), [makeTHonía] **Μακεδονία** *Macedonia* (2.3 million), [pelopónisos] **Πελοπόννησος** *Peloponnese* (1 million), [thesalía] **Θεσσαλία** *Thessaly* (750,000), [kríti] **Κρήτη** *Crete* (550,000), [nisiá eghéu] **Νησιά Αιγαίου** *the Aegean Islands* (500,000), [ípiros] **Ήπειρος** *Epirus* (350,000), [thráki] **Θράκη** *Thrace* (350,000) and [nisiá ioníu] **Νησιά Ιονίου** *the Ionian Islands* (200,000). You can see these areas on the map.

Can you name Greece's largest city, highest mountain and biggest island?

# Vocabulary builder

**1** 02.01 **Listen a couple of times to the names of the geographical areas while looking at the map and familiarizing yourself with their location. Then listen again and repeat them out loud.**

**2** 02.02 **Listen to the audio and study the chart below. Then listen once again and repeat the names of the countries, cities and languages after the speaker. Which places have you visited and which languages can you speak?**

| City | Country | Language |
|---|---|---|
| [i athína] | [i eláTHa] | [ta eliniká] |
| **η Αθήνα** | **η Ελλάδα** | **τα Ελληνικά** |
| *Athens* | *Greece* | *Greek* |
| [to lonTHíno] | [i anglía] | [ta angliká] |
| **το Λονδίνο** | **η Αγγλία** | **τα Αγγλικά** |

| City | Country | Language |
|---|---|---|
| *London* | *England* | *English* |
| [to parísi] | [i galía] | [ta galiká] |
| **το Παρίσι** | **η Γαλλία** | **τα Γαλλικά** |
| *Paris* | *France* | *French* |
| [i rómi] | [i italía] | [ta italiká] |
| **η Ρώμη** | **η Ιταλία** | **τα Ιταλικά** |
| *Rome* | *Italy* | *Italian* |
| [to verolíno] | [i yermanía] | [ta yermaniká] |
| **το Βερολίνο** | **η Γερμανία** | **τα Γερμανικά** |
| *Berlin* | *Germany* | *German* |
| [i maTHríti] | [i ispanía] | [ta ispaniká] |
| **η Μαδρίτη** | **η Ισπανία** | **τα Ισπανικά** |
| *Madrid* | *Spain* | *Spanish* |
| [i néa iórki] | [i amerikí] | [ta angliká] |
| **η Νέα Υόρκη** | **η Αμερική** | **τα Αγγλικά** |
| *New York* | *America* | *English* |
| [to síTHnei] | [i afstralía] | [ta angliká] |
| **το Σίδνεϋ** | **η Αυστραλία** | **τα Αγγλικά** |
| *Sydney* | *Australia* | *English* |

Did you notice that all city names, country names and languages are preceded by the definite article in Greek? Unlike in English, the definite article in Greek has many different forms, sometimes as individual words and sometimes combined with a preposition. The three articles used here are:

- [i] **η** before feminine nouns
- [to] **το** before neuter nouns.
- [ta] **τα** before neuter nouns.

**Circle these three articles in the table below. The translation for all three remains *the*.**

| Masculine article | Feminine article | Neuter article |
|---|---|---|
| Singular | | |
| ο | η | το |
| Plural | | |
| οι | οι | τα |

**3** 02.03 **Here are some typical questions and answers about where someone is from. Listen to the audio as you read the text. Then listen once again and repeat after the speaker.**

| | | |
|---|---|---|
| [apó poo íse]? | **Από πού είσαι;** | *Where are you from?* |
| [apó pya póli]? | **Από ποια πόλη;** | *From which city?* |
| [apó pya hóra]? | **Από ποια χώρα;** | *From which country?* |
| [íme apó tin néa iórki]. | **Είμαι από τη Νέα Υόρκη.** | *I'm from New York.* |
| [apó to parísi]. | **Από το Παρίσι.** | *From Paris.* |
| [íme apó tin anglía]. | **Είμαι από την Αγγλία.** | *I'm from England.* |
| [apó to lonTHíno]. | **Από το Λονδίνο.** | *From London.* |
| [íme apó tin athína]. | **Είμαι από την Αθήνα.** | *I'm from Athens.* |
| [íme apó tin eláTHa]. | **Είμαι από την Ελλάδα.** | *I'm from Greece.* |

Did you notice that the feminine article takes a new form, either **τη** or **την**, after the preposition *from*? There is a phonetic rule which stipulates whether the final letter **-ν** remains or is dropped in certain Greek words. It is recommended that you always use the final letter **-ν** as even some Greek speakers do this when they're talking very quickly. If you are from *Scotland* [i skotía] you can say [íme apó tin skotía] **Είμαι από την Σκωτία** *I'm from Scotland*. [íme apó tin oo-alía] **Είμαι από την Ουαλία** means *I'm from Wales* and [íme apó tin irlanTHía] **Είμαι από την Ιρλανδία** means *I'm from Ireland*. The neuter article **το** remains unchanged.

**Είμαι από το Μάντσεστερ. Είμαι από το Μπρίστολ. Είμαι από το Κάρντιφ.** Can you work out the names of these three cities in English?

**4** **02.04 In these early stages when you cannot yet express yourself fluently in Greek you may well want to ask people if they speak English. Here are some questions and answers relating to speaking and understanding. Listen and repeat each one after the speaker. If you want to challenge yourself a little more, read each example out loud first and then listen to the audio to check your pronunciation.**

| | | |
|---|---|---|
| [milás/miláte angliká]? | Μιλάς/Μιλάτε Αγγλικά; | *Do you* (infml/fml) *speak English?* |
| [katalavénis/ katalavénete]? | Καταλαβαίνεις/ Καταλαβαίνετε; | *Do you understand?* (infml/fml) |
| [xéris/xérete eliniká]? | Ξέρεις/Ξέρετε Ελληνικά; | *Do you* (infml/fml) *know Greek?* |
| [ne], [miláo angliká]. | Ναι, μιλάω Αγγλικά. | *Yes, I speak English.* |
| [THen katalavéno]. | Δεν καταλαβαίνω. | *I don't understand.* |
| [óchi] [THén xéro elliniká]. | Όχι, δεν ξέρω Ελληνικά. | *No, I don't know Greek.* |

**LANGUAGE TIP**

The word **Δεν/δε** and sometimes **Δε/δε** is a negative particle and is used before Greek verbs to show negation. It does not have different forms compared to English, such as *don't, doesn't, didn't, hasn't*, etc.

The two verbs **καταλαβαίνω** and **ξέρω** are conjugated exactly like **κάνω** and **περιμένω** in Unit 1. The verb **μιλάω/μιλώ** belongs to another verb group and is fully conjugated for you later on in this unit.

# Conversation 1 Do you speak Greek?

**02.05 Listen to the words and expressions that are used in the conversation. Note their meaning.**

| | | |
|---|---|---|
| [po-po]! | πω, πω! | *Wow!* |
| [ne] | ναι | *yes* |
| [líga] | λίγα | *a little* |
| [esí] | εσύ | *you* |
| [egó] | εγώ | *I* |
| [brávo] | μπράβο | *bravo* |

**02.06** *Anna is surprised at how well John and Mary speak Greek.*

1 **Listen to the conversation once or twice without looking at the text. Can you list the languages you hear?**

| | | |
|---|---|---|
| **Anna** | [efharistó], [efharistoóme], [po-po]! [miláte eliniká]? | *Thanks, thank you! Wow! Do you speak Greek?* |
| **John** | [ne], [angliká] [ke líga] [eliniká]. [esí]? | *Yes, English and some Greek. And you? (lit. you?)* |
| **Mary** | [egó miláo eliniká], [angliká] [ke líga] [yermaniká]. | *I speak Greek, English and some German.* |
| **Anna** | [brávo]! | *Bravo!* |

| | |
|---|---|
| **Άννα** | Ευχαριστώ, ευχαριστούμε! Πω, πω! Μιλάτε Ελληνικά; |
| **John** | Ναι. Αγγλικά και λίγα Ελληνικά. Εσύ; |
| **Mary** | Εγώ μιλάω Ελληνικά, Αγγλικά και λίγα Γερμανικά. |
| **Άννα** | Μπράβο! |

2 **Now read the conversation and answer the questions.**

**a** What languages does John speak?

**b** What languages does Mary speak?

3 **Listen again and pay special attention to the words which run together. Practice speaking the part of John or Mary and pay particular attention to your pronunciation.**

# Language discovery 1

1 **There are two personal pronouns in this conversation. Can you find the Greek words for the following?**

**a** I **b** you

2 **Find the Greek words for the following three languages that are mentioned in the conversation. Do you notice anything special about the endings of the words?**

**a** Greek **b** English **c** German

## 1 PERSONAL PRONOUNS

Personal pronouns are important building blocks for any conversation. Two of them [egó] **εγώ** *I* and [esí] **εσύ** *you* were used in the conversation. See the table below for the rest of them.

| | | |
|---|---|---|
| [egó] | **εγώ** | *I* |
| [esí] | **εσύ** | *you* (sing/infml) |
| [aftós] | **αυτός** | *he* |
| [aftí] | **αυτή** | *she* |
| [aftó] | **αυτό** | *it* |
| [emís] | **εμείς** | *we* |
| [esís] | **εσείς** | *you* (pl/fml) |
| [aftí] | **αυτοί** | *they* (m or m + f) |
| [aftés] | **αυτές** | *they* (f only) |
| [aftá] | **αυτά** | *they* (n) |

## 2 THE VERB *TO SPEAK*

Another useful verb you met in the conversation above is [miláo] **μιλάω** *to speak/I speak/I am speaking*. Remember you learned in Unit 1 that you do not usually need to use personal pronouns such as *I*, *you* and *they* before the verb because the different verb endings tell you which person is being referred to. Here, however, the personal pronouns are given in brackets before the verb to give you a little extra help.

| | | |
|---|---|---|
| [egó] [miláo/miló] | **(εγώ) μιλάω/μιλώ** | *to speak/I speak/I am speaking* |
| [esí] [milás] | **(εσύ) μιλάς** | *you speak* |
| [aftós/-tí/-tó] [milái/milá] | **(αυτ-ός/-ή/-ό) μιλάει/ μιλά** | *he/she/it speaks* |
| [emís] [miláme] | **(εμείς) μιλάμε** | *we speak* |
| [esís] [miláte] | **(εσείς) μιλάτε** | *you speak* |
| [aftí/-és/tá] [milán(e)/ miloón(e)] | **(αυτ-οί/-ές/-ά) μιλάν(ε)/ μιλούν(ε)** | *they speak* |

**LANGUAGE TIP**

There are three instances where you see two different forms above, e.g. **μιλάω/μιλώ**. There is no difference between them in meaning and Greek speakers often use both forms interchangeably.

# Conversation 2 Are you from London?

**02.07 Listen to the words and expressions that are used in the conversation and note their meaning. Then listen again and repeat after the speaker.**

| | | |
|---|---|---|
| [íste]? | Είστε; | *Are you?* (pl/fml) |
| [tin] [afstralía] | την Αυστραλία | *Australia* |
| [óhi] | όχι | *no* |
| [ki] | κι | *and* |
| [amerikí] | Αμερική | *America* |
| [íse]? | Είσαι; | *Are you?* (sing/infml) |
| [ton] [póro] | τον Πόρο | *Poros* (Greek island) |
| [alá] | αλλά | *but* |
| [tóra] | τώρα | *now* |
| [méno] | μένω | *I live* |

02.08 *Anna is trying to find out where John and Mary come from.*

**1 Listen to their conversation a couple of times without looking at the text. Which countries do John and Mary come from?**

| | | |
|---|---|---|
| **Anna** | [íste] [apó to lonTHíno]? | *Are you from London?* |
| **John** | [óhi], [íme] [apó tin afstralía]. | *No, I'm from Australia.* |
| **Mary** | [ki egó] [apó tin amerikí]. [esí]? [íse] [apó tin athína]? | *And I am from America. And you? Are you from Athens?* |
| **Anna** | [óhi], [íme] [apó ton póro], [alá tóra] [méno stin athína]. | *No, I'm from Poros but now I live in Athens.* |

| | |
|---|---|
| **Άννα** | Είστε από το Λονδίνο; |
| **John** | Όχι, είμαι από την Αυστραλία. |
| **Mary** | Κι εγώ, από την Αμερική. Εσύ; Είσαι από την Αθήνα; |
| **Άννα** | Όχι. Είμαι από τον Πόρο, αλλά τώρα μένω στην Αθήνα. |

**2 Now read the conversation and answer the questions.**

**a** Where does Anna come from?

**b** Where does she live now?

**3 Listen again and pay special attention to the words which run together. Practice speaking the part of John or Mary and pay particular attention to your pronunciation.**

# Language discovery 2

**1 The conversation has three different forms of the definite article (*the*) following the preposition *from*. Can you find them and work out why the different forms are used?**

**2 All the verbs were used without personal pronouns in the conversation. Add the corresponding pronouns for each verb form?**

**a** *you are* (sing) _____ **c** *I am* _____

**b** *you are* (pl) _____ **d** *I live* _____

**3 This unit introduced two important words in Greek: *yes* and *no*. Can you write these words in Greek script and say them out loud?**

### THE DEFINITE ARTICLE *THE*

As mentioned before, the word *the* in Greek has various forms compared to English. It is also used more than in English, notably with the names of people, cities or countries. The table below will give you a better overview.

| | Masculine article | Feminine article | Neuter article |
|---|---|---|---|
| Nominative case | **ο** | **η** | **το** |
| | **ο Πόρος** [o póros] | **η Αυστραλία** [i afstralía] | **το Λονδίνο** [to lonTHíno] |
| Accusative case | **τον** | **την** | **το** |
| | Είμαι **από τον** Πόρο. [íme apó ton póro] | Είμαι **από την** Αυστραλία.[íme apó tin afstralía] | Είμαι **από το** Λονδίνο. [íme apó to lonTHíno] |
| | Μένω **στον** Πόρο. [méno ston póro] | Μένω **στην** Αυστραλία. [méno stin afstalía] | Μένω **στο** Λονδίνο. [méno sto lonTHíno] |
| Nominative and accusative case | **Ο Άγγελος** είναι **από τον Πόρο** αλλά τώρα μένει **στον Καναδά.** | **Η Άννα** είναι **από την Αγγλία** αλλά μένει τώρα **στην Ελλάδα.** | Αυτό **το παιδί** είναι **από το Βέλγιο** αλλά μένει **στο Μπρίστολ** τώρα. |

# Language discovery 3

**1 There are two new countries in the table above, Καναδάς and Βέλγιο. Can you first work out the countries in English and then write them in nominative case with the appropriate article and in Greek script? Do you notice anything?**

**2 παιδί is also a new word. Could you perhaps associate it with the word *paediatrics* or *paediatrician* and guess its meaning?**

**3 The word [tóra] τώρα now (a time adverb) appears in the last three examples. Where is it placed (the beginning, middle or end of the sentence)?**

**LANGUAGE TIP**

In the last three examples the preposition **σε** *at/in/to* is combined with the articles **τον**, **την** and **το** to form one word. It is incorrect to say **σε τον**, **σε την** or **σε το** as two separate words.

# Practice

**1 You are in Patras, a bustling harbor in the Western Peloponnese, where many visitors arrive by boat from Italy. You see some cars with the following nationality stickers. Complete the table using transliteration and/or Greek script with the correct country and language relating to each sticker.**

| Symbol | Country | Language |
|---|---|---|
| GR | a ______ | ______ |
| E | b ______ | ______ |
| I | c ______ | ______ |
| F | d ______ | ______ |
| GB | e ______ | ______ |

**2 Match each question with the most appropriate answer.**

**a** [apó poo íse]? Από πού είσαι; **1** [stin athína]. Στην Αθήνα.
**b** [apó pia póli]? Από ποια πόλη; **2** [lonTHíno]. Λονδίνο.
**c** [miláte italiká]? Μιλάτε Ιταλικά; **3** [óhi]. Όχι.
**d** [poo ménete]? Πού μένετε; **4** [apó tin anglía]. Από την Αγγλία.

**3 Monster words! The following sentences have not been separated into their individual words. Insert spaces in the appropriate places to make proper sentences. Use capital letters if necessary. Then translate each sentence into English.**

**a** [íneapótinthesaloníki]. είναιαπότηνθεσσαλονίκη
**b** [alátóraménostinpátra]. αλλάτώραμένειστηνπάτρα
**c** [miláoitalikákelígaispaniká]. μιλάωιταλικάκαιλίγαισπανικά
**d** [iathínaínestineláTHa]. ηαθήναείναιστηνελλάδα
**e** [ketoparísisistingalía]. καιτοπαρίσιστηνγαλλία

4 **The six largest cities and towns in Greece are listed below, with their approximate populations in brackets. Can you find them on the map?**

**a** [i athína] η Αθήνα (4,000,000)
**b** [i thesaloniki] η Θεσσαλονίκη (1,000,000)
**c** [i pátra] η Πάτρα (170,000)
**d** [to iráklio] το Ηράκλειο (125,000)
**e** [i lárisa] η Λάρισα (120,000)
**f** [o vólos] ο Βόλος (80,000)

5 **Choose the correct form of the Greek word for *the* in each of the following cases. Then rewrite each sentence using Greek script.**

| | | 1 | 2 | 3 |
|---|---|---|---|---|
| **a** | [íme apó] ______ [lonTHíno]. | **1** [o] | **2** [to] | **3** [sto] |
| **b** | [méno] ______ [lonTHíno]. | **1** [o] | **2** [to] | **3** [sto] |
| **c** | [íme apó] ______ [amerikí]. | **1** [i] | **2** [tin] | **3** [stin] |
| **d** | [apó] ______ [néa iórki]. | **1** [i] | **2** [tin] | **3** [stin] |
| **e** | ______ [néa iórki íne stin amerikí]. | **1** [i] | **2** [tin] | **3** [stin] |
| **f** | ______ [lonTHíno íne stin anglía]. | **1** [o] | **2** [to] | **3** [sto] |

**6** 02.09 **Listen again to Conversation 2 and fill in the missing words using the words in the box. Note that one of the words is used twice! Then write out each sentence using Greek script.**

| [alá] [apó] [esí] [egó] [óhi] |
|---|

| | |
|---|---|
| **Anna** | [íste] **a** _____ [to lonTHíno]? |
| **John** | **b** _____. [íme] [apó tin afstralía]. |
| **Mary** | [ki] **c** _____ [apó tin amerikí]. **d** _____? [íse] [apó tin athína]? |
| **Anna** | **e** _____. [íme] [apó ton póro]. **f** _____ [tóra] [méno stin athína]. |

**7** 02.10 **Look at the three business cards, then listen to the dialogue and decide which business card it relates to.**

# Test yourself

1. How would you ask which country someone is from?
2. How do you ask someone *Where do you live now?* in Greek?
3. How would you say *I'm from Cardiff but I live in Manchester now*?
4. Give the Greek words for three European languages.
5. Give the names of three European cities in Greek.

## SELF CHECK

| | I CAN... |
|---|---|
| • | ... ask where someone comes from and where they live now. |
| • | ... ask which languages someone speaks. |
| • | ... give personal information about where I come from and where I live. |
| • | ... say which languages I speak. |
| • | ... say the names of some cities and countries. |

3

**In this unit you will learn how to:**

» talk about different jobs and professions.
» ask someone what their job is and say what your own job is.
» say the names of different professions.
» make sentences negative and turn a statement into a question.

# Τι δουλειά κάνεις;

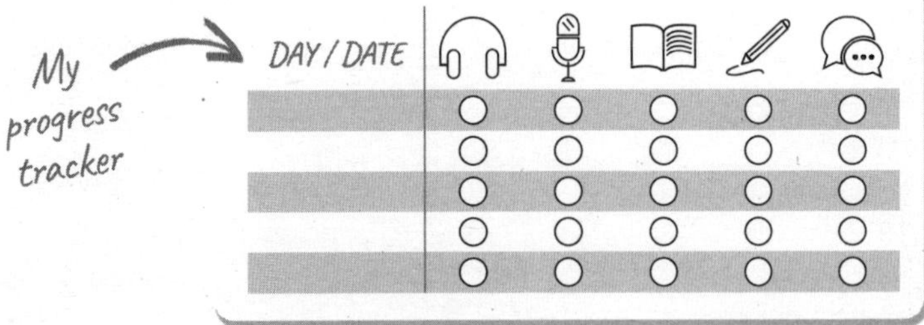


## Employment in Greece

Many Greeks are [iTHiotikós ipálilos] **ιδιωτικός υπάλληλος** *self-employed*. Others become [THimósios ipálilos] **δημόσιος υπάλληλος** *civil servants* in the hope of long-term job security. Shipping has a long tradition in Greece and employs a large number of [ergátis (m) – ergátria (f)] **εργάτης-εργάτρια** *workers*. Equally important for the Greek economy is the tourist industry, which generates around one-eighth of the gross national income. Greece is also an agricultural country, producing olive oil, wine, milk products, fruit, vegetables and cereals, and this sector also creates many part-time and full-time jobs. Unfortunately, several economic recessions that began in 2010 caused vast numbers of job losses, leaving many in Greece unemployed. The word [ánergos] (m) **άνεργος** or [ánergi] (f) **άνεργη** *unemployed* or the phrase [horís ergasía] **χωρίς εργασία** *without work* are often heard or read nowadays. Working in the civil service no longer provides the job security it once did and job prospects are not very promising for the near future.

There is a common stem, namely **-εργ-**, in the following three words: **εργάτης / εργάτρια, άνεργος, εργασία.** With that as a starting point, can you guess what the Greek verb **εργάζομαι** means?

# Vocabulary builder

## ΕΠΑΓΓΕΛΜΑΤΑ *PROFESSIONS*

**1** 03.01 **Listen as you look at the following list of professions and complete the English translations in your book. Then listen again and try to imitate the speakers.**

| **Masculine** | **Feminine** |
|---|---|
| [o arhitéktonas] | [i arhitéktonas] |
| **ο αρχιτέκτονας** | **η αρχιτέκτονας** |
| *architect* | *architect* |
| [o moosikós] | [i moosikós] |
| **ο μουσικός** | **η μουσικός** |
| *musician* | ________ |
| [o pianístas] | [i pianístria] |
| **ο πιανίστας** | **η πιανίστρια** |
| *pianist* | *pianist* |
| [o servitóros] | [i servitóra] |
| **ο σερβιτόρος** | **η σερβιτόρα** |
| *waiter/waitress/server* | ________ |
| [o yiatrós] | [i yiatrós] |
| **ο γιατρός** | **η γιατρός** |
| *doctor* | *doctor* |
| [o THáskalos] | [i THaskála] |
| **ο δάσκαλος** | **η δασκάλα** |
| *teacher* | *teacher* |
| [o sigraféas] | [i sigraféas] |
| **ο συγγραφέας** | **η συγγραφέας** |
| *writer* | *writer* |
| [o ithopi-ós] | [i ithopi-ós] |
| **ο ηθοποιός** | **η ηθοποιός** |
| *actor* | ________ |
| [o trapezítis] | [i trapezítria] |
| **ο τραπεζίτης** | **η τραπεζίτρια** |
| *banker* | *banker* |

**LANGUAGE TIP**

Although it's too early for you to come to terms with many new and unique differences between these two languages, we urge you to become a careful 'detective' and attempt to see some similarities instead of obvious differences. If you go back to this list of professions you can easily see, apart from word endings and pronunciations, that many professions do have a common base in both languages. Architect, musician, or pianist are more obvious but waiter/waitress from *serve* or writer from *graphology, graphics* can give us a small hint. Don't you agree?

| | |
|---|---|
| [o chrimatistís] | [i chrimatístria] |
| **ο χρηματιστής** | **η χρηματίστρια** |
| *stockbroker* | *stockbroker* |
| [o nosokómos] | [i nosokóma] |
| **ο νοσοκόμος** | **η νοσοκόμα** |
| *nurse* | *nurse* |

**2 Was your profession listed above? And if not, have you already looked it up in a dictionary? Write it here now: ______________!**

## ΜΙΛΩΝΤΑΣ ΓΙΑ ΔΟΥΛΕΙΑ *QUESTIONS AND ANSWERS ABOUT WORK*

**3 03.02 Without looking at the text, listen to the recording in which people talk about work. Then, listen again and repeat after the speaker, concentrating on your pronunciation.**

| | | |
|---|---|---|
| [ti THooliá kánis/kánete]? | Τι δουλειά κάνεις/κάνετε; | *What's your job?* |
| [poo THoolévis/THoolévete]? | Πού δουλεύεις/δουλεύετε; | *Where do you work?* |
| [ergházese/ergházeste]? | Εργάζεσαι/Εργάζεστε; | *Do you work?* |
| [THoolévo se énan yiatró/mía tavérna/éna ghrafío]. | Δουλεύω σε έναν γιατρό/μία ταβέρνα/ένα γραφείο. | *I work in a doctor's office/a taverna/an office.* |
| [THen THoolévo tóra]. | Δεν δουλεύω τώρα. | *I'm not working at the moment.* |
| [THoolévo ston kípo/stin koozína/sto nosokomío]. | Δουλεύω στον κήπο/στην κουζίνα/στο νοσοκομείο. | *I work in the garden/kitchen/hospital.* |
| [ergházome gia ton kósta/tin etería ion]. | Εργάζομαι για τον Κώστα/την εταιρία ΙΟΝ. | *I work for Kostas/the ION company.* |
| [íme THaskála sto skolío aghía ána]. | Είμαι δασκάλα στο σχολείο «Αγία Άννα» | *I am a teacher at St Anna's School.* |

Did you notice above the use of the indefinite article, *a* or *an*, with the preposition [se] **σε** *at/in/to*? [se énan yiatró] (m), [se mía tavérna] (f), [se éna grafío] (n). Unit 4 will explain more about these important words.

# Conversation 1 I'm a teacher

## NEW WORDS AND EXPRESSIONS 1

**03.03 Listen to the words and expressions that will be used in the next conversation. Then listen again and repeat after the speaker.**

| | | |
|---|---|---|
| [ménete] | μένετε | *you live* (pl/fml) |
| [sto] | στο | *in the* |
| [THoolévo] | δουλεύω | *I work* |
| [gráfo] | γράφω | *I write* |
| [pediká] | παιδικά | *children's* |
| [vivlía] | βιβλία | *books* |
| [THooliá] | δουλειά | *work* |

03.04 *Anna finds out about John's and Mary's professions.*

**1 Listen to their conversation a couple of times without looking at the text. What does Anna do for a living?**

| | | |
|---|---|---|
| **Anna** | [ti]? [afstralía]? [amerikí]? [ke tóra] [ménete sto lonTHíno]? | *What? Australia? America? And now you live in London?* |
| **John** | [ne]. [THoolévo] [sto lonTHíno]. [íme arhitéktonas]. | *Yes. I work in London. I'm an architect.* |
| **Mary** | [ki' egó] [íme sigraféas]. [gráfo pediká vivlía]. [esí]? [ti THooliá kánis]? | *And I'm a writer. I write children's books. How about you? What do you do for a living?* |
| **Anna** | [íme THaskála]. | *I'm a teacher.* |

| | |
|---|---|
| **Άννα** | Τι; Αυστραλία; Αμερική; Και τώρα μένετε στο Λονδίνο; |
| **John** | Ναι. Δουλεύω στο Λονδίνο. Είμαι αρχιτέκτονας. |
| **Mary** | Κι εγώ είμαι συγγραφέας. Γράφω παιδικά βιβλία. Εσύ; Τι δουλειά κάνεις; |
| **Άννα** | Είμαι δασκάλα. |

**2 Now read the conversation and answer the questions.**

**a** Where does John live now?
**b** What does he do for a living?
**c** What is Mary's job?
**d** Is Anna a writer?

**3 Listen again and pay special attention to the words which run together. Practice speaking the part of Mary or Anna and pay particular attention to your pronunciation.**

## Language discovery 1

**1 The following three professions are all mentioned in the conversation. Find them and write them in Greek script. Which profession has a different form for its male and female counterpart?**

**a** architect **b** writer **c** teacher

**LANGUAGE TIP**

In Greek, when you say what your job is you do not use the indefinite article *a/an*. *I am an architect* = [íme arhitéktonas] **είμαι αρχιτέκτονας**.

**2 Look at the conversation once again and find four main verbs. Write them in Greek script. Then say all the verbs out loud.**

**a** I live. **b** I work. **c** I write. **d** I am.

### 1 PROFESSIONS

As you have seen, professions may have different forms for masculine and feminine, or the same word may be used for both sexes. Compared to English, Greek tends to have many more professions with two words instead of one. Here are some examples divided into two groups.

| Group I (same word for both sexes) | Group II (two different words) |
|---|---|
| **ο αρχιτέκτον-ας/η αχιτέκτον-ας** *architect*<br>**ο γιατρ-ός/η γιατρ-ός** *doctor*<br>**ο δικηγόρ-ος/η δικηγόρ-ος** *lawyer* | **ο πιανίστ-ας/η πιανίστ-ρια** *pianist*<br>**ο φοιτητ-ής/η φοιτήτ-ρια** *student*<br>**ο δάσκαλ-ος/η δασκάλ-α** *teacher* |

**Go back through all the professions mentioned so far and decide whether they belong to Group I or Group II.**

## 2 VERB GROUPS

As you have seen, conversation 1 features four common verbs: **μένω** *I live*, **δουλεύω** *I work*, **γράφω** *I write* and **είμαι** *I am*. This unit also introduced the verb [ergázome] **εργάζομαι** *I work / I'm employed*. Let's remember some key points about Greek verbs. Decide if the following statements are true (NAI) or false (OXI):

| | NAI | OXI |
|---|---|---|
| 1 The infinitive is also the first-person singular of the simple present or present continuous, namely [**gráfo**] **γράφω** is *to write*, *I write*, and *I am writing*. | | |
| 2 Greek verbs usually omit their personal pronouns, words like *you*, *she*, *we*, etc. because the verb ending shows this information. | | |
| 3 Nevertheless, you can always use personal pronouns with Greek verbs, especially when emphasis is needed. | | |
| 4 Unit 1 introduced two different verb groups, one for the verb [**íme**] **είμαι** to be and one for the verb [**káno**] **κάνω** *to do*. | | |
| 5 Unit 2 introduced a third verb group, namely the verb [**miláo / miló**] **μιλάω / μιλώ** *to speak*. | | |
| 6 It is very helpful to know that all active Greek verbs have an **-ω** ending like **κάν-ω** and all passive verbs a **-μαι** ending like **εργάζο-μαι**. | | |
| 7 Unit 3 will introduce a fourth verb group, giving a full conjugation of the verb [**ergázome**] **εργάζο-μαι** *to work*. | | |
| 8 The full conjugation for each verb group helps learners to have a better overview and sort out major/minor verb differences. | | |

## 3 THE VERB *TO WORK / TO BE EMPLOYED*

This unit has introduced two verbs meaning to work, [THoolévo] **δουλεύω** (informal) and [ergázome] **εργάζομαι** (formal). The first can copy the full conjugation of [káno] **κάνω** found in Unit 1. The full conjugation for the second verb is given below.

| | | |
|---|---|---|
| [**ergázome**] | **εργάζ-ομαι** | *to work / I work / I'm working* |
| [**ergázese**] | **εργάζ-εσαι** | *you work / you're working* |
| [**ergázete**] | **εργάζ-εται** | *s/he, it works / is working* |
| [**ergazómaste**] | **εργαζ-όμαστε** | *we work / we are working* |
| [**ergazósaste**] [**ergázeste**] | **εργαζ-όσαστε / εργάζ-εστε** | *you work / you are working* |
| [**ergázonte**] | **εργάζ-ονται** | *they work / they are working* |

# Conversation 2 Where do you live?

## NEW WORDS AND EXPRESSIONS 2

**03.05 Listen to the words and expressions that are used in the next conversation and note their meaning.**

| | | |
|---|---|---|
| [kséris] | ξέρεις | *you know* (sing/infml) |
| [THen] | δεν | *not* |
| [kséro] | ξέρω | *I know.* |
| [poo] | πού | *where* |
| [kondá] | κοντά | *near, close to* |

**03.06** *John and Mary now ask Anna some questions.*

**1 Listen to their exchange a couple of times without looking at the text. Does Anna live close to Angelos?**

| | | |
|---|---|---|
| **John** | [ána], [kséris to lonTHíno]? | *Anna, do you know London?* |
| **Anna** | [óhi] [THen kséro to lonTHíno]. [kséro móno tin athína]. | *No, I don't know London. I only know Athens.* |
| **Mary** | [poo ménis]? [ménis kondá ston ángelo]? | *Where do you live? Do you live near Angelos?* |
| **Anna** | [ne]. [méno kondá ston ángelo]. | *Yes. I live near Angelos.* |

**John** Άννα, ξέρεις το Λονδίνο;
**Άννα** Όχι, δεν ξέρω το Λονδίνο. Ξέρω μόνο την Αθήνα.
**Mary** Πού μένεις; Μένεις κοντά στον Άγγελο;
**Άννα** Ναι. Μένω κοντά στον Άγγελο.

**2 Now read the conversation and answer the questions.**

**a** Does Anna know London or Athens better?

**b** Did you pick up the two words for *yes* and *no* in Greek?

**3 Listen again and pay special attention to the words which run together. Practice speaking the part of Anna and pay particular attention to your pronunciation.**

# Language discovery 2

1 **Can you find the Greek for the following English phrases in the conversation? Do the Greek questions also contain two verbs? Why do you think that is?**

**a** ... do you know? **b** Where do you live? **c** Do you live ... ?

2 **The last two conversations include two words with a double γγ: συγγραφέας and Άγγελο. Would you guess that these two words have a similar or different sound for this double letter? To help you decide, listen to both conversations once again and just focus on the pronunciation of these two words.**

## ASKING QUESTIONS

Asking questions in Greek is very simple: all you do is raise the intonation of your voice at the end of the sentence to make it sound like a question. There is no auxiliary verb in Greek and no inversion of subject and verb, e.g. *you are well* ⟶ *are you well?* The written form, therefore, is exactly the same whether it is a statement or a question, apart from the question mark at the end (;).

| | | |
|---|---|---|
| [ménis stin athína]. | **Μένεις στην Αθήνα.** | *You live in Athens.* |
| [ménis stin athína]? | **Μένεις στην Αθήνα;** | *Do you live in Athens?* |
| [íste THaskála]. | **Είστε δασκάλα.** | *You are a teacher.* |
| [íste THaskála]? | **Είστε δασκάλα;** | *Are you a teacher?* |

Listen carefully once again to the conversations in the past three units, paying particular attention to how the questions are formulated and the intonation of the speaker.

## QUESTION WORDS

You already know five question words in Greek: [poo]? **πού;** *where?*, **[ti]? τι;** *what?*, [pos]? **πώς;** *how?*, [yatí] **γιατί** why? and [p-ya]? **ποια;** *who?/which?/what?* Practice using these words with the verbs that you have learned in order to form questions in Greek. For instance:

| | | |
|---|---|---|
| [poo ménis]? | **Πού μένεις;** | *Where do you live?* |
| [ti gráfis]? | **Τι γράφεις;** | *What do you write?/ What are you writing?* |
| [pos íse]? | **Πώς είσαι;** | *How are you?* |
| [p-ja kséris]? | **Ποια ξέρεις;** | *Who* (female) *do you know?* |
| [yatí íse eTHó]? | **Γιατί είσαι εδώ;** | *Why are you here?* |

### NEGATIVE STATEMENTS

To make a sentence negative in Greek, simply put the negative word [THen] **δεν** before the verb.

| | | |
|---|---|---|
| [ménoome stin athína]. | **Μένουμε στην Αθήνα.** | *We live in Athens.* |
| [THen] [ménoome stin pátra]. | **Δεν μένουμε στην Πάτρα.** | *We don't live in Patra.* |
| [íme sigraféas]. | **Είμαι συγγραφέας.** | *I am a writer.* |
| [THen] [íme arhitéktonas]. | **Δεν είμαι αρχιτέκτονας.** | *I am not an architect.* |
| [kséri anglikáa] | **Ξέρει Αγγλικά.** | *He knows English.* |
| [THen] [kséri italiká]. | **Δεν ξέρει Ιταλικά.** | *He doesn't know Italian.* |

# Practice

**1 Complete each sentence using one of the words from the box. In some cases there is more than one possible correct answer. The first one has been done for you. Once you have completed all the sentences, try to write them out in Greek script.**

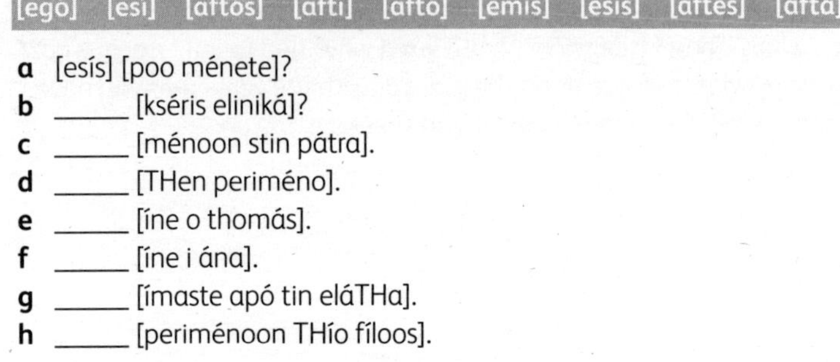

[egó] [esí] [aftós] [aftí] [aftó] [emís] [esís] [aftés] [aftá]

**a** [esís] [poo ménete]?
**b** ______ [kséris eliniká]?
**c** ______ [ménoon stin pátra].
**d** ______ [THen periméno].
**e** ______ [íne o thomás].
**f** ______ [íne i ána].
**g** ______ [ímaste apó tin eláTHa].
**h** ______ [periménoon THío fíloos].

2 **Change the following positive statements into negative ones by replacing the words after each verb with the alternatives given in the second brackets. Once you have finished, translate each of the negative sentences into English. Look at the example:**

[miláo galiká]. [eliniká] [THen miláo eliniká].

a [miláme angliká]. [yermaniká]

b [kséro ton yiáni]. [ángelo]

c [ksérete tin ioána]. [ána]

d [periméni THío fíloos]. [tris fíloos]

e [ménoon stin athína]. [sta yánena]

f [íme apó tin anglía]. [amerikí]

g [íne apó tin eláTHa]. [italía]

3 **Change the following sentences into questions and then write them in Greek script, as in the example:**

[kséro yermaniká]. [esí] [esí kséris yermaniká]? Εσύ ξέρεις Γερμανικά;

a [ménoome stin yermanía]. [esís]

b [aftós íne apó tin afstralía]. [aftí]

c [kséroon líga eliniká]. [esí]

d [aftí periménoon THío fíloos]. [aftés]

e [miláo angliká]. [esí]

f [THen miláme ispaniká]. [esís]

g [ímaste apó tin anglía]. [esís]

4 **Look at the pictures and write down the appropriate jobs in transliteration and Greek script. The third one has been done for you.**

a  

____________

____________

b 

____________

____________

c 

[nosokóma]

νοσοκόμα

d  e  f 

______________ ______________ ______________

______________ ______________ ______________

**5 Read the following sentences. According to the pictures in the previous exercise, is each one true or false?**

**a** Αυτός δεν είναι γιατρός.
**b** Αυτή είναι δασκάλα.
**c** Αυτή δεν είναι νοσοκόμα.
**d** Αυτή είναι γραμματέας.
**e** Αυτός δεν είναι σερβιτόρος.
**f** Είναι αρχιτέκτονας.

**6 03.07 Listen to this short conversation between two people in which they talk about what they do for a living. Match their jobs or professions with two of the six images in exercise 4.**

**a** The man's job ______________________________

**b** The woman's job ____________________________

**7 Match each question with the most appropriate answer.**

**a** [íse arhitéktonas]?
**b** [íste yiatrós]?
**c** [o yiánis íne servitóros]?
**d** [i ána íne sigraféas]?
**e** [o ángelos íne THáskalos]?

**1** [óhi], [íne pianístas].
**2** [óhi], [íne servitóra].
**3** [ne, íne THáskalos].
**4** [óhi, íme moosikós].
**5** [ne, íme yiatrós].

**8 Decide which of the three options is correct in each case. Then, translate the statements into English.**

| | | | | |
|---|---|---|---|---|
| **a** | [ksério] ______ [lonTHíno kalá]. | **1** [o] | **2** [to] | **3** [sto] |
| **b** | ______ [thomás íne yiatrós]. | **1** [o] | **2** [i] | **3** [to] |
| **c** | ______ [ioána íne arhitéktonas]. | **1** [o] | **2** [i] | **3** [to] |
| **d** | [méno]______ [pátra tóra]: | **1** [i] | **2** [tin] | **3** [stin] |
| **e** | [alá íme apó] ______ [yiánena]. | **1** [to] | **2** [ta] | **3** [sta] |

**9 Monster words! The following sentences have not been separated into their individual words. Insert spaces in the appropriate places to make proper sentences. Then write out each sentence in Greek script.**

**a** [ímeservitóraTHenímepianístria].
**b** [THenímesigraféas].
**c** [ísteyiatrósóhiímemoosikós].
**d** [ménokondástinthesaloníki].
**e** [THenímasteapótinanglía].

**10** 03.08 **Listen again to Conversation 2 and fill in each blank using one of the words in the box. Then write out the conversation in Greek script.**

[ne] [óhi] [poo]
[móno] [kondá] [kséris]

| | |
|---|---|
| **John** | [ána], **a** _____ [to lonTHíno]? |
| **Anna** | **b** _____ [THen kséro to lonTHíno]. [kséro] **c** _____ [tin athína]. |
| **Mary** | **d** _____ [ménis]? [ménis] **e** _____ [ston ángelo]? |
| **Anna** | **f** _____ [méno] **e** _____ [ston ángelo]. |

**11 Read the two business cards and decide which two Greek letters represent the following sounds.**

**a** /u/ as in *put*
**b** /i/ as in *pin*
**c** /g/ as in *get* or /ng/ as in *angel*

**12 Although this unit introduced some professions, your profession may not have been included. Fill out or circle all relevant personal information in this questionnaire. Get help from a Greek dictionary or a Greek friend.**

| | |
|---|---|
| **a** [ti THooliá kánis/kánete]?<br>Τι δουλειά κάνεις/κάνετε; | [íme ...]<br>Είμαι ... |
| **b** [poo THoolévis/THoolévete]?<br>Πού δουλεύεις/δουλεύετε; | [THoolévo se ...] / [THe THoolévo tóra]<br>Δουλεύω σε ... / Δεν δουλεύω τώρα. |
| **c** [ergázese / ergázeste]?<br>Εργάζεσαι; / Εργάζεστε; | [ne, ergázome] / [óhi, THen ergázome]<br>Ναι, εργάζομαι. / Όχι, δεν εργάζομαι. |
| **d** [íse/íste ánergos/ánergi]?<br>Είσαι / Είστε άνεργος / άνεργη; | [ne íme] / [óhi THen íme]<br>Ναι είμαι. / Όχι δεν είμαι. |

# Test yourself

1 How would you ask someone what their job is?
2 How would you say *I'm a teacher*?
3 If someone tells you [íme sigraféas] what is their job?
4 What is the difference between [méno sto Manchester] and [méno kondá sto Manchester]?
5 What is the difference between [íse apó tin anglía]? and [íste apó tin anglía]?
6 How would you translate these question words: [ti], [pos], [poo], [pia]?

## SELF CHECK

| | I CAN... |
|---|---|
| • | ... talk about different jobs and professions. |
| • | ... ask someone what their job is and say what my own job is. |
| • | ... say the names of different professions. |
| • | ... say which languages I speak. |
| • | ... make sentences negative and turn a statement into a question. |

# R1 Revision Test 1

1 **Which greeting would you use at the following times?** *(5 points)*
**a** 8:30 **b** 12:30 **c** 16:10 **d** 21:00 **e** 23:40

2 **Take part in the following conversation using the English as a prompt.** *(10 points)*

| | | |
|---|---|---|
| **Από εδώ ο Νίκος!** | **You** | Say *Hello Nikos! Nice to meet you!* |
| **Καλώς όρισες στη Ελλάδα!** | **You** | Say *Thanks. Nice to have met you* |
| **Είσαι από την Ελλάδα;** | **You** | Say *No, I'm from Liverpool.* |

3 **Can you come up with the appropriate question for each of the following answers?** *(10 points)*
**a** Περιμένω δύο φίλους.
**b** Είμαι καλά. Εσύ;
**c** Με λένε Άρη.
**d** Μιλάω λίγο Ελληνικά.
**e** Τώρα μένω στην Αθήνα.

4 **Match each question with the most appropriate answer. Then translate each profession mentioned into English.** *(10 points)*

| | |
|---|---|
| **a** Είσαι αρχιτέκτονας; | **1** Όχι, είναι πιανίστας. |
| **b** Είστε γιατρός; | **2** Όχι, είναι σερβιτόρα. |
| **c** Ο Γιάννης είναι σερβιτόρος; | **3** Ναι, είναι δάσκαλος. |
| **d** Η Άννα είναι συγγραφέας; | **4** Όχι, είμαι μουσικός. |
| **e** Ο Άγγελος είναι δάσκαλος; | **5** Ναι, είμαι γιατρός. |

5 **Look at the car stickers and name the countries and their corresponding languages.** *(10 points)*

| Symbol | Country | Language | Symbol | Country | Language |
|---|---|---|---|---|---|
| USA | a _____ | 1 _______ | IT | d _____ | 4 _______ |
| D | b _____ | 2 _______ | GR | e _____ | 5 _______ |
| F | c _____ | 3 _______ | | | |

6 **Choose the correct forms of the Greek word for** *the* **and** *in the* **to complete the following sentences.** *(10 points)*

| | | | |
|---|---|---|---|
| **a** [íme apó] _____ [athína]. | **1** [i] | **2** [tin] | **3** [stin] |
| **b** _____ [athína íne stin eláTHa]. | **1** [i] | **2** [tin] | **3** [stin] |
| **c** _____ [lonTHíno íne stin anglía]. | **1** [o] | **2** [to] | **3** [sto] |

d [méno] _____ [lonTHíno]. **1** [o] **2** [to] **3** [sto]

e [méno] _____ [athína]. **1** [i] **2** [tin] **3** [stin]

**7 Here are some cities in Greek. What is their correct transliteration?** *(12 points)*

| | | | | |
|---|---|---|---|---|
| **a** | ΑΘΗΝΑ: | **1** [aTHína] | **2** [athína] | **3** [athiná] |
| **b** | ΒΕΡΟΛΙΝΟ: | **1** [berolíno] | **2** [verolinó] | **3** [verolíno] |
| **c** | ΜΑΔΡΙΤΗ: | **1** [maTHríti] | **2** [mathríti] | **3** [máTHriti] |
| **d** | ΡΩΜΗ: | **1** [rómi]] | **2** [rómi] | **3** [rómh] |
| **e** | ΛΟΝΔΙΝΟ: | **1** [lonTHíno] | **2** [lonthíno] | **3** [loTHíno] |
| **f** | ΠΑΡΙΣΙ: | **1** [parísi] | **2** [papísi] | **3** [parízi] |

**8 Can you solve the crossword puzzle by translating the clues into Greek? The shaded vertical word spells out the word for architect.** *(13 points)*

**a** writer
**b** waitress
**c** pleased (to meet you)
**d** London
**e** doctor
**f** USA
**g** musician
**h** Madrid
**i** I work
**j** near
**k** pianist
**l** teacher

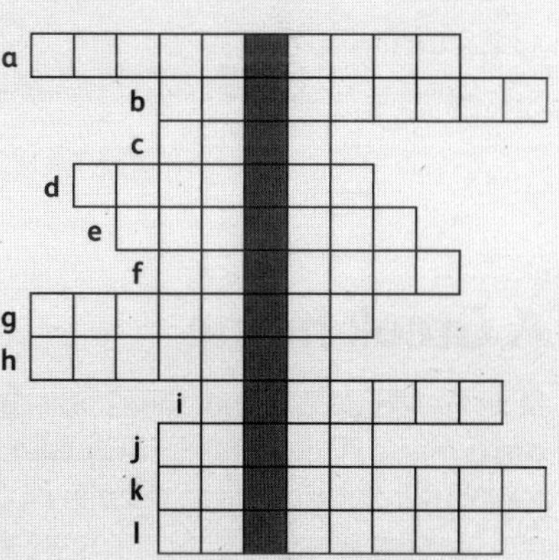

**9 Take part in the following conversation using the English as a prompt.** *(20 points)*

**Maria** [na sas sistíso] [apo'THó i maría].
**You** Say *Hi Maria! Pleased to meet you!*
**Maria** [ki'egó]. [apó poo íse]?
**You** Say *From the States. From New York. You?*
**Maria** [apó tin thesaloníki] [alá tóra méno stin athína]. [esí]?
**You** Say *I also live in Athens now and I work in an office. How about you? Do you work?*

**TOTAL: 100 POINTS**

Check your score now. Have you scored more than 60 points? If yes, congratulations! If not, reviewing the last three units might clear up any problematic points.

# 4

**In this unit you will learn how to:**

» talk about different types of accommodation.
» describe your own home.
» count from 0 to 10.
» use the plural forms of some Greek nouns.

# Μένω σε διαμέρισμα

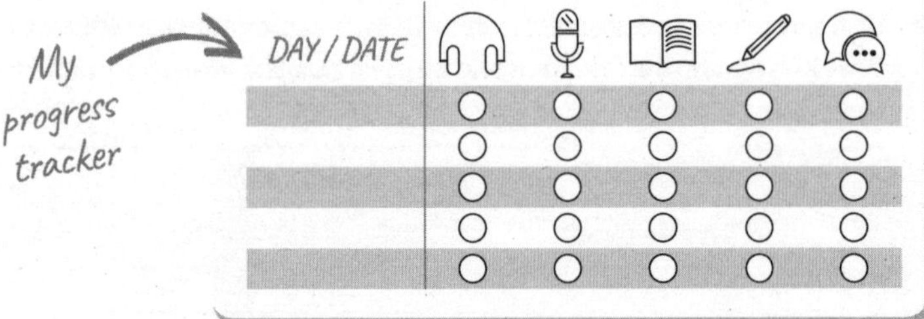


## A Greek home

Most Greeks used to own their home. Building or buying one's own [spíti] **σπίτι** *house* [THiamérizma] **διαμέρισμα** *flat/apartment* is still a dream for many in spite of the increase in property taxes and the cost of land and building permits. More and more young families rent nowadays.

Greek homes come in different architectural styles, with [sínhrona ktíria] **σύγχρονα κτίρια** *modern buildings* coexisting alongside [neoklasiká ktíria] **νεοκλασσικά κτίρια** *neoclassical buildings*. Modern apartments have fewer dividing walls, open-plan kitchens, more bathrooms, larger balconies and more colors. Building methods, however, are sometimes old-fashioned and not very time- or cost-effective. [Betón] **Μπετόν** *Concrete* is still the predominant building material compared to [xílo] **ξύλο** *wood*, [túvlo] **τούβλο** *brick*, [pétra] **πέτρα** *stone* or [métalo] **μέταλλο** *metal*. Flat, sloping and, increasingly, red-tiled roofs can be seen atop houses with white, pink, blue and other colorful facades. Local styles prevail in the countryside and on the islands, such as the famous whitewashed houses in the Cyclades or the stone houses built of gray slate in the Zagori villages in Epirus.

1 **Read the text and say if you live in a flat or a house.**
**[méno se éna] Μένω σε ένα** ______________________

2 **Give the Greek words for two building materials.**

3 **Can you associate the Greek words for μέταλλο, ξύλο with any English words?**

# Vocabulary builder

**ΚΑΤΟΙΚΙΕΣ ΚΑΙ ΔΩΜΑΤΙΑ** *TYPES OF ACCOMMODATION AND ROOMS*

1 04.01 **Listen a couple of times to the recording while you read the list of types of accommodation. Then listen again and repeat them out loud.**

***Types of accommodation***

| | | |
|---|---|---|
| [i katikía] | η κατοικία | *residence* |
| [to spíti] | το σπίτι | *house/home* |
| [to THiamérizma] | το διαμέρισμα | *apartment/flat* |
| [i garsoniéra] | η γκαρσονιέρα | *studio/bedsit* |
| [to retiré] | το ρετιρέ | *penthouse/top floor flat* |
| [i monokatikía] | η μονοκατοικία | *detached house* |
| [i polikatikía] | η πολυκατοικία | *apartment building/ block of flats* |

**LANGUAGE TIP**

Another important piece of vocabulary: [to ktírio] **το κτίριο** means *building*.

2 04.02 **Now listen to the audio while you read the words for different rooms in a house. Then listen again and repeat each word out loud.**

***Rooms***

| | | |
|---|---|---|
| [to salóni] | το σαλόνι | *living room* |
| [to kathistikó] | το καθιστικό | *sitting room* |
| [i koozína] | η κουζίνα | *kitchen* |
| [i trapezaría] | η τραπεζαρία | *dining room* |
| [to ipnoTHomátio] | το υπνοδωμάτιο | *bedroom* |
| [to bán-yo] | το μπάνιο | *bathroom* |
| [i tzamaría] | η τζαμαρία | *conservatory* |

**3 04.03 Listen carefully to the audio. You will hear different people telling you where they live. Now give each sentence a letter from a to d according to the order in which you heard the descriptions. Then listen again and repeat each sentence out loud.**

_____ [eghó méno se mya monokatikía] Εγώ μένω σε μια μονοκατοικία.

_____ [eghó méno se éna THiamérizma] Εγώ μένω σε ένα διαμέρισμα.

_____ [eghó méno se éna spíti] Εγώ μένω σε ένα σπίτι.

_____ [eghó méno se mya polikatikía] Εγώ μένω σε μια πολυκατοικία.

# Conversation 1 In a house?

## NEW WORDS AND EXPRESSIONS 1

**04.04 Listen to the words and expressions that are used in the conversation. Note their meaning.**

| | | |
|---|---|---|
| [se] | σε | *in* |
| [mía] | μία | *a, an/one* |
| [éhi] | έχει | *it has* |
| [tésera] | τέσσερα | *four* |
| [THomátia] | δωμάτια | *rooms* |
| [éna] | ένα | *a/an, one* |
| [kéna] | κι ένα | *and a/an/one* |
| [mikró] | μικρό | *small* |
| [hol] | χωλ / χολ | *hallway* |
| [megálo] | μεγάλο | *big, large* |

04.05 *Anna describes her flat to John and Mary.*

**1 Listen to the conversation a couple of times. How many rooms does Anna have?**

| | | |
|---|---|---|
| **Mary** | [ménis] [se spíti]? | *Do you live in a house?* |
| **Anna** | [óhi], [méno] [se THiamérizma] [se mía polikatikía]. [éhi] [tésera THomátia], [mía koozína], [éna bánio] [kéna mikró hol]. | *No, I live in an apartment in a block of flats. It has four rooms, a kitchen, a bathroom and a small hallway.* |
| **Mary** | [po-po], [íne megálo]! | *Wow, it's big!* |

**Mary** Μένεις σε σπίτι;

**Άννα** Όχι, μένω σε διαμέρισμα σε μία πολυκατοικία. Έχει τέσσερα δωμάτια, μία κουζίνα, ένα μπάνιο, κι ένα μικρό χωλ.

**Mary** Πω, πω, είναι μεγάλο!

**2 Now read the conversation again and answer the questions.**

**a** Can you name two rooms in Anna's flat?

**b** To help you memorize the new words and expressions, can you think of any English words that sound like the Greek words for *big* and *small*?

**3 Listen again to the conversation and pay special attention to the words which run together. Practice speaking the part of Anna and pay particular attention to your pronunciation.**

# Language discovery 1

**1 In Conversation 1 there are different indefinite articles (similar to the English *a* or *an*). Read or listen to the conversation again and decide which Greek article is used in each case.**

**a** a hallway

**b** a bathroom

**c** a kitchen

**d** a block of flats

**2 The Greek words for *a* or *an* are also used to say the number *one*. Read or listen to the conversation again and try to find the numbers *one* and *four* as follows.**

**a** one (for neuter nouns)
**b** one (for feminine nouns)
**c** four (for neuter nouns)

Did you solve the last two exercises in Language discovery 1 without any problems?

## 1 THE INDEFINITE ARTICLE

In Conversation 1 Anna says [mía koozína] **μία κουζίνα** *a kitchen* and [éna bánio] **ένα μπάνιο** *a bathroom*. All you need to remember for now is that [mía] **μία** goes with feminine nouns and [éna] **ένα** goes with neuter nouns. The following table will give you an overview of the different forms of the indefinite article:

| | Masculine | Feminine | Neuter |
|---|---|---|---|
| Nominative | **ένας** | **μία/μια** | **ένα** |
| | **Ένας γιατρός μένει σε ένα σπίτι.** *A doctor lives in a house.* | **Μία δασκάλα γράφει βιβλία.** *A teacher writes books.* | **Ένα μεγάλο σπίτι δεν είναι για μένα.** *A big house is not for me.* |
| Accusative | **έναν** | **μία/μια** | **ένα** |
| | **Ξέρω έναν γιατρό.** *I know a doctor.* | **Μένω σε μία πολυκατοικία.** *I live in a block of flats.* | **Έχω ένα μεγάλο σαλόνι.** *I have a big living room.* |

In contrast to English, where *a* changes to *an* according to the sound of the word that follows the article, in Greek the four different forms of the indefinite article are used according to grammatical rules, i.e. the gender and case of the noun that follows.

## 2 THE NUMBERS 1–10

04.06 You are going to listen to the numbers 1–10. Listen carefully a couple of times and pay special attention to the numbers *one*, *three* and *four*, which have more than one form. Then listen again and repeat out loud.

| | | |
|---|---|---|
| [énas]<br>[mía]<br>[éna] | **ένας** (m)<br>**μία** (f)<br>**ένα** (n) | *one* |

| [THío] | **δύο** | *two* |
|---|---|---|
| [tris]<br>[tría] | **τρεις** (m/f)<br>**τρία** (n) | *three* |
| [téseris]<br>[tésera] | **τέσσερις** (m/f)<br>**τέσσερα** (n) | *four* |
| [pénde] | **πέντε** | *five* |
| [éksi] | **έξι** | *six* |
| [eptá]/[eftá] | **επτά/εφτά** | *seven* |
| [októ]/[ohtó] | **οκτώ/οχτώ** | *eight* |
| [enéa]/[eniá] | **εννέα/εννιά** | *nine* |
| [THéka] | **δέκα** | *ten* |

**LANGUAGE TIP**

[miTHén] **μηδέν** stands for null or zero. The numbers *one, three* and *four* have more than one form because they have to agree with the gender (masculine, feminine or neuter) of the noun. The numbers *seven, eight* and *nine* have two different pronunciations; both are frequently used but the second is more informal than the first. Have you also noticed that some of these Greek numbers are hidden in English words? Can you guess which number is behind the following words: *decathlon, duet, pentagon or trigonometry?*

# Conversation 2 Big house!

## NEW WORDS AND EXPRESSIONS 2

**04.07 Listen to the words and expressions that are used in the conversation and note their meaning. Then listen again and repeat after the speaker.**

| | | |
|---|---|---|
| [sálo] | σ' άλλο | *in a different* (lit. *another*) |
| [pósa] | πόσα | *how many* |
| [mazí me] | μαζί με | *along with* |
| [vesé] | WC | *guest toilet* |
| [pénde] | πέντε | *five* |

04.08 *Angelos now describes his new house to his friends.*

**1 Listen to the conversation a couple of times. Can you say how many bedrooms there are?**

| | | |
|---|---|---|
| **Angelos** | [ksérete] [egó méno] [sálo spíti tóra]. [íne mía monokatikía]. | *You know, I live in a different house now. It's a detached house.* |
| **Mary** | [pósa THomátia éhi]? | *How many rooms does it have?* |
| **Angelos** | [éhi] [éna megálo salóni], [mazí me mía trapezaría], [éna bánio] [kéna vesé], [ke pénde ipnoTHomátia]. | *It has one big living room, along with a dining room, a bathroom and a guest toilet, and five bedrooms.* |
| **Mary** | [megálo spíti]! | *Big house!* |
| **John** | [polí megálo spíti]! | *Very big house!* |

| | |
|---|---|
| **Άγγελος** | Ξέρετε, εγώ μένω σ' άλλο σπίτι τώρα. Είναι μία μονοκατοικία. |
| **Mary** | Πόσα δωμάτια έχει; |
| **Άγγελος** | Έχει ένα μεγάλο σαλόνι, μαζί με μία τραπεζαρία, ένα μπάνιο κι ένα WC και πέντε υπνοδωμάτια. |
| **Mary** | Μεγάλο σπίτι! |
| **John** | Πολύ μεγάλο σπίτι! |

**2 Now read the conversation and answer the questions.**

**a** What kind of house is it?

**b** Can you list all the rooms in the house?

**3 Listen again to the conversation and pay special attention to the words which run together. Practice speaking the part of Angelos and pay particular attention to your pronunciation.**

# Language discovery 2

**1 The two conversations in this unit include the following four phrases in which Greek adjectives are used. Find the Greek for these four phrases. What do you notice about the adjective endings?**

**a** big house
**b** different house
**c** small hallway
**d** big living room

**2** **You have already learned the plural forms of two neuter nouns (δωμάτι-ο ⟶ δωμάτι-α and βιβλί-ο ⟶ βιβλί-α). Can you use what you have learned to work out the plural forms of the following neuter nouns in this unit?**

**a** μπάνι-ο
**b** κτίρι-ο
**c** ξύλ-ο
**d** μέταλλ-ο

**3** **The word for *and* is either *και* or *κι* in Greek. Both conversations in this unit had an example with the second word, namely *κι ένα μικρό χολ* and *κι ένα WC*. Can you guess if the meaning will change if we replace *κι* with *και* or the pronunciation of the words which run together?**

## 1 ADJECTIVES

If you look up an adjective in a Greek dictionary, you will find three different forms: masculine, feminine and neuter. This may seem like a lot to learn but you may find it easier if you learn each adjective as part of an adjective + noun combination, as in Language discovery exercise 1. Here is how you might find the adjectives for that exercise listed in a dictionary:

**άλλος, άλλη, άλλο** or **άλλ-ος/-η/-ο**

**μικρός, μικρή, μικρό** or **μικρ-ός/-ή/-ό**

**μεγάλος, μεγάλη, μεγάλο** or **μεγάλ-ος/-η/-ο**

Apart from these three examples one can come up with other adjective groups which have different endings. Nevertheless, this adjective group is the most important one. The Grammar section at the back of the book will give you a better overall view.

## 2 PLURAL FORMS

Nouns follow certain rules regarding their plural formation. The following list allows you to learn three plural endings as a first step. The list is not exhaustive but the three plural endings, **-οι, -ες, -α**, presented here are important and very common to many nouns.

***Masculine nouns***

| | | | | | | |
|---|---|---|---|---|---|---|
| [o fílos] | **ο φίλος** | *friend* | ⟶ | [i fíli] | **οι φίλοι** | *friends* |
| [o THáskalos] | **ο δάσκαλος** | *teacher* | ⟶ | [i THáskali] | **οι δάσκαλοι** | *teachers* |

*Feminine nouns*

| | | | | | | |
|---|---|---|---|---|---|---|
| [i THaskála] | **η δασκάλα** | *teacher* | ⟶ | [i THaskáles] | **οι δασκάλες** | *teachers* |
| [i koozína] | **η κουζίνα** | *kitchen* | ⟶ | [i koozínes] | **οι κουζίνες** | *kitchens* |

*Neuter nouns*

| | | | | | | |
|---|---|---|---|---|---|---|
| [to vivlío] | **το βιβλίο** | *book* | ⟶ | [ta vivlía] | **τα βιβλία** | *books* |
| [to ktírio] | **το κτίριο** | *building* | ⟶ | [ta ktíria] | **τα κτίρια** | *buildings* |

## 3 ONE WORD, TWO MEANINGS?

It is easy to assume that every word has just one meaning but, as you will know from English, this is not always the case! There are two words in this unit which you met in Unit 1; here, however, they have a different meaning:

| | | |
|---|---|---|
| [pos se léne]? | **Πώς σε λένε;** | *What's your name?* (lit. *How do they call you?*) |
| [méno se éna THiamérizma]. | **Μένω σε ένα διαμέρισμα.** | *I live in an apartment.* |
| [me léne ána]. | **Με λένε Άννα.** | My name is Anna (lit. *They call me Anna*). |
| [... me trapezaría] | **... με τραπεζαρία** | ... *with dining room* |

These two words, **σε** and **με**, function both as pronouns, meaning *you* and *me* respectively, and as prepositions, meaning *in* and *with* respectively. As a rule of thumb, when these words function as pronouns they are usually with verbs, i.e. **με λένε, σε λένε**, etc. and when they function as prepositions they are usually with nouns, i.e. **με μία κουζίνα, σε ένα σπίτι**.

## 4 CONTRACTIONS

You will already be familiar with English contractions (such as *do not* ⟶ *don't*; *I have* ⟶ *I've*). These exist in Greek too and you have already encountered some in the previous units.

### Unit 1

[sto] **στο** = [se] + [to] *at the*

[stin] **στην** = [se] + [tin] *in the*

### Unit 2

[kegó] or [ki egó] **κι εγώ** = [ke] + [egó] **και εγώ** *and I/me too*

### Unit 3

[ston] **στον** = [se] + [ton] *at/in/to the*

### Unit 4

[kéna] or [ki éna] **κι ένα** = [ke] + [éna] **και ένα** *and one*

[sálo] **σ'άλλο** = [se] [álo] **σε άλλο** *in another*

**LANGUAGE TIP**

It is not possible to use the uncontracted forms [se] + [to], [se] + [tin] and [se] + [ton].

# Practice

**1 Match each word on the left with a word that means either the same or the opposite on the right.**

| | |
|---|---|
| **a** [kondá] | **1** [THiamérizma] |
| **b** [spíti] | **2** [kathistikó] |
| **c** [salóni] | **3** [megálo] |
| **d** [koozína] | **4** [makriá] (*far*) |
| **e** [mikró] | **5** [trapezaría] |

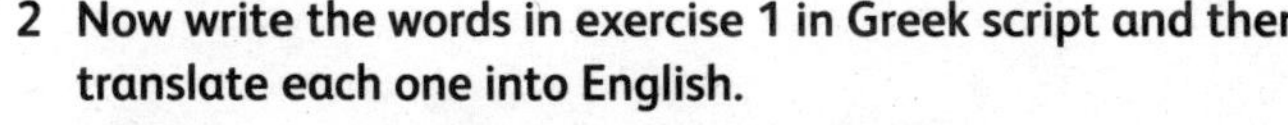

**2 Now write the words in exercise 1 in Greek script and then translate each one into English.**

**3 Match each question with its corresponding answer.**

| | |
|---|---|
| **a** [poo ménete]? Πού μένετε; | **1** [óhi], [alá íne kondá]. Όχι, αλλά είναι κοντά. |
| **b** [íne megálo]? Είναι μεγάλο; | **2** [óhi], [íne mikró]. Όχι, είναι μικρό. |
| **c** [íne] [stin athína]? Είναι στην Αθήνα; | **3** [i rafína] [íne] [éna limáni] Η Ραφήνα είναι ένα λιμάνι. |
| **d** [poo íne]? Πού είναι; | **4** [méno] [se THiamérizma]. Μένω σε διαμέρισμα. |
| **e** [ti íne] [i rafína]? Τι είναι η Ραφήνα; | **5** [íne sti rafína] Είναι στη Ραφήνα. |

**INSIGHT**

[rafína] **Ραφήνα** is a [limáni] **λιμάνι** *port* on the Aegean coast. Boats leave from there to many islands in the Cyclades, such as Andros, Tinos and Mykonos.

**4 Put these sentences in the correct order to form a dialogue.**

a ______ [éna salóni] [kéna ipnoTHomátio]. Ένα σαλόνι κι ένα υπνοδωμάτιο.
b ______ [pósa THomátia éhi]? Πόσα δωμάτια έχει;
c ______ [éhis megálo spíti]? Έχεις μεγάλο σπίτι;
d ______ [móno THío THomátia]. Μόνο δύο δωμάτια.
e ______ [óhi polí megálo]. Όχι πολύ μεγάλο.
f ______ [ti THomátia]? Τι δωμάτια;

**5 Here is a plan of an apartment. Can you write the name of each room?**

a ________________ d ________________
b ________________ e ________________
c ________________ f ________________

**6 Learning numbers is an essential part of studying a language. Here is a list of emergency numbers in Greece. Can you read them out loud, number by number? The number 1 reads as [éna] ένα.**

**a** 100 – Police
**b** 112 – European Emergency Number
**c** 134 – Phone Operator
**d** 166 – Emergency Medical Assistance
**e** 169 – International Operator
**f** 171 – Tourist Police
**g** 199 – Fire Department

**7 The answers to the following puzzle are different types of homes and rooms. Can you solve it? The vertical shaded word spells out the Greek for living room. Write the words in a phonetic representation and not in Greek script.**

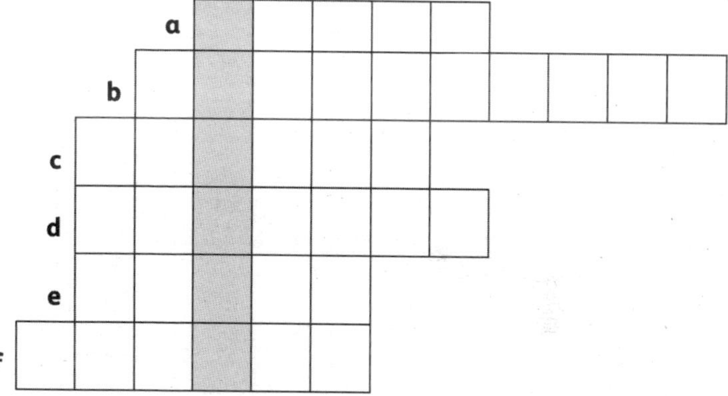


**a** house/home
**b** flat/apartment
**c** living room
**d** kitchen
**e** bathroom
**f** penthouse/top floor flat/ apartment

**8 Now write each word from the puzzle in Greek script.**

**a** ____________________
**b** ____________________
**c** ____________________
**d** ____________________
**e** ____________________
**f** ____________________
**g** (shaded word) ____________________

**9** 04.09 **Listen again to Conversation 2 of this unit. Choose a word from the box to complete each line of the conversation.**

| [megálo] [sálo] [polí][mazí] [pénde] [pósa] |
|---|

| | |
|---|---|
| **Angelos** | [ksérete] [egó méno] **a** _____ [spíti tóra]. [íne mía monokatikía]. |
| **Mary** | **b** _____ [THomátia éhi]? |
| **Angelos** | [éhi] [éna] **c** _____ [salóni], **d** _____ [me mía trapezaría], [éna bánio] [kéna vesé], [ke] **e** _____ [ipnoTHomátia]. |
| **Mary** | [megálo spíti]! |
| **John** | **f** _____ [megálo spíti]! |

**10 Work out the correct form of the following adjectives in context.**

| | |
|---|---|
| **a μεγάλ-ος/-η/-ο κουζίνα** | **c καλ-ός/-ή/-ό δασκάλα** |
| **b μικρ-ός/-ή/-ό σπίτι** | **d άλλ-ος/-η/-ο σερβιτόρος** |

**11 Which indefinite article (*ένας, μία/μια, ένα, έναν*) completes each sentence?**

**a** _________________ δασκάλα γράφει βιβλία.
**b** Μένω σε _________________ μονοκατοικία.
**c** Ξέρετε _________________ καλό γιατρό.
**d** Δουλεύετε σε _________________ ταβέρνα;
**e** _________________ φίλος μου έχει σπίτι στην Πάτρα.
**f** Μένουμε σε _________________ μεγάλο διαμέρισμα.

# Test yourself

**1 You are now at the end of Unit 4. Let's see how easy the following questions are for you.**

- **a** What are the three Greek words for *bathroom*, *toilet* and *guest toilet*?
- **b** Name four rooms in a house (not counting the words in question 1 above).
- **c** Name four different types of home.
- **d** How do you say *I live in a detached house in Belfast*?
- **e** Give the opposites of [megálo], [kondá] and [monokatikía].
- **f** Give words that mean the same as [salóni], [bánio] and [spíti].

**2 Here is an advert for ΔΕΗ (Δημόσια Εταιρία Ηλεκτρισμού), Greece's state-run electricity company. Can you find the Greek words for** *electricity* **and** *programmes*? **Can you also guess the meaning of [THímos] in the words [THimósia] δημόσια above as *public* or [THimokratía] δημοκρατία as *democracy*?**

**3 Fill out the table below with the singular and/or plural form of the following nouns.**

| Masculine | Feminine | Neuter |
|---|---|---|
| a **ο φίλος** | c **η τζαμαρία** | e **το σπίτι** |
| b **οι δάσκαλοι** | d **οι κουζίνες** | f **τα μπάνια** |

## SELF CHECK

| | I CAN... |
|---|---|
| • | ... talk about different types of accommodation. |
| • | ... describe my own home. |
| • | ... count from 0 to 10. |
| • | ... use the plural forms of some Greek nouns. |

# 5

**In this unit you will learn how to:**

» ask questions about family and children.
» describe your own family.
» ask how old someone is and say how old you are.
» count from 11 to 100.

# Μια μεγάλη οικογένεια

My progress tracker

| DAY / DATE | | | | | |
|---|---|---|---|---|---|
| | ○ | ○ | ○ | ○ | ○ |
| | ○ | ○ | ○ | ○ | ○ |
| | ○ | ○ | ○ | ○ | ○ |
| | ○ | ○ | ○ | ○ | ○ |
| | ○ | ○ | ○ | ○ | ○ |

## Greek names

Greek names often have a particular meaning, e.g. [elpíTHa] **Ελπίδα** *Elpida* means *hope*, [aghápi] **Αγάπη** *Aghapi* means *love*, [zoí] **Ζωή** *Zoe* means *life*, [sotíris] **Σωτήρης** *Sotiris* means *saviour* and [ángelos] **'Αγγελος** Angelo means *bearer of news*.

When Greeks are named after saints, that saint's day becomes the person's name day. Name days are observed and celebrated more in Greece than people's actual birthdays. The dates of several name days are very widely known, such as [vasílis] **Βασίλης** *Bill* on 1 January, [yiánis] **Γιάννης** *John the Baptist* on 7 January and [yioryía] **Γιωργία** *Georgia* on 23 April. Most birthdays will pass by unnoticed except perhaps for children's birthdays, which are often celebrated at fast-food restaurants or special playgrounds. Adults will usually only celebrate their name day.

It is still customary to name a child after its grandparents. Even the order of name giving is set, starting with the grandparents on the paternal side. Of course, there are always exceptions, which can lead to a serious objection from the grandparent concerned! Most Greek children are baptized, the majority in the Greek Orthodox faith. Greek saints' names are still dominant, in order to respect traditional name-giving conventions and to satisfy religious views. The words [moró] **μωρό** *baby* or [bébis] **μπέμπης** *baby boy* and [béba] **μπέμπα** *baby girl* are used for unbaptized children. So, any unbaptized child, whatever their age, will be addressed as *baby* until the holy day of baptism!

Another interesting cultural point here is that most first names have a *nickname* alternative. Sometimes the nickname can be deciphered from the main name but often not! Some examples here include: Πάνος from Παναγιώτης, Γιώτα from Παναγιώτα, Γωγώ from Γεωργία, or Άλκης from Αλκιβιάδης.

---

**What are the Greek words for *love*, *hope* and *life*? Do you still remember that male names take a special form when addressing someone directly? Some examples here include: Άρη not ΄Αρης, Γιώργο not Γιώργος, Γιάννη not Γιάννη, or Άγγελε not Άγγελος.**

---

# Vocabulary builder

**ΟΙΚΟΓΕΝΕΙΑΚΟ ΔΕΝΤΡΟ** *FAMILY TREE*

**1** 05.01 **Anna describes her family. Read the words in the family tree as you listen carefully a couple of times and then listen once again and repeat.**

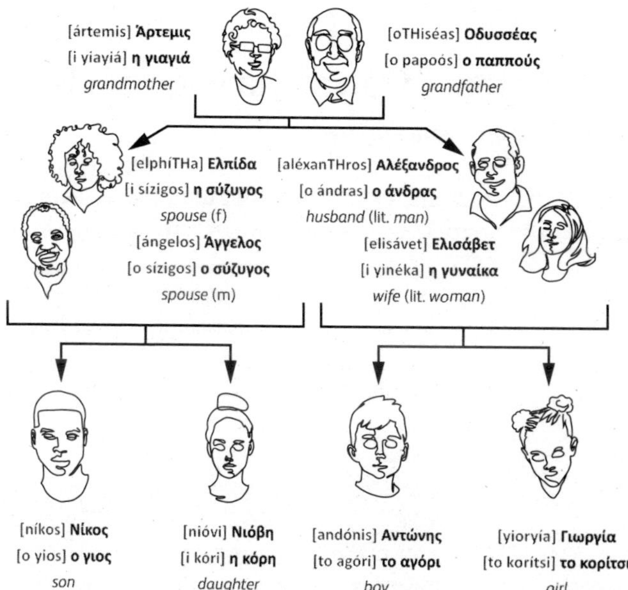

**2** **05.02 Look at the words and complete the missing translations. Then listen and try to imitate the pronunciation of the speaker.**

| Masculine | Feminine | Neuter |
|---|---|---|
| [o patéras] | [i mitéra] | [to peTHí] |
| **ο πατέρας** | **η μητέρα** | **το παιδί** |
| *father* | __________ | *child* |
| [o papoós] | [i yiayiá] | |
| **ο παππούς** | **η γιαγιά** | |
| __________ | *grandmother* | |
| [o yios] | [i kóri] | [to moró] |
| **ο γιος** | **η κόρη** | **το μωρό** |
| *son* | *daughter* | *baby* |
| [o egonós] | [i egoní] | [to egóni] |
| **ο εγγονός** | **η εγγονή** | **το εγγόνι** |
| __________ | *granddaughter* | *grandchild* |
| [o aTHelfós] | [i aTHelfí] | |
| **ο αδελφός** | **η αδελφή** | |
| *brother* | __________ | |
| [o (e)ksáTHelfos] | [i (e)ksaTHélfi] | |
| **ο (ε)ξάδελφος** | **η (ε)ξαδέλφη** | |
| *cousin* (m) | *cousin* (f) | |

**LANGUAGE TIP**

Words for diverse families nowadays include: [thetós patéras] **θετός πατέρας** *stepfather*, [thetí mitéra] **θετή μητέρα** *stepmother*, [eterothalís aTHelfós] **ετεροθαλής αδελφός** *stepbrother*; [eterothalí saTHelfí] **ετεροθαλής αδελφή** *stepsister*; or [o/i síndrofos] **ο/η σύντροφος** *partner (m/f)*.

# Conversation 1 Do you have a family?

## NEW WORDS AND EXPRESSIONS 1

**05.03 Read the words and expressions that are used in the next conversation and note their meanings. Then listen and repeat after the speaker.**

| | | |
|---|---|---|
| [páme] | πάμε; | *Shall we go?* (lit. *we go*) |
| [misó leptó] | μισό λεπτό | *just a minute* (lit. *half a minute*) |
| [áli] | άλλη | *another* |
| [erótisi] | ερώτηση | *question* |
| [éhete] | έχετε; | *Do you have?* (pl/fml) |
| [peTHiá] | παιδιά | *children* |
| [éhoome] | έχουμε | *we have* |
| [agóri] | αγόρι | *boy* |
| [pénde hronón] | πέντε χρονών | *five years old* (lit. *five of years*) |
| [trión hronón] | τριών χρονών | *three years old* (lit. *three of years*) |

| | | |
|---|---|---|
| [éhis] | έχεις; | *Do you have?* (sing/infml) |
| [ikoyénia] | οικογένεια | *family* |
| [ého] | έχω | *I have* |
| [megáli] | μεγάλη | *large, big* |

05.04 *Anna is trying to get some personal information about Mary and John.*

**1 Listen to the conversation a couple of times. Do they have any children?**

| | | |
|---|---|---|
| **Angelos** | [páme spíti tóra]? | *Shall we go home now?* |
| **Anna** | [misó leptó]. [áli mía erótisi]: [éhete peTHiá]? | *Just a minute. One more question: Do you have any children?* |
| **Mary** | [ne]. [éhoome] [THío peTHiá]: [éna agóri], [pénde hronón], [kéna korítsi], [trión hronón]. | *Yes. We have two children: one boy, five years old, and one girl, three years old.* |
| **John** | [esí]? [éhis ikoyénia]? | *How about you? Do you have a family?* |
| **Anna** | [ne]. [ého] [mía megáli ikoyénia]. | *Yes. I have a big family.* |

| | |
|---|---|
| **Άγγελος** | Πάμε σπίτι τώρα; |
| **Άννα** | Μισό λεπτό. Άλλη μία ερώτηση: έχετε παιδιά; |
| **Mary** | Ναι. Έχουμε δύο παιδιά: ένα αγόρι, πέντε χρονών, κι ένα κορίτσι, τριών χρονών. |
| **John** | Εσύ; Έχεις οικογένεια; |
| **Άννα** | Ναι. Έχω μία μεγάλη οικογένεια. |

**2 Read the conversation and answer the questions.**

**a** Find the Greek phrase that means *Just a minute*.

**b** How old is Mary and John's son?

**c** And how old is their daughter?

**3 Listen again and pay special attention to the words which run together. Practice speaking the part of Anna or Mary and pay particular attention to your pronunciation.**

# Language discovery 1

**1 Find the following phrases in the conversation. What do you notice about the underlined words?**

**a** Do you have a family?

**b** five years old

**c** Just a moment.

**d** Do you have any children?

**2 Find the following numbers in the conversation. Which one has something different about it compared to what you learned in Unit 4?**

**a** one

**b** two

**c** three

**d** five

**3 Find the following neuter nouns in the conversation. Can you work out their singular or plural form? One is already given in the plural.**

| | |
|---|---|
| **a** house/home ________________ | houses/homes ________________ |
| **b** boy ________________ | boys ________________ |
| **c** girl ________________ | girls ________________ |
| **d** child ________________ | children ________________ |

**4 The conversation included four different verb forms of [ého] έχω *to have*. First, write them out. Which two verb forms were not in the conversation?**

### 1 WORD FOR WORD

When you learn another language, it is natural to try to translate everything word for word and to find an equivalent for each word in the other language. As you may already have realized, language does not always work out as conveniently as that! In past units you have encountered extra Greek words that are not present in the English, e.g. [íme i ána] **Είμαι η Άννα** *I am (the) Anna* or [íme apó to lonTHíno] **Είμαι από το Λονδίνο** *I am from (the) London*. In this unit, you will learn structures containing extra English words that are not present in Greek, for instance in the four examples of the first Language discovery activity. Keep an eye open for more of these in future units and be aware that it will be easier to learn them as chunks of language rather than to attempt a word-for-word translation into English.

## 2 SAYING YOUR AGE

Be careful if you are saying an age that includes any of the numbers one, three or four. In these cases, you should use the words [enós] **ενός** *one*, [trión] **τριών** *three* and [tesáron] **τεσσάρων** *four* respectively. Only these numbers will change. Look at the following examples.

| | | |
|---|---|---|
| [íme triánda hronón] | **Είμαι τριάντα χρονών.** | *I'm 30 years old.* |
| [íme triánda enós hronón]. | **Είμαι τριάντα ενός χρονών.** | *I'm 31 years old.* |
| [íme triánda THío hronón]. | **Είμαι τριάντα δύο χρονών.** | *I'm 32 years old.* |
| [íme triánda trión hronón]. | **Είμαι τριάντα τριών χρονών.** | *I'm 33 years old.* |
| [íme triánda tesáron hronón]. | **Είμαι τριάντα τεσσάρων χρονών.** | *I'm 34 years old.* |
| [íme triánda pénde hronón]. | **Είμαι τριάντα πέντε χρονών.** | *I'm 35 years old.* |

**LANGUAGE TIP**

When saying your age, remember that the word *old*, as in *I'm 30 years old*, is not used in Greek. You simply say *I'm 30 years*.

## 3 NEUTER PLURAL

When you completed exercise 3 in Language discovery 1 you will have seen that the plural of neuter nouns is normally formed by adding the ending **-α** to the noun. The four words used in this exercise are:

**σπίτι ⟶ σπίτια**

**αγόρι ⟶ αγόρια**

**κορίτσι ⟶ κορίτσια**

**παιδί ⟶ παιδιά**

Note that the sound of the letter **ι** changes when it becomes part of the plural ending. In the singular form it has an /i/ sound as in the word *pin*. When the letter **α** is added to make the plural form, it changes its sound to /y/. Look at the transliteration of the four words and their plural forms:

[spíti] ⟶ [spit-ya]

[aghóri] ⟶ [aghór-ya]

[korítsi] ⟶ [koríts-ya]

[peTHí] ⟶ [peTH-ya]

This phonetic rule also sometimes applies to other vowel combinations. Some examples here include: [bán-yo] **μπάνιο** *bathroom*, [bán-ya] **μπάνια** *bathrooms*, [ya-yá] **γιαγιά** *grandmother*, [yos] **γιος** *son*, [yá-nis] **Γιάννης** John/Yannis, [ya] **γεια** hello, etc. As with many other rules, this one unfortunately comes with its exceptions. Some examples here are: [yor-gí-a] **Γιωργία** *Georgia*, [ktí-ri-o] **κτίριο** *building*, [ktí-ri-a] **κτίρια** *buildings*, [vi-vlí-o] **βιβλίο** *book*, [vi-vlí-a] **βιβλία** *books*, etc. The vowel combinations in the second set of examples are pronounced separately. When in doubt, ask a Greek speaker about the right pronunciation.

# Conversation 2 How old are they?

## NEW WORDS AND EXPRESSIONS 2

**05.05 Read the words and expressions that are used in the next conversation and note their meanings. Then listen and repeat after the speaker.**

| | | |
|---|---|---|
| [ándras] | άντρας | *husband* |
| [moo] | μου | *my* |
| [servitóros] | σερβιτόρος | *server* |
| [ton léne] | τον λένε | *his name is* (lit. *they call him*) |
| [agória] | αγόρια | *boys* |
| [ta] | τα | *the* (used with neuter plural nouns) |
| [ta onómatá toos] | τα ονόματά τους | *their names* |
| [póson hronón] | πόσων χρονών | *how old* |
| [THóTHeka] | δώδεκα | *twelve* |
| [THéka] | δέκα | *ten* |
| [eptá] | επτά | *seven* |
| [ah]! | αχ! | *Oh!* |
| [yiatí]? | γιατί; | *Why?* |
| [févyete] | φεύγετε; | *Are you leaving?* (pl/fml) |
| [thélo na] | θέλω να | *I want to.* |
| [sas] | σας | *you* |
| [ksanaTHó] | ξαναδώ | *see again* |
| [na sas ksanaTHó] | να σας ξαναδώ | *to see you* (pl) *again* |

**05.06** *Anna describes her family to Mary and John and hopes to see them again soon.*

**1 Listen to the conversation a couple of times. How many children does Anna have?**

| | | |
|---|---|---|
| **Anna** | [o ándras moo] [íne servitóros]. [ton léne] [yiórgo]. [éhoome] [tría peTHiá]: [THío agória] [kéna korítsi]. [ta onómata toos] [íne] [yiánis], [THéspina] [ke níkos]. | *My husband is a waiter. His name is Yiorgos. We have three children: two boys and one girl. Their names are Yiannis, Despina and Nikos.* |
| **Mary** | [póson hronón íne]? | *How old are they?* |
| **Anna** | [o yiánis] [íne THóTHeka], [I THéspina] [íne THéka] [ke o níkos] [íne eptá]. [ah]! [yiatí févyete]? [thélo] [na sas ksanaTHó]! | *Yiannis is twelve, Despina is ten and Nikos is seven. Oh! Why are you leaving? I want to see you again!* |

**Άννα** Ο άντρας μου είναι σερβιτόρος. Τον λένε Γιώργο. Έχουμε τρία παιδιά: δύο αγόρια κι ένα κορίτσι. Τα ονόματά τους είναι Γιάννης, Δέσποινα και Νίκος.

**Mary** Πόσων χρονών είναι;

**Άννα** Ο Γιάννης είναι δώδεκα, η Δέσποινα είναι δέκα κι ο Νίκος είναι επτά. Αχ! Γιατί φεύγετε; Θέλω να σας ξαναδώ!

**2 Read the conversation and answer the questions.**

**a** What does Anna's husband do?

**b** How old are her two sons?

**c** And how old is Anna's daughter?

**3 Listen again and pay special attention to the words which run together. Practice speaking the part of Anna and pay particular attention to your pronunciation.**

# Language discovery 2

**1 Find the following phrases in the conversation. What do you notice about the word order? Is an article necessary in Greek?**

**a** my husband **b** their names

**2 Phrases a and c are from Conversation 2. One word has been replaced in each to create phrases b and d. Can you translate all four phrases? What role do the underlined words play?**

**a** <u>Τον</u> λένε Γιώργο.

**b** <u>Σας</u> λένε Γιώργο.

**c** Θέλω να <u>σας</u> ξαναδώ!

**d** Θέλω να <u>τον</u> ξαναδώ!

**3 Find the following numbers in the conversation. Which number has more than one possible form in Greek?**

**a** seven **b** ten **c** twelve

## 1 POSSESSIVE PRONOUNS

You learned about subject or personal pronouns (*I*, *you*, *they*, etc.) in Unit 2. This unit introduces possessive pronouns, which are words such as *my*, *your*, *his*, *our*, etc. There are two important differences to note between Greek and English:

**a** In Greek these words come after the noun they modify, whereas in English they come before the noun, i.e. [to spíti moo] **το σπίτι μου** *my house* /my home.

**b** An article is used before the noun in Greek. Look at the examples:

| Masculine | Feminine | Neuter |
|---|---|---|
| [o ándras moo]<br>**ο άντρας μου**<br>*my husband* | [i yinéka moo]<br>**η γυναίκα μου**<br>*my wife* | [to spíti moo]<br>**το σπίτι μου**<br>*my house* |
| [o papoós moo]<br>**ο παππούς μου**<br>*my grandfather* | [i yiayiá moo]<br>**η γιαγιά μου**<br>*my grandmother* | [to THomátió moo]<br>**το δωμάτιό μου**<br>*my room* |
| [o yios moo]<br>**ο γιος μου**<br>*my son* | [i kóri moo]<br>**η κόρη μου**<br>*my daughter* | [to peTHí moo]<br>**το παιδί μου**<br>*my child* |

Study the table to become familiar with the full list of possessive pronouns. Note that the word for *his* and *its* is the same in Greek: [too] **του**.

| | | |
|---|---|---|
| [moo] | **μου** | *my* |
| [soo] | **σου** | *your* (sing/infml) |
| [too] | **του** | *his, its* |
| [tis] | **της** | *her* |
| [mas] | **μας** | *our* |
| [sas] | **σας** | *your* (pl/fml) |
| [toos] | **τους** | *their* |

## 2 PERSONAL PRONOUNS

One of the first things you learned to say in Greek was [pos se léne]? **Πώς σε λένε;** *What's your name?* (lit. *What do they call you?*) and its answer [me léne] ... **Με λένε ...** *My name is ...* (lit. *They call me ...*). In this unit you met a similar phrase: [ton léne yiórgo] **Τον λένε Γιώργο** *His name is Yiorgos* (lit. *They call him Yiorgos*). Unit 2 also introduced a different set of personal pronouns, which were in the nominative case. A new set below is in the accusative case. Study the table and come back to it whenever needed.

| Personal pronouns in nominative | Personal pronouns in accusative |
|---|---|
| εγώ, εσύ,<br>αυτός/αυτή/αυτό<br>εμείς, εσείς,<br>αυτοί/αυτές/αυτά | *(εμένα) με, (εσένα) σε,*<br>*(αυτόν) τον/(αυτήν) την/(αυτό) το*<br>*(εμάς) μας, (εσάς) σας,*<br>*(αυτούς) τους/(αυτές) τις, (αυτά) τα* |

The personal pronouns in parenthesis are usually left out and only when emphasis is needed can one use them. An example to clarify that is: [me léne ána] **Με λένε Άννα**. *My name's Anna / They call me Anna*. The information here is about a name and not about where the use of the second personal pronoun might be necessary, as in [eména me léne ána] **Εμένα με λένε Άννα**. *My name's Anna / They call me Anna* (and perhaps not another girl).

## 3 TWO SPECIAL VERBS: *TO GO AND TO CALL*

Notice below the full conjugation of two verbs which do not conform to the standard conjugation of verbs such as [ého] **έχω** *to have*, [káno] **κάνω** *to do*, or [méno] **μένω** *to live* etc. Pay attention not only to the special verb endings of the verb *to go* but also to the usage of different personal pronouns for the verb *to call* compared to all other verbs learned up to this unit.

| The verb *to go* | The verb *to call* |
|---|---|
| (εγώ) πάω, (εσύ) πας,<br>(αυτός/αυτή/αυτό) πάει<br>(εμείς) πάμε, (εσείς) πάτε,<br>(αυτοί/αυτές/αυτά) πάνε | *(εμένα) με λένε, (εσένα) σε λένε,*<br>*(αυτόν) τον λένε/(αυτήν) την λένε/(αυτό) το λένε*<br>*(εμάς) μας λένε, (εσάς) σας λένε,*<br>*(αυτούς) τους λένε/(αυτές) τις λένε, (αυτά) τα λένε* |

## 4 THE NUMBERS 11–20

**05.07 You are going to listen to the numbers 11 to 20. Try to listen a couple of times without looking at the numbers. Then listen once again and repeat after the speaker.**

| | | |
|---|---|---|
| [éndeka] | **έντεκα** | *eleven* |
| [THóTHeka] | **δώδεκα** | *twelve* |
| [THekatrís] | **δεκατρείς** (m/f) | *thirteen* |
| [THekatría] | **δεκατρία** (n) | |
| [THekatéseris] | **δεκατέσσερις** (m/f) | *fourteen* |
| [THekatésera] | **δεκατέσσερα** (n) | |
| [THekapénde] | **δεκαπέντε** | *fifteen* |
| [THekaéksi] | **δεκαέξι** | *sixteen* |
| [THekaeftá] | **δεκαεφτά** | *seventeen* |
| [THekaohtó] | **δεκαοχτώ** | *eighteen* |
| [THekaeniá] | **δεκαεννιά** | *nineteen* |
| [íkosi] | **είκοσι** | *twenty* |

The numbers 17, 18 and 19 have two interchangeable forms (like 7, 8 and 9). The alternative forms are [THekaeptá] **δεκαεπτά**, [THekaoktó] **δεκαοκτώ** and [THekaenéa] **δεκαεννέα** respectively.

## 5 THE NUMBERS 21–100

**05.08** Now listen to the numbers 21–100. If you want, you can first say each number and then compare your pronunciation with the audio.

| | | |
|---|---|---|
| [íkosi éna] | **είκοσι ένα** | *twenty-one* |
| [íkosi THío] | **είκοσι δύο** | *twenty-two* |
| [triánda] | **τριάντα** | *thirty* |
| [triánda éna] | **τριάντα ένα** | *thirty-one* |
| [saránda] | **σαράντα** | *forty* |
| [penínda] | **πενήντα** | *fifty* |
| [exínda] | **εξήντα** | *sixty* |
| [evTHomínda] | **εβδομήντα** | *seventy* |
| [oghTHónda] | **ογδόντα** | *eighty* |
| [enenínda] | **ενενήντα** | *ninety* |
| [ekató] | **εκατό** | *one hundred* |

### 6 DOUBLE ACCENTS?

Let's review fast what we have learned about Greek accents. Decide whether the statements below are true or false.

| | | NAI | OXI |
|---|---|---|---|
| **a** | Most one syllable words do not have an accent mark, i.e. **η**, **τον**, **στην**, **ναι**, **γεια**, **μπαρ** | | |
| **b** | Very few one syllable words have an accent mark to differentiate their meaning to one without an accent mark, i.e. **η** *the* and **ή** *or* | | |
| **c** | Greek words with more than one syllable will always have an accent mark when written in small letters, i.e. **σπίτι**, **πάμε**, **βιβλίο** | | |
| **d** | The stress mark will always fall on one of the last three syllables, i.e. **εφτά**, **δέκα**, **δώδεκα** | | |
| **e** | Greek words written in capitals will never have an accent mark, i.e. **ΑΝΝΑ**, **ΣΠΙΤΙ**, **ΠΑΜΕ** | | |
| **f** | Initial words or proper names starting with a capital letter will have an accent mark if the capital letter is stressed, i.e. **Άννα**, **Άρης**, **Όλγα** | | |
| **g** | Double accents are used in certain circumstances. We have seen two examples so far, namely: **το δωμάτιό μου**, **τα ονόματά τους** | | |
| **h** | All the above statements focus on correct spelling. The most important aspect for you is to learn the correct pronunciation of words. | | |

# Practice

**1 Match the following words with their English translation. What words do you need in order to introduce your own family?**

**a** [o patéras moo] **1** my sister
**b** [i mitéra moo] **2** my mother
**c** [i aTHelfí moo] **3** my cousin
**d** [o yios moo] **4** my father
**e** [i kóri moo] **5** my daughter
**f** [o exáTHelfós moo] **6** my son

**2 Match each question with the most appropriate answer.**

| | |
|---|---|
| **a** [éhete peTHiá]? | **1** [ton léne yiórgo]. |
| **b** [éhis ikoyénia]? | **2** [íme THóTHeka]. |
| **c** [pos léne ton ándra soo]? | **3** [óhi], [THen ého]. |
| **d** [pos léne tin sízigó soo]? | **4** [ne], [ého éna peTHí]. |
| **e** [póson hronón íse]? | **5** [tin léne ioána]. |

**3** 05.09 **Some schoolchildren are asked how old they are. Listen to the audio and then work ou how old each child is.**

**a** [yiórgos] Γιώργος
**b** [panayiótis] Παναγιώτης
**c** [kóstas] Κώστας
**d** [elpíTHa] Ελπίδα
**e** [ioána] Ιωάννα
**f** [ariána] Αριάννα

**4** 05.10 **Two friends are telling each other their phone number** [sto spíti] **στο σπίτι** *at home* **and** [stin THooliá] **στη δουλειά** *at work*. **Listen to the audio and write down both numbers.**

**a** [spíti] στο σπίτι ____________________
**b** [THooliá] στη δουλειά ______________

**5 Translate the following phrases into Greek.**

**a** his flat
**b** our home
**c** their grandfather
**d** her mother
**e** my room
**f** your husband

**6 Let's have some fun now! How many Greek words can you find in this word search? There are ten words to find and they read across, up and down.**

| | | | | | | |
|---|---|---|---|---|---|---|
| p | a | p | o | o | s | y |
| a | n | p | l | h | e | i |
| m | y | i | n | e | k | a |
| e | o | a | e | n | a | y |
| k | o | r | i | t | s | i |
| k | m | i | t | e | r | a |

**7 Now write out the words from the word search in Greek.**

____________________ ____________________
____________________ ____________________
____________________ ____________________
____________________ ____________________
____________________ ____________________

**8** 05.11 **Listen again to Conversation 2 and complete each sentence below by choosing one word from the box.**

| [níkos] [ándras] [korítsi] [peTHiá] [ton] [hronón] [yiatí] [eptá] [THéka] [THóTHeka] |
|---|

| | |
|---|---|
| [ána] | [o **a** _____ moo] [íne servitóros]. **b** _____ [léne] [yiórgo]. [éhoome] [tría] **c** _____: [THío agória] [kéna] **d** _____ [ta onómatá toos] [íne] [yiánis], [THéspina] [ke] **e** _____. |
| Mary | [póson] **f** _____ [íne]? |
| [ána] | [o yiánis [íne] **g** _____, [i THéspina] [íne] **h** _____ [ki-o] **e** _____ [íne] **i** _____. [ah]! **j** _____ [févyete]? [THélo] [na sas ksanaTHó] ... |

# Test yourself

**1** Give six Greek words for different members of the family.

**2** How do you say the numbers 11, 12, 14, 17, 19 and 20 in Greek?

**3** Can you describe your own family in Greek?

**4** How do you ask someone how old they are?

**5** *What is it called in Greek?* is an important question. How do you say it?

## SELF CHECK

| | **I CAN...** |
|---|---|
| • | ... ask questions about family and children. |
| • | ... describe my own family. |
| • | ... ask how old someone is and say how old I am. |
| • | ... count from 11 to 100. |

# 6

**In this unit you will learn how to:**

- » welcome people and reply to people when they welcome you.
- » ask for or offer drinks.
- » read and understand items on a drinks menu.
- » thank people and reply when they thank you.

# Καλώς ορίσατε!

My progress tracker

DAY / DATE

## Ordering drinks

[frapés] **Φραπές** *iced coffee* is the most popular drink consumed during the summer months. You can always order [nes] **νες** or [nes kafé] **νες καφέ**, which is a cup of hot instant coffee, or [elinikós kafés] **ελληνικός καφές** *Greek coffee* which is a small cup of strong black coffee. When ordering Greek coffee at a [kafenío] **καφενείο** *traditional café* or [kafetéria] **καφετέρια** *café*, you should specify how sweet you would like it to be: [skéto] **σκέτο** *no sugar*, [métrio] **μέτριο** *medium*, i.e., with one teaspoonful of sugar or [glikó] **γλυκό** *sweet*, i.e., with two spoons of sugar. This is also true when ordering [frapés / frapé] **φραπές / φραπέ**. You can specify if you'd like the coffee [me gála] **με γάλα** *with milk* or [horís gála] **χωρίς γάλα** *without milk*. [frédo] [frédo espréso] *Freddo Espresso* and [frédo kaputsíno] *Freddo Cappuccino* or regular espresso and cappuccino are other popular coffee orders in Greece.

Some popular cold drinks are [lemonáTHa] **λεμονάδα** *lemonade*, [portokaláTHa] **πορτοκαλάδα** *orangeade* and, of course, all international soft drinks. You can always ask for [neró] **νερό** *water*, or more precisely [emfialoméno neró] **εμφιαλωμένο νερό** *bottled water*, or [éna potíri neró] **ένα ποτήρι νερό** *a glass of water*. Bottled water often comes [horís anthrakikó] **χωρίς ανθρακικό** *non-carbonated* but you can also order [me anthrakikó] **με ανθρακικό** *carbonated/sparkling*. Some drinks come in a [bookáli] **μπουκάλι** *bottle* and others in a [kootí] **κουτί** *can*, so you can ask for [éna bookáli kóka kóla]/[éna kootí kóka kóla] **ένα μπουκάλι κόκα κόλα/ένα κουτί κόκα κόλα** *a bottle/can of Coke*. [karáfa] **καράφα** *carafe / jar* is also used with water or other refreshments and [karafáki] **καραφάκι** a *small carafe* often for [oózo] **ούζο** *ouzo*.

---

**1 How many words can you find with the word *coffee* as a separate word or as a prefix in the text?**

**2 What are the alternative ways that you can order a Greek coffee?**

---

# Vocabulary builder

## ΚΑΤΑΛΑΒΑΙΝΩ ΤΟΝ/ΤΗΝ ΣΕΡΒΙΤΟΡ-Ο/-Α *UNDERSTANDING THE SERVER*

**1 06.01 Listen to some typical questions a server might ask and write down the order you hear them in. Then listen again and repeat.**

**a** Καλημέρα, τι θέλετε παρακαλώ;
**b** Καλημέρα, τι θα πάρετε παρακαλώ;
**c** Καλημέρα, τι θα πιείτε παρακαλώ;
**d** Καλημέρα, τι θα θέλατε παρακαλώ;

## ΔΙΝΩ ΠΑΡΑΓΓΕΛΙΑ *PLACING AN ORDER*

**2 06.02 Look at the following phrases you might need when you order a drink and fill in the missing English words. Then listen and try to imitate the pronunciation of the speakers.**

| | |
|---|---|
| Θέλω έναν σκέτο παρακαλώ. | *I'd like* (lit. *I want) a _______, please.* |
| Θα πάρω έναν φραπέ γλυκό με γάλα. | *I'm going to have* (lit. *I'll take) an iced _______ with milk.* |
| Εγώ θα πιω μια πορτοκαλάδα. | *I'm going to have an _______.* |
| Θα 'θελα μια λεμονάδα. | *I'd like a _______.* |
| Έναν μέτριο ελληνικό για μένα! | *A _______ Greek coffee for me!* |
| Μου φέρνετε ένα νες καφέ παρακαλώ; | *Could you bring me a _______, please?* |
| Φέρτε μου ένα(ν) φραπέ σκέτο χωρίς γάλα. | *Can you bring me an iced coffee without sugar and _______ milk.* |

## ΔΕΥΤΕΡΟ ΡΗΜΑΤΙΚΟ ΘΕΜΑ *SECOND VERB STEM*

**3** The previous two activities introduced some useful verbs when trying to understand a server or placing an order. Unlike in English, some verb forms, particularly with a particle like the word for *will* [tha] **θα** in Greek, will often require a second verb stem. Both verb stems are necessary in order to build verb tenses for past, present or future. Unfortunately, most dictionaries do not include the second verb stem in their entries which is an integral component when learning Greek. The table below will give you a better overview regarding this aspect of the two verb stems.

| Verbs with the same verb stems | Verbs with two different (but similar) stems | Verbs with two completely different verb stems |
|---|---|---|
| έχω – έχω *to have*, κάνω – κάνω *to do*, ξέρω – ξέρω *to know* ... | φέρνω – φέρω *to bring*, πίνω – πιω *to drink*, γράφω – γράψω *to write* ... | βλέπω – δω *to see*, παίρνω – πάρω *to take*, εργάζομαι – εργαστώ *to work* ... |

Most Greek verbs fall into the second group, although the first and the third group also contain important verbs used in everyday speech. Starting with this unit, both verb stems will be written for all new verbs introduced and it will definitely help you if you learn them as a set. More information can be found in the Grammar section at the back of the book.

## ΚΑΤΑΛΟΓΟΣ *MENU ITEMS AND PRICES*

**4** 06.03 **Read the menu as you listen and repeat the words and expressions. Try to work out what the following items mean in English. You can check your answers in the key.**

| ΖΕΣΤΑ ΡΟΦΗΜΑΤΑ | | ΑΝΑΨΥΚΤΙΚΑ | | ΠΟΤΑ | |
|---|---|---|---|---|---|
| Ελληνικός καφές | 2,00 | Πορτοκαλάδα | 2,20 | Μπίρα | 3,20 |
| Φραπές | 3,50 | Λεμονάδα | 2,20 | Ποτήρι κρασί | 4,30 |
| Τσάι | 2,40 | Χυμός (ανανάς) | 3,00 | Μπουκάλι Ρετσίνα | 11,00 |
| Ζεστή σοκολάτα | 3,00 | Νερό (μικρό) | 1,00 | Καραφάκι Ούζο | 6,00 |

## ΚΑΤΑΛΑΒΑΙΝΩ ΜΙΑ ΠΑΡΑΓΓΕΛΙΑ *UNDERSTANDING AN ORDER*

**4** 06.04 **Now listen to two friends ordering from the same menu. Listen carefully and decide which the correct option is in each case.**

**a** **1** Φραπές μέτριος με γάλα **2** Φραπές μέτριος χωρίς γάλα
**b** **1** Νερό μικρό **2** Νερό μεγάλο
**c** **1** Ποτήρι Ρετσίνα **2** Μπουκάλι Ρετσίνα

# Conversation 1 Welcome!

## NEW WORDS AND EXPRESSIONS 1

06.05 **Listen to the words and expressions that are used in the next conversation and note their meaning.**

| | | |
|---|---|---|
| [hérome] | χαίρομαι | *I'm glad.* |
| [poo] | που | *that* |
| [ksanavlépo] | ξαναβλέπω | *to see again* |
| [kalós se vríkame]. | Καλώς σε βρήκαμε. | *Glad to be here again* (lit. *Good to have found you*). |
| [kírie] | κύριε = κ. | *Mr* |
| [kiría] | κυρία = κα. | *Mrs* |

06.06 *Angelos drives them home now. Elpida, his wife, and Andonis and Yioryía, his children, are there waiting for Mary and John.*

**1 Listen to the conversation a couple of times. What does John say in reply to Elpida's welcome?**

| | | |
|---|---|---|
| **Elpida** | [kalós orísate]! [hérome] [poo sas ksanavlépo]! | *Welcome! Glad to see you again!* |
| **John** | [yiásoo elpíTHa]. [kalós se vríkame]. | *Hi, Elpida. Glad to be here again.* |
| **Mary** | [yiásoo elpíTHa], [yiásas peTHiá]. | *Hi, Elpida, hi kids.* |
| **Andonis** | [yiásas] [kírie John]. [yiásas] [kiría Mary]. | *Hello, Mr John. Hello, Mrs Mary.* |
| **Yioryía** | [yiásas] | *Hello.* |

**Ελπίδα** Καλώς ορίσατε! Χαίρομαι που σας ξαναβλέπω!
**John** Γεια σου, Ελπίδα. Καλώς σε βρήκαμε.
**Mary** Γεια σου, Ελπίδα. Γεια σας, παιδιά.
**Αντώνης** Γεια σας, κύριε John. Γεια σας, κυρία Mary.
**Γιωργία** Γεια σας.

2 **Now read the conversation and answer the questions.**

**a** What are the names of Angelos' children? Can you write the names in Greek?

**b** What are the words for *Mr* and *Mrs* in Greek?

**c** Conversation 2 in Unit 5 used the verb **ξαναδώ** and here we meet the verb **ξαναβλέπω**, both of which mean *see you again*. How is this related to the first and second verb stem introduced earlier in this unit. And where is the word *again* hidden?

3 **Listen again to the conversation. Practice speaking the parts of Elpida and Mary.**

# Language discovery 1

1 **The conversation includes a phrase used when welcoming people. Complete the list below with the phrase *Welcome!* and decide which phrases are used formally and which informally.**

**a** Καλώς ήλθες!

**b** Καλώς ήλθατε!

**c** Καλώς όρισες!

**d** ________

2 **The phrase Γεια σας was used four times in the conversation. Fill out the two columns below.**

| Who uses the phrase? | Whom were they addressing? |
|---|---|
| ________________ | ________________ |
| ________________ | ________________ |

### WELCOMING SOMEONE

There are many expressions used in Greek to welcome someone. The phrases [kalós órises] **Καλώς όρισες** and [kalosórises] **Καλωσόρισες** both mean *welcome* and are used to address one person informally. The following expressions are used when addressing one person formally or more than one person: [kalós orísate]! **Καλώς ορίσατε!** or [kalosorísate]! **Καλωσορίσατε!** There are two alternative phrases which mean the same: [kalós ílthes]! **Καλώς ήλθες!** and [kalós ílthate]! **Καλώς ήλθατε!** The most typical replies to these expressions are [kalós se vríka]! **Καλώς σε βρήκα!**, used by one person to reply informally to another person, and [kalós sas vríka]! **Καλώς σας βρήκα!** when one person replies to more than one person or formally to one person. Finally, [kalós se vríkame] **Καλώς σε βρήκαμε!** is used when two or more people reply to only one person, whereas [kalós sas vríkame] **Καλώς σας βρήκαμε!** is used when two or more people reply to two or more people or only to one person but formally. The closest translation for all these phrases is *Nice to see/meet you* or *Nice to be here.*

# Conversation 2 Would you like a coffee?

## NEW WORDS AND EXPRESSIONS 2

**06.07 Listen to the words and expressions that are used in the next conversation and note their meanings.**

| | | |
|---|---|---|
| [eláte] | ελάτε | *come* |
| [kathíste] | καθίστε | *have a seat, sit down* |
| [kanapé] | καναπέ | *sofa* |
| [páre] | πάρε | *take* |
| [karékla] | καρέκλα | *chair* |
| [kondá] [moo] | κοντά μου | *close to me* |
| [efharistó] | ευχαριστώ | *thanks* |
| [oréo] | ωραίο | *nice, beautiful* |
| [pináte]? | Πεινάτε; | *Are you hungry?* |
| [THipsáte]? | Διψάτε; | *Are you thirsty?* |
| [thélete]? | Θέλετε; | *Would you like?* (lit. *Do you want?*) (pl/fml) |
| [kafé] | καφέ | *coffee* |
| [kóka kóla] | κόκα κόλα | *Coke* |
| [éhis] | έχεις | *Do you have?* |
| [portokaláTHa] | πορτοκαλάδα | *orangeade* |
| [frapé] | φραπέ | *iced coffee* |
| [yia] [ména] | για μένα | *for me* |

**06.08** *Elpida is trying to find out what her guests might like to drink.*

**1 Listen to the conversation. What does Elpida offer them first?**

| | | |
|---|---|---|
| **Angelos** | [eláte], [kathíste ston kanapé]. [John], [pare mia karékla] [kondá moo]. | *Come on in, have a seat on the sofa. John, take a chair close to me.* |
| **John** | [efharistó]. | *Thanks.* |
| **Mary** | [oréo spíti], [polí oréo] [ke polí megálo]. | *Nice house, very nice and very big.* |
| **Elpida** | [pináte]? [THipsáte]? [Thélete] [énan kafé], [mia kóka kóla]? | *Are you hungry? Are you thirsty? Would you like a coffee, a Coke?* |
| **Mary** | [éhis portokaláTHa]? | *Do you have orangeade?* |
| **John** | [énan frapé] [yia ména]. | *An iced coffee for me.* |

**Άγγελος** Ελάτε, καθίστε στον καναπέ. John, πάρε μια καρέκλα κοντά μου.
**John** Ευχαριστώ.
**Mary** Ωραίο σπίτι, πολύ ωραίο και πολύ μεγάλο.
**Ελπίδα** Πεινάτε; Διψάτε; Θέλετε έναν καφέ, μια κόκα κόλα;
**Mary** Έχεις πορτοκαλάδα;
**John** Έναν φραπέ για μένα.

**2 Now read the conversation and answer the questions.**

**a** What does Mary say about the house?

**b** What would Mary and John like to drink?

**3 Listen again to the conversation and pay special attention to the words which run together. Practice speaking the parts of Angelos and Mary.**

## Language discovery 2

**1 Angelos uses three verbs to request something from his guests. Find them and complete the gaps. Can you guess why there are two verb forms in Greek?**

**a** έλα / ________ **b** κάθισε / ________ **c** ________ / πάρτε

**2 Mary uses three verbs to ask her guests something. Find them and complete the gaps.**

**a** πεινάς ________ **b** διψάς ________ **c** θέλεις ________

**3 The conversation includes the names of four drinks. Find them and decide whether you would use ένανν or μία *a/an* for each one. Does the choice of article depend on the sound of the word that follows, as it does in English?**

**a** Θέλω ________ **c** Θέλω ________

**b** Θέλω ________ **d** Θέλω ________

**4 What is extremely important for you to watch out for when you use many verbs with the indefinite article έναν and masculine nouns? Choose the correct alternative.**

**a** Θέλω έναν χυμός/χυμό.

**b** Έχω έναν καναπές/καναπέ.

**c** Ξέρω έναν γιατρός/γιατρό.

## 1 IMPERATIVES

When giving orders or making requests, a special verb form is used. This is called the imperative. Imperative verb forms should be learned by heart as they are not usually the same as the infinitive form, as they are in English. Look at the answers you gave to the first exercise. If they are correct you will see the singular verb form (used when speaking informally to one person) and the plural verb form (used when speaking to more than one person, or formally to one person) of the imperative. Here are the main verb forms and the corresponding imperatives of these three verbs:

| Main verb form: | **έρχομαι** *to come* | **κάθομαι** *to sit* | **παίρνω** *to take* |
|---|---|---|---|
| Imperative form: | **έλα-ελάτε** | **κάθισε-καθίστε** | **πάρε-πάρτε** |

## 2 THE GREEK VERB ΘΕΛΩ *TO WANT*

When addressing someone directly in Greek, always remember to decide on the appropriate form of the word for *you* (**εσύ** or **εσείς**). For example, *Do you want ...?* would be **θέλεις** (or **θες** – an everyday alternative form) if asking a friend, and **θέλετε** if asking a stranger or someone you have a more formal relationship with. Remember that the personal pronouns **εσύ** and **εσείς** will be usually left out.

[thélo] **θέλω** is a very common verb in Greek. Although it essentially means *want*, it is used to express all manner of nuances including *I want it here and now!*, *I want it if possible*, *I would like* or even *I'd love to!* Pay attention to the speaker's intonation if you hear this verb in order to understand which nuance of meaning is implied. Look at the forms of the verb:

### Verb group 1

| | | |
|---|---|---|
| [thélo] | **θέλω** | *I want* |
| [thélis/thes] | **θέλεις – θες** | *you want* (sing/infml) |
| [théli] | **θέλει** | *he/she/it wants* |
| [théloome] | **θέλουμε** | *we want* |
| [thélete] | **θέλετε** | *you want* (pl/fml) |
| [théloon(e)] | **θέλουν(ε)** | *they want* |

This important verb is part of verb group 1 and its conjugation is identical, in terms of verb endings, to many other verbs you were introduced to in the last few units, including **κάνω** *to do*, **έχω** *to have*, **μένω** *to live*.

## 3 GREEK VERBS ΔΙΨΑΩ *TO BE THIRSTY* AND ΠΕΙΝΑΩ *TO BE HUNGRY*

Conversation 2 has two new verbs which are part of verb group 2. Look at their full conjugation below and compare the endings with the verb **θέλω** *to want* above.

### Verb group 2

| [THipsáo] **διψάω** to be thirsty | [pináo] **πεινάω** to be hungry |
|---|---|
| (εγώ) διψάω-διψώ<br>(εσύ) διψάς<br>(αυτός / αυτή / αυτό) διψάει-διψά<br>(εμείς) διψάμε<br>(εσείς) διψάτε<br>(αυτοί / αυτές / αυτά) διψούν (ε) - διψάνε | (εγώ) πεινάω-πεινώ<br>(εσύ) πεινάς<br>(αυτός / αυτή / αυτό) πεινάει-πεινά<br>(εμείς) πεινάμε<br>(εσείς) πεινάτε<br>(αυτοί / αυτές / αυτά) πεινούν (ε) – πεινάνε |

As you can see, there are some alternative forms that can be used interchangeably without changing the meaning of the verb. Most dictionary entries will include these verbs from verb group 2 with both forms. Unit 2 introduced the verb [miláo-miló] **μιλάω – μιλώ** *to speak* which also falls under this verb group.

## 4 THE INDEFINITE ARTICLE

The Greek indefinite article, the words for *a* or *an*, was first introduced in Unit 4. The different forms of this article are often used when ordering something, as shown in the examples below.

| (masculine) έναν | (feminine) μια | (neuter) ένα |
|---|---|---|
| **Θέλω έναν καφέ.**<br>*I'd like a (cup of) coffee.* | **Θέλω μια πορτοκαλάδα.**<br>*I'd like an orangeade.* | **Θέλω ένα ποτήρι νερό.**<br>*I'd like a glass of water.* |

**LANGUAGE TIP**

When ordering or requesting items which are masculine in gender, then the final [s] **ς** is dropped from the noun:

**Θέλω έναν καφέ/φραπέ/χυμό.** *I'd like a coffee/iced coffee/juice.*

The main form of these three nouns is **ο καφές/ο φραπές/ο χυμός**.

## 5 THANKING SOMEONE

No matter how little you can converse in another language, being able to exchange pleasantries will go a long way. If you can thank someone or respond when they *thank you*, Greek speakers will appreciate your courtesy. [efharistó] **ευχαριστώ** *thanks* (lit. *I thank)*, [efharistó polí] **ευχαριστώ πολύ** *thanks a lot*, [parakaló] **παρακαλώ** *you're welcome* (lit. *I please*) and [típota] **τίποτα** *don't mention it* (lit. *nothing)* will all be useful phrases when making simple conversation.

### 6 THE VERBS ΕΥΧΑΡΙΣΤΩ *TO THANK* AND ΠΑΡΑΚΑΛΩ *TO PLEASE*

Now is a good opportunity to introduce verb group 3. Looking at the conjugations below, how are these verbs different to those in verb group 1 or verb group 2?

**Verb group 3**

| [efharistó] ευχαριστώ *to thank* | [parakaló] παρακαλώ *to please* |
|---|---|
| (εγώ) ευχαριστώ<br>(εσύ) ευχαριστείς<br>(αυτός / αυτή / αυτό) ευχαριστεί<br>(εμείς) ευχαριστούμε<br>(εσείς) ευχαριστείτε<br>(αυτοί / αυτές / αυτά) ευχαριστούν(ε) | (εγώ) παρακαλώ<br>(εσύ) παρακαλείς<br>(αυτός / αυτή / αυτό) παρακαλεί<br>(εμείς) παρακαλούμε<br>(εσείς) παρακαλείτε<br>(αυτοί / αυτές / αυτά) παρακαλούν(ε) |

# Practice

1 **Mateo has taken out a family photo and talks about the people in it. Fill out in the text below for each person (1-6).**

[eTHó íne i ikoghénia moo] [aftós íne o babás moo (1) ______, aftí íne i mamá moo (2) _____ ke THípla tis íne i kóri moo (3) _____] [o aTHelfós moo (4) _____ íne anámesa ston babá moo ke tin mama moo] [THípla ston babá moo ine o síndrofos (5) _____ too aTHelfoó moo] [ke THípla too íne o y-os (ghios) moo (6) ______.]

a [o papoós moo]
b [i yiayiá moo]
c [o aTHelfós moo]
d [i eksaTHélfi moo]
e [o yios moo]
f [o ándras moo]

2 **Match each question with the most appropriate answer.**

| | | | |
|---|---|---|---|
| **a** | [éhis oréo spíti]? | **1** | [óhi], [mía lemonáTHa]. |
| **b** | [thélis énan kafé]? | **2** | [éna tsái], [efharistó]. |
| **c** | [thélis mía portokaláTHa]? | **3** | [óhi], [pináme]! |
| **d** | [THipsáte]? | **4** | [polí oréo ke polí megálo]. |
| **e** | [ti thélis]? | **5** | [ne], [énan frapé skéto me ghála]. |

3 **Rearrange these lines to make a dialogue.**

**a** [ti thélis] [na pyis]? Τι θέλεις να πιεις;

**b** [éna himó] [se parakaló] Ένα χυμό σε παρακαλώ.

**c** [ángele], [THipsás]? Άγγελε, διψάς;

**d** [THen kséro]. [ti éhi]? Δεν ξέρω. Τι έχει;

**e** [ne polí] [mitéra]. Ναι πολύ, μητέρα.

**f** [éhi himó lemonáTHa] [ke fisiká kafé]. Έχει χυμό, λεμονάδα και φυσικά καφέ.

4 **Translate your part of the conversation to complete the following dialogue.**

**[fílos]** [páre mía karékla] [kondá moo].

**You** Say *Close to you? Why?*

**[fílos]** [yiatí] [thélo na miláme] [angliká].

**You** Say *English? I want to speak Greek!*

**[fílos]** [eliniká]? [oréa]! [kafé stin arhí]?

**You** Say *Why not? Coffee to start with* (lit. *in the beginning*). *An iced coffee for me, milk, no sugar.*

5 06.09 **Listen again to Conversation 2 of this unit and fill in the blanks using the words from the box. Then try to write out the whole conversation in Greek script.**

[pináte] [kanapé] [énan] [ména] [eláte] [mia] [yia] [karékla] [éhis]

**Angelos** **a** _______. [kathíste ston] **b** _______. [John], [páre mia] **c** _______ [kondá moo].

**John** [efharistó].

**Mary** [oréo spíti], [polí oréo] [ke polí megálo].

**Elpida** **d** _______? [THipsáte]? [thélete] **e** _______ [kafé], **f** _______ [kóka kóla]?

**Mary** **g** _______ [portokaláTHa]?

**John** [éna frapé] **h** _______ **i** _______.

**6 Ask for the following.**

**a** I'd like a small bottle of water.

**b** I'd like a big bottle of water.

**c** I'd like a bottle of mineral water.

**d** I'd like a glass of water.

**7 You are in a café and would like to order the following drinks. Fill in the missing words to complete your order.**

**a** Θέλω ________ παρακαλώ. *I'd like a Greek coffee without sugar, please.*

**b** ________ έναν φραπέ γλυκό με γάλα. *I'm going to have an iced coffee with sugar and milk.*

**c** ________ μια πορτοκαλάδα. *I'm going to have an orangeade.*

**d** Θα ΄θελα ________. *I'd like a lemonade.*

**e** Έναν μέτριο ελληνικό ________! *A Greek coffee with one sugar for me!*

**f** ________ ένα νες καφέ παρακαλώ; *Could you bring me a hot instant coffee, please?*

**g** Φέρτε μου έναν φραπέ ________; *Can you bring me an iced coffee without sugar or milk?*

**8 Read the menu and order the following drinks. Remember what you have learned about the use of the indefinite article έναν / μία-μια / ένα but also about dropping the final -ς, i.e. καφές – καφέ.**

**a** a sweet Greek coffee

**b** an iced coffee with milk but no sugar

**c** a small bottle of water

**d** a small carafe of ouzo

**e** a beer

**f** a hot chocolate

**9 This unit introduced two important verb groups, namely verb groups 2 and 3. Below is a clear revision of all 4 verb groups which all end in -*ω* but have different conjugations. Fill out the '*you-form*' both singular / informal or plural / formal.**

Greek verbs ending in -ω, -άω/ώ, -ώ, or special -ω conjugations

| Verb group 1 | Verb group 2 | Verb group 3 | Verb group 4 |
|---|---|---|---|
| Ending in **-ω** | Ending in **-άω/ώ** | Ending in **-ώ** | Special **-ω** verbs |
| **θέλω** | **διψάω-διψώ** | **παρακαλώ** | **πάω** |
| ______ | ______ | ______ | ______ |
| **θέλει**<br>**θέλουμε** | **διψάει-διψά**<br>**διψάμε** | **παρακαλεί**<br>**παρακαλούμε** | **πάει**<br>**πάμε** |
| ______ | ______ | ______ | ______ |
| **θέλουν(ε)** | **διψούν(ε) - διψάνε** | **παρακαλούν(ε)** | **παν / πάνε** |

**10 Read the sentences about Greek verbs. Tick '*YES*-NAI' if the sentence is true and '*NO*-OXI' if it's false.**

| | NAI | OXI |
|---|---|---|
| **a** There are four major verb groups which include most verbs ending in **-ω**, **-άω/-ώ**, **-ώ**, and a few other special **-ω** verbs. | | |
| **b** The first three verb groups have a standard conjugation which helps us to identify which verb belongs to which group. | | |
| **c** Verb endings normally help us identify the person in focus, i.e. *I*, *you*, *we*, *they* etc., and so personal pronouns are often left out. | | |
| **d** The base form of many verbs can serve three different functions: entry word in a dictionary, i.e. [**méno**] **μένω** to live, simple present, i.e. [**méno**] **μένω** I live, and present continuous, i.e. [**méno**] **μένω** I am living. | | |
| **e** This base form is also called stem 1 and together with stem 2 they are the two most important parts you need to build all possible verb tenses in past, present or future. | | |
| **f** Although stem 1 and stem 2 can be identical, this is usually not the case and you have to learn them together as a set if possible. | | |

## Test yourself

1 Give the names of five drinks in Greek. [kóka kóla] doesn't count!

2 How do you say *Come and sit next to me?*

3 Ask *Do you have an orangeade or a juice?*

4 How do you say *Have a seat!*

### SELF CHECK

| | **I CAN...** |
|---|---|
| • | ... welcome people and reply to them when they welcome me. |
| • | ... ask for and offer drinks. |
| • | ... read and understand items on a drinks menu. |
| • | ... thank people and reply when they thank me. |

# Revision test 2

**1 Do you remember the words for each room in a house? The first one is a new word and has been done for you.** *(6 points)*

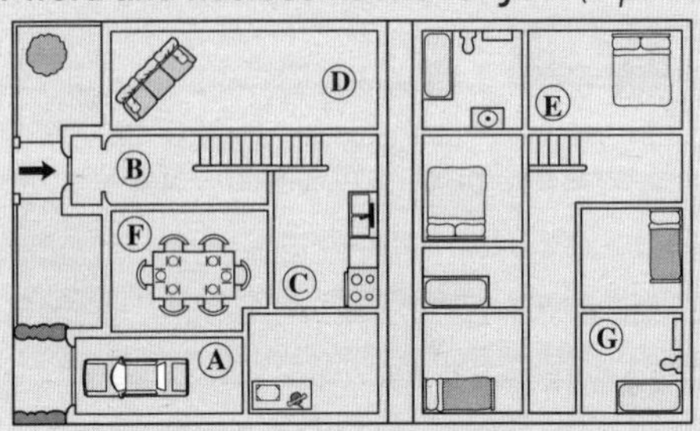


a [garáz] γκαράζ

b ______

c ______

d ______

e ______

f ______

g ______

**2 A friend is showing you some family pictures hanging on the wall. Match each phrase to the correct picture.** *(10 points)*

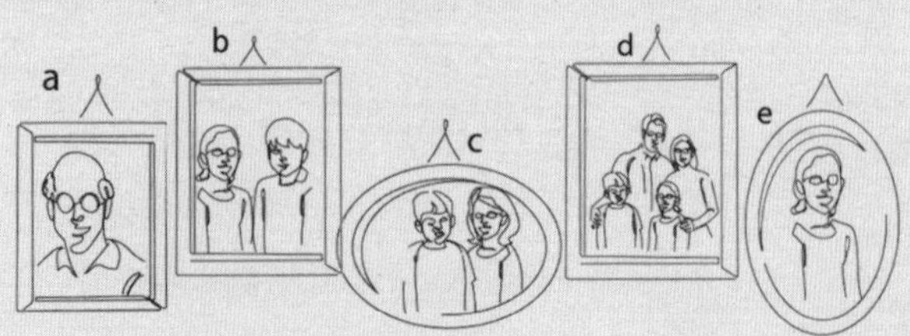


1 [eghó ki i stéla] Εγώ κι η Στέλλα.
2 [i ikoyenía papá]. Η οικογένεια Παππά.
3 [i stéla][íne i aTHelfí moo] Η Στέλλα είναι η αδελφή μου.
4 [o papoós moo] [o yiánis]. Ο παππούς μου ο Γιάννης.
5 [o ksáTHelfos ke i ksaTHélfi moo]. Ο ξάδελφος και η ξαδέλφη μου.

**3 Some numbers are missing in the grid. Can you write them out in words? Then try to say them out loud.** *(10 points)*

| a | 1 | 2 | | 4 | |
|---|---|---|---|---|---|
| b | 6 | | 8 | 9 | |
| c | | | 13 | | 15 |
| d | | 17 | 18 | | |

**4 Can you match each image to the correct English heading? There are at least five words that you should be able to translate into English. Can you find them and translate them?** *(10 points)*

**1** underground/metro
**2** book/Kostas
**3** restaurant/café
**4** ticket/Athens
**5** pastry shop/sugar

5 **Read the text and check whether the statements are true or false.** *(10 points)*

Ο Γιώργος μένει σε ένα μικρό διαμέρισμα σε μια μεγάλη πολυκατοικία. Έχει μόνο ένα δωμάτιο και το μπάνιο είναι μικρό αλλά βολικό. Αυτό είναι μεγάλο πρόβλημα γιατί ο Κοσμάς ο φίλος του, θέλει να μείνει με τον Γιώργο και ο Γιώργος δεν δουλεύει τώρα.

**a** Το διαμέρισμα είναι μεγάλο.
**b** Η πολυκατοικία είναι μικρή.
**c** Το διαμέρισμα έχει δύο δωμάτια.
**d** Το μπάνιο δεν είναι βολικό.
**e** Ο Γιώργος δουλεύει τώρα.

6 **Match each Greek word in the left-hand column to its correct translation in the right-hand column. Then add the correct article to each Greek word.** *(14 points)*

| | | | |
|---|---|---|---|
| **a** | _______ κατοικία | **1** | studio/bedsit |
| **b** | _______ σπίτι | **2** | detached house |
| **c** | _______ διαμέρισμα | **3** | residence |
| **d** | _______ γκαρσονιέρα | **4** | apartment building/block of flats |
| **e** | _______ ρετιρέ | **5** | house/home |
| **f** | _______ μονοκατοικία | **6** | penthouse |
| **g** | _______ πολυκατοικία | **7** | apartment/flat |

7 **Nikos is showing you a family photo and explains who everyone is. Read the phrases and translate them into English.** *(20 points)*

**a** Από εδώ η γιαγιά μου η Άρτεμις και ο παππούς μου ο Οδυσσέας.
**b** Τη σύζυγό μου τη λένε Ελπίδα.
**c** Έχουμε δύο παιδιά. Ένα αγόρι και ένα κορίτσι.
**d** Τον γιο μας τον λένε Άγγελο και την κόρη μας τη λένε Νιόβη.
**e** Μένουμε σε μια μεγάλη μονοκατοικία.

8 **Can you come up with an appropriate question for each of the following answers?** *(10 points)*

**a** Ο άντρας μου δεν δουλεύει τώρα.
**b** Έχουμε τρία παιδιά.
**c** Ναι, έχω μια μεγάλη οικογένεια.
**d** Τη γυναίκα μου τη λένε Άννα.
**e** Ναι, μιλάω λίγα Ελληνικά!

**9 Take part in the following conversation using the English as a prompt.** *(10 points)*

| | |
|---|---|
| **Maria** | Ελάτε, καθίστε στον καναπέ. |
| **You** | Say *Thanks. That's a nice big house!* |
| **Maria** | Πεινάτε; Διψάτε; Θέλετε έναν καφέ; |
| **You** | Say *That's a good idea. A coffee for me please!* |
| **Maria** | Τι καφέ θέλετε; Ένα φραπέ ίσως; |
| **You** | Say *Yes. An iced coffee, medium without milk. And some water, please.* |
| **Maria** | Ένα ποτήρι ή ένα μπουκάλι; |
| **You** | Say *A glass of water, please.* |
| **Maria** | Με ή χωρίς ανθρακικό; |
| **You** | Say *I don't understand! What is that in English?* |
| **Maria** | *Sparkling or non-sparkling water.* |

**TOTAL: 100 POINTS**

Have you scored than more than 60 points? If yes, congratulations! If not, it might be a good idea to review the last three units and focus on any lexical and/or grammatical points that pose a challenge to you.

7

**In this unit you will learn how to:**

» agree or disagree with someone.
» say if you like or dislike something.
» use more Greek nouns in singular and plural form.
» use adjectives.
» use words for color and furniture.

# Τι ωραία πολυθρόνα!

My progress tracker

| DAY / DATE | | | | | |
|---|---|---|---|---|---|
| | ○ | ○ | ○ | ○ | ○ |
| | ○ | ○ | ○ | ○ | ○ |
| | ○ | ○ | ○ | ○ | ○ |
| | ○ | ○ | ○ | ○ | ○ |
| | ○ | ○ | ○ | ○ | ○ |

## Greek hospitality

People often talk about Greek [filoxenía] **φιλοξενία** *hospitality*. This is a compound word from [fílos] **φίλος** *friend* and [xénos] **ξένος** *guest/stranger*. Generally speaking, Greeks are hospitable people; they open their homes to friends and acquaintances and entertain generously. Of course, hospitality in its broadest sense can be interpreted differently. You need to experience it in order to realize what it is like and what lies between the reality and the myth. What is generally unthinkable for many of us, e.g. sleeping three or four people in one [THomátio] **δωμάτιο** *room*, in the [avlí] **αυλή** *yard* or on the [tarátsa] **ταράτσα** *roof*, used to be offered as part of Greek hospitality in the past. High unemployment rates, low salaries, and very low pensions make many people more reserved nowadays. Nevertheless, we do hope that you will experience Greek hospitality and have a pleasant [paramoní/THiamoní] **παραμονή/διαμονή** (longer/shorter) stay there.

**There are some Greek compound words (two words together) in the text with different prefixes, e.g. φίλ-, παρα-, and δια-. Can you find a couple of words with one of these prefixes from past units?**

## Επίπλωση στο σπίτι *Furniture*

You learned about different types of houses in Unit 4. Now it's time to learn the words for different items found inside the home. When you learn the name of a room, try to learn the words for items that may be found in that room. Certain associations can be made as follows: [koozína] **κουζίνα** *kitchen* with [pángos] **πάγκος** *counter*, [trapézi] **τραπέζι** *table*, [nerochítis] **νεροχύτης** *sink*, [karékla] **καρέκλα** *chair*, [psighío] **ψυγείο** *refrigerator* and [foórnos] **φούρνος** *stove*; [ipnoTHomátio] **υπνοδωμάτιο** *bedroom* with [kathréftis] **καθρέφτης** *mirror*, [kreváti] **κρεβάτι** *bed* and [doolápa] **ντουλάπα** *wardrobe*; [bánio] **μπάνιο** *bathroom* with [baniéra] **μπανιέρα** *bathtub* and [niptíras] **νιπτήρας** *washbasin*; and [salóni] **σαλόνι** *living room* with [polithróna] **πολυθρόνα** *armchair* and [kanapés] **καναπές** *sofa*. Some other useful words are [balkóni] **μπαλκόνι** *balcony/porch*, [paráthiro] **παράθυρο** *window*, [pórta] **πόρτα** *door* and [avlí] **αυλή** *courtyard*.

**Now look at the picture and see how many items of furniture you can label in Greek.**

# Vocabulary builder

### ΣΕ ΕΝΑ ΣΑΛΟΝΙ *IN A LIVING ROOM*

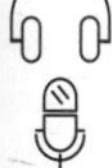

1 07.01 **The following table includes all the items that you can see in the picture. Listen carefully to Nikos as he will list only what he has in his living room. Tick the items you hear. Then listen again and repeat the sentences after the speaker.**

| Το παράθυρο | | Η κουρτίνα | | Το κάδρο | |
|---|---|---|---|---|---|
| Η βιβλιοθήκη | | Η καρέκλα | | Η πόρτα | |
| Το τηλέφωνο | | Η πολυθρόνα | | Ο καναπές | |
| Το τραπεζάκι | | Η πρίζα | | Η τηλεόραση | |

**2** 07.02 **Without using a dictionary, can you work out which words on the list in exercise 1 correspond to the English words? Decide which is the correct word in each case and then listen and compare your answers.**

**a** curtain **b** television **c** phone
**d** coffee table **e** door **f** sofa

## ΕΠΙΠΛΑ *FURNITURE*

**3** 07.03 **Look at the following items of furniture and sort them according to their gender (masculine, feminine or neuter). Then listen to the audio and compare your answers. Finally, listen again and repeat after the speaker.**

πάγκος τραπέζι νεροχύτης καρέκλα καθρέφτης κρεβάτι ντουλάπα μπανιέρα τραπεζάκι νιπτήρας πολυθρόνα κάδρο

| Masculine | Feminine | Neuter |
|---|---|---|
| | | |

## ΗΛΕΚΤΡΙΚΕΣ ΣΥΣΚΕΥΕΣ *ELECTRICAL APPLIANCES*

**4** 07.04 **Look at the list of electrical appliances and complete the missing English expressions. Then listen and try to imitate the pronunciation of the speaker.**

| | |
|---|---|
| Το ψυγείο | ______ |
| Το πλυντήριο πιάτων | *dishwasher* |
| Το πλυντήριο ρούχων | *washing* ______ |
| Ο φούρνος | ______ |
| Ο φούρνος μικροκυμάτων | ______ |
| Η καφετιέρα | ______ *machine* |
| Ο βραστήρας νερού | *kettle* |
| Η τηλεόραση | *television* |

# Conversation 1 Here's the kitchen

## NEW WORDS AND EXPRESSIONS 1

**07.05 Listen to the words and expressions that are used in the next conversation and note their meanings.**

| | | |
|---|---|---|
| [éla na soo THíkso] | έλα να σου δείξω | *Let me show you.* (lit. *come to show you*) |
| [páme] | Πάμε | *Let's go.* |
| [oréa] | ωραία | *beautiful* |
| [polithróna] | πολυθρόνα | *armchair* |
| [hóro] | χώρο | *space, area* |
| [karékles] | καρέκλες | *chairs* |
| [vlépo] | βλέπω | *I see.* |

Starting with this unit, both verb stems will be written out for you. [THíhno/THíkso] **δείχνω / δείξω** *to show*, [pighéno (páo)/páo] **πηγαίνω (πάω) / πάω** *to go*, and [vlépo/Tho] **βλέπω / δω** *to see / to watch*. Stem 1 for the verb *to go* is officially **πηγαίνω** but its short form **πάω** is also used not only as stem 2 but also as stem 1 in everyday speech.

07.06 *Elpida is proud of their new house and shows Mary around.*

**1 Listen to the conversation a couple of times. Which room does she take Mary to first?**

| | | |
|---|---|---|
| **Elpida** | Mary [éla na soo THíkso] [to spíti]. | *Mary, let me show you the house.* |
| **Mary** | [ne] [to thélo polí]. [páme]. | *Yes, I'd like that a lot. Let's go.* |
| **Elpida** | [eTHó íne to ipnoTHomátió mas]. | *Here's our bedroom.* |
| **Mary** | [ti oréa polithróna] [ke ti megálo krevàti]! | *What a beautiful armchair and what a big bed!* |
| **Elpida** | [eTHó íne i koozína]. [éhi megálo pángo] [ke hóro yia megálo trapézi] [ke polés karékles]. | *Here's the kitchen. It has a long worktop and space for a big table and many chairs.* |
| **Mary** | [vlépo], [vlépo]. [brávo, elpíTHa]. | *I see, I see. Bravo, Elpida.* |

**Ελπίδα** Mary, έλα να σου δείξω το σπίτι.
**Mary** Ναι, το θέλω πολύ. Πάμε.
**Ελπίδα** Εδώ είναι το υπνοδωμάτιό μας.
**Mary** Τι ωραία πολυθρόνα και τι μεγάλο κρεβάτι!
**Ελπίδα** Εδώ είναι η κουζίνα. Έχει μεγάλο πάγκο και χώρο για μεγάλο τραπέζι και πολλές καρέκλες.
**Mary** Βλέπω, βλέπω. Μπράβο, Ελπίδα.

**2 Now read the conversation and answer the questions.**

**a** What items of furniture did Mary see in the bedroom?

**b** Can a big table fit into the kitchen without a problem?

**3 Listen again and pay special attention to the words which run together. Practice speaking the part of Mary and pay particular attention to your pronunciation.**

# Language discovery 1

**1 The conversation includes five adjectives. Find them and fill in the gaps.**

| | |
|---|---|
| **a** many chairs | _______ karékles |
| **b** long worktop | _______ pángo |
| **c** beautiful armchair | _______ polithróna |
| **d** big table | _______ trapézi |
| **e** big bed | _______ kreváti |

**2 Are you a good word detective? Read the conversation again carefully and try to find the following words hidden as words or parts of a word in the text.**

| | | |
|---|---|---|
| **a** bravo | **b** mega- | **c** hypno- |
| **d** cuisine | **e** poly- | **f** trapezoid |

### 1 ADJECTIVES

Adjectives were first introduced in Unit 4. Adjectives are words which describe people or things, giving more information about the noun they modify. Greek adjectives, like nouns, have a gender (masculine, feminine or neuter) and different singular or plural forms, which makes them a little more challenging to learn. If you look up a Greek adjective in the dictionary you will see it listed with all three gender forms in the singular, e.g. **μεγάλ-ος/μεγάλ-η/μεγάλ-ο** or **μεγάλ-ος/-η/-ο.**

When you learn a new adjective, try to learn the word for its opposite at the same time. This is a good way of expanding your vocabulary. Try, for example, to learn these three word pairs by heart:

| | | |
|---|---|---|
| [polés – líghes] | **πολλές – λίγες** | *many – few* |
| [meghálo – mikró] | **μεγάλο – μικρό** | *big – small* |
| [oréa – áschimi] | **ωραία – άσχημη** | *beautiful – ugly* |

An overview of three adjective groups is given in the table below:

| Endings | Endings | Irregular endings |
|---|---|---|
| **-ος/-η/-ο** | **-ος/-α/-ο** | |
| μικρός, μικρή, μικρό | ωραίος, ωραία, ωραίο | πολύς, πολλή, πολύ |

The final example creates a small challenge not only with its endings but also with its spelling. As a first step, learn only the forms found in context in this or other units.

### 2 BEING A GOOD DETECTIVE!

Did you manage to do exercise 2? Being a good word detective, which means observing words and their sounds carefully, can help your understanding when you are having a real conversation with a Greek speaker. Remember the influence Greek has had on English – you will recognize many Greek words that have become part of the English language, often as prefixes or suffixes. Two of the words above have given us *oligarchy* (*government by a few*) [lígh-os/-i/-o] **λίγ-ος/-η/-ο** *little, a few* and *microscope (small+see)* [mikr-ós/-í/-ó] ***μικρ-ός/-ή/-ό*** small.

# Conversation 2 Do you like it?

### NEW WORDS AND EXPRESSIONS 2

**07.07 Listen to the words and expressions that are used in the next conversation. Note their meanings.**

| | | |
|---|---|---|
| [praktikó] | πρακτικό | *practical* (with neuter noun) |
| [ótan] | όταν | *when* (not as a question) |
| [anángi] | ανάγκη | *necessity; necessary* |
| [vévea] | βέβαια | *of course, naturally* |
| [lootró] | λουτρό | *bath; bathroom* |
| [soo arési]? | Σου αρέσει; | *Do you like?* (sing/infml) |
| [hrómata] | χρώματα | *colors* |
| [strongilós] | στρογγυλός | *round* |
| [kathréftis] | καθρέφτης | *mirror* |
| [mávro] | μαύρο | *black* |
| [áspro] | άσπρο | *white* |
| [antíthesi] | αντίθεση | *contrast* |
| [simfonó] | συμφωνώ | *I agree* |
| [THíkio] | δίκιο | *right* |

**07.08** *Elpida takes Mary further around the house.*

**1 Listen to the conversation a couple of times. Which is the next room that she takes Mary to?**

| | | |
|---|---|---|
| **Elpida** | [eTHó] [íne to vesé]. [íne lígo mikró] [alá polí praktikó] [ótan íne anángi]. | *Here's the toilet. It's a little bit small but very practical when necessary.* |
| **Mary** | [ne], [vévea]. | *Yes, of course.* |
| **Elpida** | [apo'THó to lootró]. [soo arési]? | *This is the bathroom. Do you like it?* |
| **Mary** | [moo arési polí]. [moo arésoon] [ta hrómata polí] [ke o strongilós kathréftis]. | *I like it a lot. I like the colors and the round mirror.* |
| **Elpida** | [ne] [to mávro ke áspro] [kánoon] [megáli antíthesi] [alá moo arésoon]. | *Yes, black and white create a great contrast and I like them.* |
| **Mary** | [simfonó]. [éhis THíkio]. | *I agree. You're right.* |

**Ελπίδα** Εδώ είναι το WC. Είναι λίγο μικρό αλλά πολύ πρακτικό όταν είναι ανάγκη.

**Mary** Ναι, βέβαια.

**Ελπίδα** Από ΄δω το λουτρό. Σου αρέσει;

**Mary** Μου αρέσει πολύ. Μου αρέσουν τα χρώματα πολύ και ο στρογγυλός καθρέφτης.

**Ελπίδα** Ναι, το μαύρο και άσπρο κάνουν μεγάλη αντίθεση αλλά μου αρέσουν.

**Mary** Συμφωνώ. Έχεις δίκιο.

**2 Now read the conversation and answer the questions.**

**a** What does Mary like in the bathroom?

**b** What color scheme is in the bathroom?

**3 Listen again and pay special attention to the words which run together. Practice speaking the part of Mary and pay particular attention to your pronunciation.**

# Language discovery 2

**1 The conversation includes four adjectives. Find them and fill in the gaps. If you can, you can practice writing everything in Greek script.**

**a** great contrast _______ antíthesi
**b** round mirror _______ kathréftis
**c** small toilet _______ vesé
**d** practical toilet _______ vesé

**2 The conversation includes four phrases which are used to express agreement with someone. How would you say them in Greek? Write your answers in a phonetic transliteration and/or Greek script.**

**a** You're right.
**b** Yes, of course.
**c** I agree.
**d** I like it a lot.

**3 There are three phrases that use the verb *to like* in this conversation. Can you find how to say the following in Greek? Why are two different verb forms used?**

**a** I like it a lot.
**b** I like the colors a lot.
**c** Do you like it?

## 1 MORE ADJECTIVES

Conversation 2 also includes another four adjectives. Read them and try to memorize them. As you saw earlier in this unit, with each adjective you learn it is useful to learn its opposite too, so these are also listed.

| | | |
|---|---|---|
| [meghál-os/-i/-o] | **μεγάλ-ος/-η/-ο** | *big* |
| [mikr-ós/-í/-ó] | **μικρ-ός/-ή/-ό** | *small* |
| [stroghil-ós/-í/-ó] | **στρογγυλ-ός/-ή/-ό** | *round* |
| [tetraghón-os/-i/-o] | **τετράγων-ος/-η/-ο** | *square* |
| [praktik-ós/-í/-ó] | **πρακτικ-ός/-ή/-ό** | *practical* |
| [ávol-os/-i/-o] | **άβολ-ος/-η/-ο** | *uncomfortable* |

## 2 EXPRESSING LIKES, DISLIKES, PREFERENCE AND AGREEMENT

07.09 Being able to say that you like or dislike something, that you prefer something or that you agree with someone is useful in many conversations. Read the expressions as you listen to the audio.

| Liking and agreement | Disliking and disagreement |
|---|---|
| [moo arési] **μου αρέσει** *I like.* (sing) | [antipathó] **αντιπαθώ** *I dislike.* |
| [moo arésoon] **μου αρέσουν** *I like.* (pl) | [THen marési] **δεν μ'αρέσει** *I don't like.* |
| [simfonó] **συμφωνώ** *I agree.* | [THiafonó] **διαφωνώ** *I disagree.* |
| [ého THíkio] **έχω δίκιο** *I'm right.* | [ého áTHiko] **έχω άδικο** *I'm wrong.* |
| [protimó] **προτιμώ** *I prefer.* | [THen protimó] **δεν προτιμώ** *I don't prefer.* |

Now read the following examples:

| | | |
|---|---|---|
| [ého THíkio i áTHiko]? | **Έχω δίκιο ή άδικο;** | *Am I right or wrong?* |
| [simfonó mazí soo]. | **Συμφωνώ μαζί σου.** | *I agree with you.* |
| [moo arési i éli]. | **Μου αρέσει η Έλλη.** | *I like Ellie.* |
| [protimó kafé ke óhi tsái]. | **Προτιμώ καφέ και όχι τσάι.** | *I prefer coffee to tea.* (lit. *and not tea*) |
| *[THen moo arésoon o pétros ke i réna].* | **Δε μου αρέσουν ο Πέτρος και η Ρένα.** | *I don't like Peter and Rena.* |

## 3 THE VERB *TO LIKE*

Expressing *liking* in Greek is different from the English verb *to like* as instead of saying *I like X*, you say *to me is pleasing X*. The object or person liked becomes the subject of the verb and so the verb will change according to whether the subject is singular or plural. Look at the different forms:

| I like (only one person or thing) | | | I like (more than one person or thing) | | |
|---|---|---|---|---|---|
| [moo arési] | **μου αρέσει** | *I like* | [moo arésoon] | **μου αρέσουν** | *I like* (sing/infml) |
| [soo arési] | **σου αρέσει** | *you like* (sing/infml) | [soo arésoon] | **σου αρέσουν** | *you like* |
| [too arési] | **του αρέσει** | *he/it likes* | [too arésoon] | **του αρέσουν** | *he/it likes* |
| [tis arési] | **της αρέσει** | *she likes* | [tis arésoon] | **της αρέσουν** | *she likes* |
| [mas arési] | **μας αρέσει** | *we like* | [mas arésoon] | **μας αρέσουν** | *we like* |
| [sas arési] | **σας αρέσει** | *you like* (pl/fml) | [sas arésoon] | **σας αρέσουν** | *you like* (pl/fml) |
| [toos arési] | **τους αρέσει** | *they like* | [toos arésoon] | **τους αρέσουν** | *they like* |

Have you noticed that the set of pronouns here are identical to the possessive pronouns introduced in Unit 5?

The first two forms in each case have an alternative contracted form: [marési] **μ'αρέσει** and [sarési] **σ'αρέσει**, and [marésoon] **μ'αρέσουν** and [sarésoon] **σ'αρέσουν**.

Look at the following examples:

| | | |
|---|---|---|
| [moo arési o kanapés]. | **Μου αρέσει ο καναπές.** | *I like the sofa.* |
| [moo arésoon i karékles]. | **Μου αρέσουν οι καρέκλες.** | *I like the chairs.* |
| [THen too arési o kathréftis]. | **Δεν του αρέσει ο καθρέφτης.** | *He doesn't like the mirror.* |
| [the mas arésoon ta hrómata]. | **Δε μας αρέσουν τα χρώματα.** | *We don't like the colors.* |

## 4 NOUN GROUPS

You have probably noticed that word endings play an important role in Greek.

| Masculine (ο) | Feminine (η) | Neuter (το) |
|---|---|---|
| **-ας, -ης, -ες, -ος** | **-α, -η** | **-ι, -ο, -μα** |
| νιπτήρας, νεροχύτης, καναπές, πάγκος | καρέκλα, αυλή | τραπέζι, ψυγείο, διαμέρισμα |

All examples, except **διαμέρισμα**, were taken from this unit. Can you flip through the pages and add a couple of other examples in the three groups above?

## 5 PLURAL NOUNS

As in English, there are different ways to form plural nouns in Greek. Below are the most important regular plural changes. Look at the list. You don't have to try to memorize everything at once; instead come back to it as often as necessary.

### *Masculine*

| | | |
|---|---|---|
| [o niptíras] | **ο νιπτήρας** | *sink* |
| [i niptíres] | **οι νιπτήρες** | *sinks* |
| [o pángos] | **ο πάγκος** | *counter* |
| [i pángi] | **οι πάγκοι** | *counters* |
| [o kathréftis] | **ο καθρέφτης** | *mirror* |
| [i kathréftes] | **οι καθρέφτες** | *mirrors* |

***Feminine***

| | | |
|---|---|---|
| [i avlí] | **η αυλή** | *yard* |
| [i avlés] | **οι αυλές** | *yards* |
| [i polithróna] | **η πολυθρόνα** | *armchair* |
| [i polithrónes] | **οι πολυθρόνες** | *armchairs* |
| [i koozína] | **η κουζίνα** | *kitchen* |
| [i koozínes] | **οι κουζίνες** | *kitchens* |

***Neuter***

| | | |
|---|---|---|
| [to THomátio] | **το δωμάτιο** | *room* |
| [ta THomátia] | **τα δωμάτια** | *rooms* |
| [to kreváti] | **το κρεβάτι** | *bed* |
| [ta krevátia] | **τα κρεβάτια** | *beds* |
| [to trapézi] | **το τραπέζι** | *table* |
| [ta trapézia] | **τα τραπέζια** | *tables* |

## 6 COLORS

This unit has introduced the words for two colors: [mávro] **μαύρο** *black* and [áspro] **άσπρο** *white*. Here are some more.

| | | | | | |
|---|---|---|---|---|---|
| [mov] | **μωβ** | *purple* | [ble] | **μπλε** | *blue* |
| [prásino] | **πράσινο** | *green* | [kítrino] | **κίτρινο** | *yellow* |
| [portokalí] | **πορτοκαλί** | *orange* | [kókino] | **κόκκινο** | *red* |

Many words for colors are declined as adjectives, i.e. the color [kítrino] **κίτρινο** yellow comes from **κίτριν-ος/-η/-ο**. Some other examples include **πράσινο** and **κόκκινο**. There are also several other words for colors which are not declined and have only one form. Some examples include μωβ/μοβ, μπλε, μπεζ. These words usually come from French.

# Practice

**1 How well do you know your flags? Look at the pictures of the six flags. What colors should each of them be?**

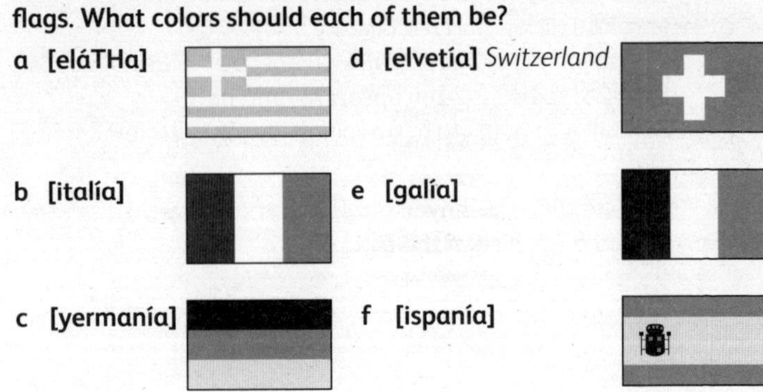

**2 Somebody wants more than one of everything. Can you change the sentences from singular to plural, following the example?**

[moo arési to trapézi] ⟶ [moo arésoon ta trapézia]

**a** [moo arési o kathréftis]
**b** [moo arési o kanapés]
**c** [moo arési i karékla]
**d** [moo arési i polithróna]
**e** [moo arési to bánio]
**f** [moo arési to kreváti]

**LANGUAGE TIP**

The word [bánio] **μπάνιο** not only means *bathroom* but also *bathtub* and *swimming.*

**3 It is useful to learn some words in pairs (either opposites or words that mean similar things). Match each word in the left-hand column with one in the right-hand column to make pairs.**

**a** [strongilós] στρογγυλός
**b** [mikrós] μικρός
**c** [oréos] ωραίος
**d** [THíkeos] δίκαιος
**e** [lígos] λίγος

**1** [áshimos] άσχημος
**2** [polís] πολύς
**3** [áTHikos] άδικος
**4** [megálos] μεγάλος
**5** [tetrágonos] τετράγωνος

**4 In the previous exercise all words were given in the masculine form. Can you change the endings to neuter following the example? Can you give the neuter and feminine forms of the adjectives in exercise 3?**

[strongilós] ⟶ [strongiló]

**a** [mikrós]
**b** [oréos]
**c** [THíkeos]
**d** [lígos]
**e** [áshimos]
**f** [polís]
**g** [áTHikos]
**h** [megálos]
**i** [tetrágonos]

**5 Rearrange these lines to make a dialogue.**

**a** [egó protimó ta mikrá spítia]. Εγώ προτιμώ τα μικρά σπίτια.
**b** [ne], [alá íne polí megálo]. Ναι, αλλά είναι πολύ μεγάλο.
**c** [THen éhis THíkio]. Δεν έχεις δίκιο.
**d** [moo arésoon ta megála spítia]. Μου αρέσουν τα μεγάλα σπίτια.
**e** [soo arési to spíti mas]? Σου αρέσει το σπίτι μας;
**f** [óhi]! [óhi]! [antipathó ta mikrá spítia]! Όχι, όχι! Αντιπαθώ τα μικρά σπίτια!

**6 07.10 Listen again to Conversation 2 of this unit and fill in the blanks using a word from the box.**

[vévea] [alá] [THíkio] [kathréftis] [áspro] [arésoon] [praktikó] [lootró]

**Elpida** [eTHó] [íne to vesé]. [íne lígo mikró] [alá polí] **a** _______ [ótan íne anángi].

**Mary** [ne], **b** _______.

**Elpida** [apó'THo to] **c** _______ [soo arési]?

**Mary** [moo arési polí]. [moo] **d** _______ [ta hrómata polí] [ke o strongilós] **e** _______

**Elpida** [ne] [to mávro ke] **f** _______ [kánoon] [megáli antíthesi]. **g** _______ [moo arésoon].

**Mary** [simfonó]. [éhis] **h** _______.

**7 Read the following conversation between Vasiliki and Olga about Greece. Then say whether each of the sentences is true or false.**

**Vasiliki** [moo arési i eláTHa] [yiatí íne mikrí].

**Olga** [THen simfonó]. [THen íne polí mikrí].

**Vasiliki** [THiafonó] [alá] ... [moo arési] [o kerós[1]] [stin eláTHa].

**Olga** [eTHó] [simfonó mazí soo]. [éhis THíkio].

**Vasiliki** [vévea], [yiatí THen protimó] [tin vrohí[2]] [sto lonTHíno].

**Olga** [THen éhis áTHiko]

[1][kerós] **καιρός** *weather*; [2] [vrohí] **βροχή** *rain*

- **a** They both believe Greece is a small country.
- **b** They both agree that Greece has nice weather.
- **c** Vasiliki dislikes rainy days in London.
- **d** Vasiliki dislikes the weather in Greece.
- **e** Olga likes the weather in Greece.

**8 Now can you translate the conversation in exercise 7?**

**9 07.11 Listen to Nikos describing his house. Look at the plan and decide whether or not it is Nikos' house.**

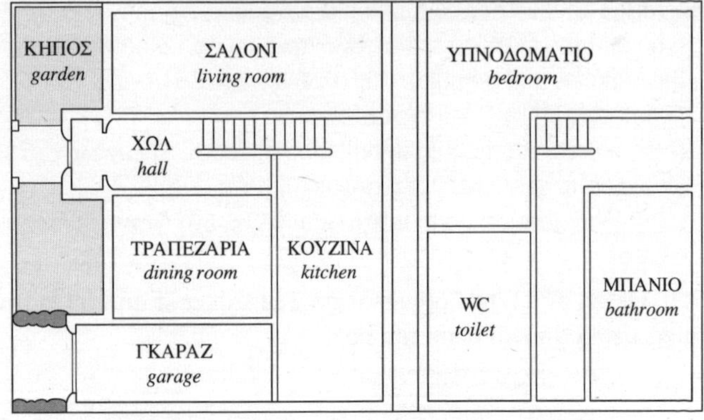

**10 Now sort all words in the above plan by gender. There are three words not of Greek origin. Which gender is your best guess?**

# Test yourself

**How did you find Unit 7? It introduced some important new vocabulary – let's see how much of it you remember.**

1 Can you name four of your favorite colors?

2 How would you say *I like*, *I agree* and *I'm right* in Greek?

3 What are the opposites of *I like*, *I agree* and *I'm right* in Greek?

4 What are the two Greek words for *dislike*?

5 Can you name five items of furniture?

6 How would you say *square*, *big* and *black* in Greek?

7 What are the opposites of *square*, *big* and *black* in Greek?

8 Name three electrical appliances.

## SELF CHECK

| | **I CAN. . .** |
|---|---|
| • | . . . agree or disagree with someone. |
| • | . . . say if I like or dislike something. |
| • | . . . use more Greek nouns in singular and plural form. |
| • | . . . use adjectives. |
| • | . . . use words for color and furniture. |

# 8

**In this unit you will learn how to:**

» talk about daily routines.
» tell the time.
» count from 101 to 1,000.
» use Greek adverbs of frequency.

# Πώς περνάς την ημέρα σου;

My progress tracker

| DAY / DATE | | | | | |
|---|---|---|---|---|---|
| | ○ | ○ | ○ | ○ | ○ |
| | ○ | ○ | ○ | ○ | ○ |
| | ○ | ○ | ○ | ○ | ○ |
| | ○ | ○ | ○ | ○ | ○ |
| | ○ | ○ | ○ | ○ | ○ |

## Breakfast, lunch and dinner

[proinó] **Πρωινό** *Breakfast* is almost non-existent in Greece, instead they usually have [kafé] **καφέ** *coffee*, [tsái] **τσάι** *tea* or [gála] **γάλα** *milk* with perhaps a [kooloóri] **κουλούρι** *sesame breadstick*, a [krooasán] **κρουασάν** *croissant* or [dimitriaká] **δημητριακά** *cereal*. Continental and cooked breakfasts are available in hotels and restaurants. As a mid-morning snack, Greek people might buy a [tirópita] **τυρόπιτα** *cheese pie*, [spanakópita] **σπανακόπιτα** *spinach pie* or [tost] **τοστ** *toasted sandwich*.

[mesimerianó] **Μεσημεριανό** *Lunch* is often a full and at times heavy meal, which definitely requires an afternoon siesta! [vraTHinó] **Βραδινό** *Dinner*, on the other hand, when eaten at home, is usually just a light snack or leftovers from lunch. Many people go out for dinner with friends or colleagues, and this meal often lasts for several hours and continues late into the night. All three words for the different meals derive from the time of day they are eaten: [proinó] **πρωινό** from [proí] **πρωί** *morning*; [mesimerianó] **μεσημεριανό** from [mesiméri] **μεσημέρι** *midday/ afternoon* and [vraTHinó] **βραδινό** from [vráTHi] **βράδυ** *evening/night*.

**Name three things Greek people might have for breakfast.**

# Vocabulary builder

## ΣΠΟΡ ΚΑΙ ΧΟΜΠΙ *SPORTS AND HOBBIES*

**1** 08.01 **Look at the phrases and complete the missing English expressions. Then listen and try to imitate the pronunciation of the speakers.**

| | |
|---|---|
| Μ' αρέσει να κάνω γυμναστική συχνά. | *I often like to work out.* |
| Δε μ' αρέσει το τένις καθόλου. | *_______ tennis at all.* |
| Ένα χόμπι μου είναι το περπάτημα. | *Walking is one _______ of mine.* |
| Βλέπω ποδόσφαιρο πάντα. | *I always watch football.* |
| Μαγειρεύω σχεδόν κάθε μέρα. | *I cook almost every _______.* |
| Δεν έχω πολύ ελεύθερο χρόνο. | *_______ much free time.* |
| Σπάνια βλέπω τηλεόραση. | *I seldom watch TV.* |
| Το αγαπημένο μου σπορ είναι το μπάσκετ. | *Basketball is my favorite _______.* |

## ΚΑΘΗΜΕΡΙΝΕΣ ΡΟΥΤΙΝΕΣ *DAILY ROUTINES*

**2** 08.02 **Listen a couple of times to two people talking about their daily routines. Then read the phrases and decide whether each one is true or false. Finally, listen again and try to imitate the pronunciation of the speakers.**

| Muhamed | Julieta |
|---|---|
| **Σηκώνομαι πολύ νωρίς.** | **Σηκώνομαι πολύ αργά.** |
| **Μαθαίνω Ελληνικά κάθε μέρα.** | **Δεν μαθαίνω Ελληνικά.** |
| **Κάνω ντους κάθε πρωί.** | **Κάνω μπάνιο κάθε βράδυ.** |
| **Πίνω λίγο καφέ.** | **Πίνω πολύ τσάι.** |
| **Επιστρέφω στο σπίτι αργά.** | **Επιστρέφω στο διαμέρισμα νωρίς.** |
| **Τελειώνω τη δουλειά στις τρεις.** | **Τελειώνω τη δουλειά στις τέσσερις.** |

**3** 08.03 **Now listen to some more daily routines and match them with the pictures. The first has been done for you. If you want to challenge yourself, cover the English translations. Then listen again and try to imitate the pronunciation of the speakers.**

[ftáno sti THooliá].

Φτάνω στη δουλειά. *I arrive at work.* 

[sikónome argá].

| | | |
|---|---|---|
| Σηκώνομαι αργά.<br>[epistréfo sto spíti argá]. | *I get up late.* | ______ |
| Επιστρέφω στο σπίτι αργά.<br>[mathéno eliniká]. | *I get home late.* | ______ |
| Μαθαίνω Ελληνικά.<br>[páo sto kreváti argá]. | *I study Greek.* | ______ |
| Πάω στο κρεβάτι αργά.<br>[páo sti THooliá]. | *I go to bed late.* | ______ |
| Πάω στη δουλειά.<br>[tró-o vraTHinó]. | *I go to work.* | ______ |
| Τρώω βραδινό.<br>[THen tró-o proinó]. | *I eat dinner.* | ______ |
| Δεν τρώω πρωινό.<br>[tró-o mesimerianó norís]. | *I don't eat breakfast.* | ______ |
| Τρώω μεσημεριανό νωρίς.<br>[káno dooz]. | *I eat lunch early.* | ______ |
| Κάνω ντους.<br>[píno polí kafé]. | *I take a shower.* | ______ |
| Πίνω πολύ καφέ.<br>[telióno ti THooliá]. | *I drink a lot of coffee.* | ______ |
| Τελειώνω τη δουλειά.<br>[pérno to asansér]. | *I finish work.* | ______ |
| Παίρνω το ασανσέρ.<br>[vlépo lígo tileórasi]. | *I use the lift.* | ______ |
| Βλέπω λίγο τηλεόραση. | *I watch some TV.* | ______ |

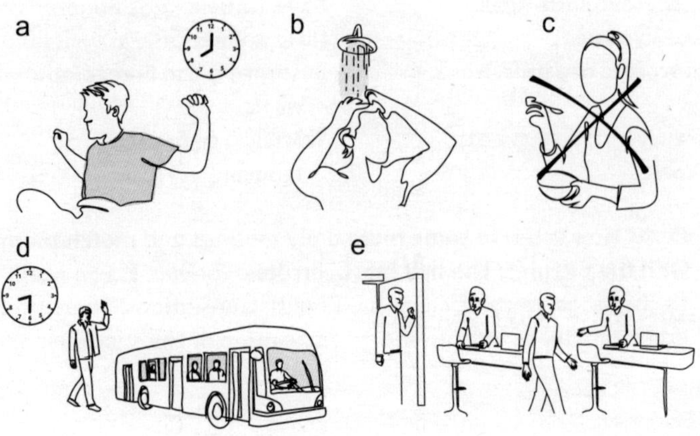

**Here are the verbs sorted according to their stems. Learn at least five by heart.**

| Stem 1 and stem 2 without change | Stem 1 and stem 2 with a small change | No obvious similarities between the two stems |
|---|---|---|
| πάω / πάω, κάνω / κάνω | φτάνω / φτάσω, επιστρέφω / επιστρέψω, πίνω / πιω, τελειώνω / τελειώσω | σηκώνομαι / σηκωθώ, μαθαίνω / μάθω, τρώω /φάω, παίρνω / πάρω, βλέπω / δω |

# Conversation 1 What time is it?

## NEW WORDS AND EXPRESSIONS 1

| Stem 1 and stem 2 without change | Stem 1 and stem 2 with a small change | No obvious similarities between the two stems |
|---|---|---|
| είμαι / είμαι | περνάω(-ώ) / περάσω, ετοιμάζω / ετοιμάσω, μαγειρεύω / μαγειρέψω | λέ(γ)ω / πω, |

**08.04 Listen to the words and expressions that are used in the next conversation. Note their meanings.**

| | | |
|---|---|---|
| [óra] | ώρα | *time* |
| [ti óra íne tóra]? | Τι ώρα είναι τώρα; | *What time is it now?* |
| [akrivós] | ακριβώς | *exactly* |
| [pes moo] | πες μου | *tell me* (sing/infml) |
| [pernás] | περνάς | *you spend* (sing/infml) |
| [norís] | νωρίς | *early* |
| [siníthos] | συνήθως | *usually* |
| [sikónome] | σηκώνομαι | *I get up.* |
| [etimázo] | ετοιμάζω | *I prepare.* |
| [pérno] | παίρνω | *I take.* |
| [sholío] | σχολείο | *school* |
| [épita] | έπειτα | *then, after that* |
| [páo] | πάω | *I go, I am going.* |
| [psónia] | ψώνια | *shopping* |
| [teliká] | τελικά | *finally* |
| [mayirévo] | μαγειρεύω | *I cook.* |
| [THistihós] | δυστυχώς | *unfortunately* |

**08.05** *Elpida tells Mary about her daily routine.*

**1 Listen to the conversation a couple of times. What time does Elpida usually get up?**

| | | |
|---|---|---|
| **Mary** | [ti óra íne tóra]? | *What time is it now?* |
| **Elpida** | [íne mía akrivós]. [yiatí ti thélis]? | *It's one o'clock exactly. Why, what do you want?* |
| **Mary** | [pes moo], [pos pernás tin iméra soo]? [ti kánis] [norís to proí]? | *Tell me, how do you spend your day? What do you do early in the morning?* |
| **Elpida** | [siníthos] [sikónome stis eptá], [etimázo proinó] [ke piyeno ta peTHiá] [sto sholío]. [épita páo yia psónia]. [teliká mayirévo] ... [THistihós]. | *I usually get up at seven, I prepare breakfast and I take the children to school. Afterwards I go shopping. Finally, I cook ... unfortunately.* |

**Mary** Τι ώρα είναι τώρα;
**Ελπίδα** Είναι μία ακριβώς. Γιατί, τι θέλεις;
**Mary** Πες μου, πώς περνάς την ημέρα σου; Τι κάνεις νωρίς το πρωί;
**Ελπίδα** Συνήθως σηκώνομαι στις επτά. Ετοιμάζω πρωινό και πηγαίνω τα παιδιά στο σχολείο. Έπειτα πάω για ψώνια. Τελικά, μαγειρεύω ... δυστυχώς.

**2 Now read the conversation and answer the questions.**

**a** Which Greek phrase means *Afterwards I go shopping*?

**b** Does Elpida sound happy about her routine? Which word tells you?

**3 Listen again and pay special attention to the words which run together. Practice speaking the part of Elpida.**

# Language discovery 1

**1 The conversation includes some words that relate to when or how often something happens. Can you find the Greek words for:**

**a** finally
**b** afterwards
**c** usually
**d** early
**e** exactly

**2 There are also some expressions relating to telling the time. Find the Greek for:**

**a** What's the time?
**b** It's one o'clock exactly.
**c** I usually get up at seven.

### 1 TELLING THE TIME

08.06 Telling the time in Greek is not very difficult. The most important thing, of course, is to remember the numbers from 1 to 60! If you are unsure, go back to Units 4 and 5 and refresh your memory before continuing. There are two different ways of telling the time: the easy way and the more challenging way! Let's start with the easy way. Read each example first before you listen to the audio, and check that you have the correct pronunciation. Alternatively, you can always listen to the audio first and then repeat after the speaker.

| | | |
|---|---|---|
| [mía ke triánda pénde] | **μία και τριάντα πέντε** | *one thirty-five* |
| [THío ke íkosi] | **δύο και είκοσι** | *two twenty* |
| [tris ke triánda] | **τρεις και τριάντα** | *three thirty* |
| [téseris ke THekapénde] | **τέσσερις και δεκαπέντε** | *four fifteen* |
| [pénde ke saránda pénde] | **πέντε και σαράντα πέντε** | *five forty-five* |

The more challenging way requires you to remember some important words:

| | | |
|---|---|---|
| [ke] | **και** | *past* (you already know this word as *and*) |
| [pará] | **παρά** | *to, before* |
| [tétarto] | **τέταρτο** | *quarter* |
| [misí] | **μισή** | *half, half past* |

Remember that the *hour* [óra] **ώρα** comes before the [leptá] **λεπτά** *minutes*. The word [ke] **και** *past* comes after the hours and before the minutes. Once again, say the times that you see and then listen to the audio and check your pronunciation.

| | | |
|---|---|---|
| [THío pará íkosi pénde] | **δύο παρά είκοσι πέντε** | *twenty-five to two* |
| [THío ke íkosi] | **δύο και είκοσι** | *twenty past two* |
| [tris ke misí] | **τρεις και μισή** | *half past three* |
| [téseris ke tétarto] | **τέσσερις και τέταρτο** | *quarter past four* |
| [éksi pará tétarto] | **έξι παρά τέταρτο** | *quarter to six* |

**Π.μ.** means *a.m.* and **μ.μ.** means *p.m.* The two letters stand for [pro mesimvrías] **προ μεσημβρίας** and [metá mesimvrías] **μετά μεσημβρίας** respectively. You should use the full forms when saying the expressions in Greek and not just the two letters, as in English.

Note too that as [óra] **ώρα** *hour* is feminine, the feminine form of [mía] **μία**, [tris] **τρεις** and [téseris] **τέσσερις** is needed.

Finally, [stis] **Στις** means *at* when telling the time, as the number is plural, except for [sti mía i óra] **στη μία η ώρα** *at one o'clock*, which uses the singular [sti] **στη**.

## 2 THE NUMBERS 101–1,000

**08.07** Talking of numbers, let's continue from where we left off in Unit 5. Note and study the new numbers from 101 to 1,000. Then listen and repeat after the speakers.

| | | |
|---|---|---|
| [ekatón éna] | **εκατόν ένα** | *one hundred and one* |
| [ekatón pénde] | **εκατόν πέντε** | *one hundred and five* |
| [ekatón evTHomínda] | **εκατόν εβδομήντα** | *one hundred and seventy* |
| [THiakósia] | **διακόσια** | *two hundred* |
| [triakósia] | **τριακόσια** | *three hundred* |
| [tetrakósia] | **τετρακόσια** | *four hundred* |
| [pendakósia] | **πεντακόσια** | *five hundred* |
| [eksakósia] | **εξακόσια** | *six hundred* |
| [eptakósia] or [eftakósia] | **επτακόσια/εφτακόσια** | *seven hundred* |
| [oktakósia] or [ohtakósia] | **οκτακόσια/οχτακόσια** | *eight hundred* |
| [eniakósia] | **εννιακόσια** | *nine hundred* |
| [híljі], [hílies], [hília] | **χίλιοι** (m), **χίλιες** (f), **χίλια** (n) | *one thousand* |

Most numbers are not declined. There are some exceptions, including the numbers 1, 3, 4 (and any combinations with these three numbers, i.e. 33, 64, 113, 524 etc.) or the number 1000 in the table above. The word for 100 is [ekató] **εκατό** but then changes to [ekatón] **εκατόν** from 101 to 199, i.e. [ekatón tría] **εκατόν τρία** 103 or [ekatón penínda] **εκατόν πενήντα** 150 etc., including the three examples in the table above. Numbers will be useful when telling the time, giving your age, saying your street number, temperatures, etc. You can always learn numbers which have personal meaning to you, i.e. your birth year and your mobile number.

# Conversation 2 I go to work

## NEW WORDS AND EXPRESSIONS 2

**08.08 Listen to the words and expressions that are used in the next conversation. Note their meanings.**

| | | |
|---|---|---|
| [iméra] | ημέρα | *day* |
| [óli tin iméra] | όλη την ημέρα | *all day* |
| [ksipnáo] | ξυπνάω | *I wake up.* |
| [dooz] | ντους | *shower* |
| [tró-o] | τρώω | *I eat.* |
| [metá] | μετά | *then, afterwards* |
| [pérno] | παίρνω | *I take* |
| [tréno] | τρένο | *train* |
| [epistréfis] | επιστρέφεις | *you return* (sing/infml) |
| [méhri] | μέχρι | *to, until* |
| [tróte] | τρώτε | *you eat* (pl/fml) |
| [vraTHinó] | βραδινό | *dinner* (n) |
| [yíro] | γύρω | *around, about* |
| [stis] | στις | *at* |
| [ékso] | έξω | *out, outside* |

There are two verbs here where the second stem is as follows: [ksipnáo (-ó)] **ξυπνάω (-ώ)** *to wake up* and [epistréfo] **επιστρέφω** *to return / to come back*: **ξυπνάω (-ώ)** / **ξυπνήσω** and **επιστρέφω** / **επιστρέψω.**

08.09 *Now Mary tells Elpida about her daily routine.*

**1 Listen to the conversation a couple of times. When does Mary usually wake up?**

| | | |
|---|---|---|
| **Elpida** | [esí ti kánis] [óli tin iméra]? | *What do you do all day?* |
| **Mary** | [ksipnáo stis eptámisi] [káno éna dooz] [ke tró-o proinó]. [metá pérno to tréno] [ke páo sti THooliá]. | *I wake up at 7:30, I take a shower and have breakfast. Then I take the train and go to work.* |
| **Elpida** | [ti óra epistréfis spíti]? | *What time do you get back home?* |
| **Mary** | [THoolévo siníthos] [apó tis THéka] [méhri tis téseris] [epistréfo spíti] [stis pendémisi]. | *I usually work from ten o'clock to four o'clock. I get back home at 5:30.* |
| **Elpida** | [ti óra] [tróte vraTHinó]? | *What time do you eat dinner?* |
| **Mary** | [yíro stis eptá] [sto spíti] [i stis októ ékso]. | *Around seven o'clock at home or at eight o'clock when eating out (lit. at eight o'clock out).* |

**Ελπίδα** Εσύ, τι κάνεις όλη την ημέρα;

**Mary** Ξυπνάω στις επτάμιση, κάνω ένα ντους και τρώω πρωινό. Μετά παίρνω το τρένο και πάω στη δουλειά.

**Ελπίδα** Τι ώρα επιστρέφεις σπίτι;

**Mary** Δουλεύω συνήθως από τις δέκα μέχρι τις τέσσερις. Επιστρέφω σπίτι στις πεντέμιση.

**Ελπίδα** Τι ώρα τρώτε βραδινό;

**Mary** Γύρω στις επτά στο σπίτι ή στις οκτώ έξω.

**2 Now read the conversation and answer the questions.**

- **a** When does Mary usually work?
- **b** When does she usually have dinner?

**3 Listen again and pay special attention to the words which run together. Practice speaking the part of Mary.**

# Language discovery 2

**1 Which expressions have to do with telling the time in this conversation? Find the Greek phrases that correspond to:**

- **a** around seven o'clock at home
- **b** from ten o'clock to four o'clock
- **c** I wake up at 7:30.

**2 The conversation also includes some useful verbs for describing daily activities. Try to give the Greek equivalents of the following English expressions without looking at the conversation. Then check and compare your answers.**

**a** I return home

**b** I usually work.

**c** I go to work.

**d** I take the train.

**e** I take a shower.

**f** I have breakfast.

**3 Can you now write both stems from the verbs in the previous exercise? Try both phonetic transliteration and Greek script!**

## 1 EXPRESSIONS OF TIME

The two conversations in this unit introduced you to a new group of words that express how often something happens. These words are called adverbs of frequency. Look at the following list:

| | | |
|---|---|---|
| [pánda] | **πάντα** | *always* |
| [sheTHón pánda] | **σχεδόν πάντα** | *almost always* |
| [sihná] | **συχνά** | *often* |
| [merikés forés] | **μερικές φορές** | *sometimes* |
| [spánia] | **σπάνια** | *rarely* |
| [sheTHón poté] | **σχεδόν ποτέ** | *hardly ever* (lit. *almost never)* |
| [poté] | **ποτέ** | *never* |

Do not confuse the word [poté] **ποτέ** *never*, with a stress on the last syllable, with the word [póte] **πότε** *when*, which is a new word for you and has the stress on the first syllable.

In this unit you have also been introduced to more words relating to time. Study them here and come back to this list whenever you need to refresh your memory.

| | | |
|---|---|---|
| [épita] | **έπειτα** | *then, later, afterwards* |
| [teliká] | **τελικά** | *finally, in the end* |
| [méhri] | **μέχρι** | *until, up to* |
| [yíro] | **γύρω** | *around, about* |
| [metá] | **μετά** | *afterwards, later* |
| [norís] | **νωρίς** | *early* |
| [argá] | **αργά** | *late* |

## THE DAILY ROUTINE

Daily routines are often universal. Here are some useful questions to ask people about how they spend their time, what hobbies they have and whether they like sport or not:

[pos pernás tin iméra]?/[échis hóbi]/[ti spor soo arésoon]

**Πώς περνάς την ημέρα σου/Έχεις χόμπι/Τι σπορ σου αρέσουν;**
*How do you spend your day?/Do you have any hobbies?/What kind of sports do you like?*

[ti kánis to proí/mesiméri/apóyevma/vráTHi]?
**Τι κάνεις το πρωί/μεσημέρι/απόγευμα/βράδυ;**
*What do you do in the morning/in the afternoon/in the evening/at night?*

There are, of course, no set answers to these questions. You might reply with one or more of the following:

[mayirévo]/[THoolévo]/[kimáme]/[tró-o]/[píno]/[perpató]/ [ého polá hóbi].
**μαγειρεύω/δουλεύω/κοιμάμαι/τρώω/πίνω/περπατώ/έχω πολλά χόμπι.**
*I cook/I work/I sleep/I eat/I drink/I walk/I have many hobbies.*

[marési to poTHósfero, to basket ke to kolímbi] .
**Μ' αρέσει το ποδόσφαιρο, το μπάσκετ και το κολύμπι.**
*I like football, basketball and swimming.*

# Practice

1 **The following sentences describe Priyanka's daily routine but in jumbled order. Rearrange the sentences into the correct order. To make it more of a challenge, cover up the transliteration column and work only with the Greek script!**

| | | |
|---|---|---|
| **a** | [ftáno sti THooliá] [stis októ]. | Φτάνω στη δουλειά στις οκτώ. |
| **b** | [sikónome norís]. | Σηκώνομαι νωρίς. |
| **c** | [epistréfo sto spíti argá]. | Επιστρέφω στο σπίτι αργά. |
| **d** | [péfto sto kreváti argá]. | Πέφτω στο κρεβάτι αργά. |
| **e** | [páo sti THooliá]. | Πάω στη δουλειά. |
| **f** | [pérno vraTHinó stis eniá]. | Παίρνω βραδινό στις εννιά. |
| **g** | [THen tró-o proinó] [móno kafé]. | Δεν τρώω πρωινό, μόνο καφέ. |
| **h** | [tró-o mesimerianó sti THooliá]. | Τρώω μεσημεριανό στη δουλειά. |
| **i** | [káno dooz]. | Κάνω ντους. |
| **j** | [píno polí kafé sti THooliá]. | Πίνω πολύ καφέ στη δουλειά. |
| **k** | [telióno ti THooliá stis éksi]. | Τελειώνω τη δουλειά στις έξι. |
| **l** | [vlépo lígo tileórasi stis THéka]. | Βλέπω λίγο τηλεόραση στις δέκα. |

2 **Can you translate the sentences in the previous exercise into English?**

3 **How do you study Greek? Use a word from the box to answer each of the following questions about how frequently you do each task. Note that there are no correct answers as such, since every learner will have their own way of learning. To make the exercise more challenging, try to write each word in Greek script.**

| [pánda] [sheTHón pánda] [siníthos] [sihná] [merikés forés] [spánia] [sheTHón poté] [poté] |
|---|

**a** I listen to the recording.
**b** I speak to Greek speakers.
**c** I use a Greek dictionary.
**d** I revise past units.
**e** I make lists of important words.
**f** I listen to Greek music.
**g** I record myself speaking Greek.

4 08.10 **Listen to some people saying at what time they do different activities. Match each time in the left-hand column with the correct activity in the right-hand column.**

**a** 8:15
**b** 9:15
**c** 13:30
**d** 16:20
**e** 16:41
**f** 17:05

**1** [THen tró-o mesimerianó stis]
**2** [pérno to tréno stis]
**3** [tró-o proinó stis]
**4** [ftáno sto spíti stis]
**5** [ftáno sti THooliá stis]
**6** [telióno ti THooliá stis]

5 08.11 **Listen to the people telling you what time it is. Can you put the times in the order you hear them?**

| 8:30 | 7:05 | 10:30 | 11:45 | 1:45 | 8:05 |
|---|---|---|---|---|---|

**a** ______
**b** ______
**c** ______
**d** ______
**e** ______
**f** ______

6 **Can you identify which option is wrong in each case?**

**a** [THoolévo]
**1** [sto spíti]
**2** [sto ble]
**3** [THistihós]
**4** [stis THéka]

**b** [epistréfo]
**1** [sto THiamérizma]
**2** [sto vraTHinó]
**3** [sti THooliá]
**4** [sto aeroTHrómio]

c [telióno]
1 [ti THooliá]
2 [ton kafé]
3 [to mesimerianó]
4 [to asansér]

d [pérno]
1 [to asansér]
2 [to proinó moo]
3 [kreváti argá]
4 [THooliá sto spíti]

**7** 08.12 **Listen again to Conversation 2 and complete each sentence by choosing one word from the box.**

| [epistréfis] [óli] [tróte] [méhri] [apó] [yíro] [tró-o] [ksipnáo] [pérno] [ékso] |
|---|

**Elpida** [esí ti kánis] **a** _______ [tin iméra]?
**Mary** **b** _______ [stis eptámisi] [káno éna dooz] [ke] **c** _______ [proinó]. [metá] **d** _______ [to tréno] [ke páo sti THooliá].
**Elpida** [ti óra] **e** _______ [spíti]?
**Mary** [THoolévo siníthos] **f** _______ [tis THéka] **g** _______ [tis téseris] [epistréfo spíti] [stis pendémisi].
**Elpida** [ti óra] **h** _______ [vraTHinó]?
**Mary** **i** _______ [stis eptá] [sto spíti] [i stis októ] **j** _______.

# Test yourself

**1** Can you say the following numbers in Greek?
**a** 104
**b** 184
**c** 231
**d** 456
**e** 827
**f** 951
**g** 1,000

**2** Can you say the following times in Greek?
**a** 7:20
**b** 8:30
**c** 9:00
**d** 11:15
**e** 1:30
**f** 4:10
**g** 5:45

**3** How do you say the following verbs in Greek?
**a** get up
**b** arrive
**c** finish
**d** come back
**e** take

**4** Translate the following sentences into Greek:

**a** I always get up at 6:15.

**b** I never arrive at work early.

**c** I sometimes finish my work late.

**d** I seldom eat out.

**e** I almost always take the train.

**5** Name three of your favorite hobbies.

## SELF CHECK

| | **I CAN...** |
|---|---|
| • | ... talk about daily routines. |
| • | ... tell the time. |
| • | ... count from 101 to 1,000. |
| • | ... use Greek adverbs of frequency. |

# 9

**In this unit you will learn how to:**

- » talk about your free time.
- » ask others about their hobbies.
- » name different kinds of Greek music and different types of books and films.
- » use loanwords in Greek.

# Έχεις χόμπι;

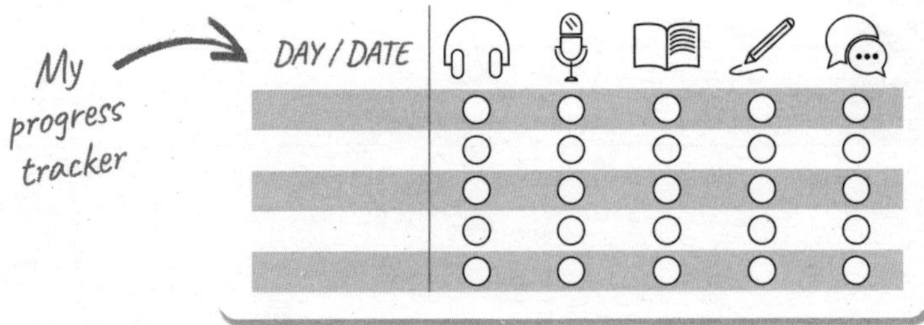


## Hobbies and Greek music

Greek people tend to enjoy reading, television, cinema and theater. Other favorite pastimes are watching and participating in sport, going to the gym, using the internet and traveling abroad. The national favorite sport is football, but basketball has recently become as popular. Outdoor activities such as [kiníghi] **κυνήγι** *hunting*, [psárema] **ψάρεμα** *fishing*, [pezoporía] **πεζοπορία** *hiking*, [orivasía] **ορειβασία** *mountain climbing* and of course [kolímbi] **κολύμπι** *swimming* are also popular. Most Greek people like listening to music and both Greek and international music can be heard every day on the radio or in bars and nightclubs. The most popular styles of traditional Greek music are [laiká] **λαϊκά** *pop music*, [elafrolaiká] **ελαφρολαϊκά** *soft pop music*, [rebétika] **ρεμπέτικα** *traditional Greek folk*, [rok] **ροκ** *rock music* and [nisiótika] **νησιώτικα** *Greek island music*. Every region has its own traditional music with local melodies and instruments. Some popular Greek instruments are the [boozoóki] **μπουζούκι** *bouzouki*, the [baglamaTHáki] **μπαγλαμαδάκι** *small bouzouki* and the [líra] **λύρα** *lyre*.

**The Greek words for some words relating to hobbies have not been provided in the text. The following are the Greek words for *television*, *gym*, computer and *traveling*. Can you work out which is which: κομπιούτερ, γυμναστήριο, ταξίδι, τηλεόραση?**

# Vocabulary builder

**ΜΟΥΣΙΚΗ, ΦΙΛΜ, ΒΙΒΛΙΑ, ΣΠΟΡ** *MUSIC, FILMS, BOOKS, SPORT*

**1** 09.01 **Look at the words and complete the missing English expressions. Then listen and try to imitate the pronunciation of the speakers.**

LANGUAGE TIP

This unit can be used as a starting point for you to come up with different word lists in groups. For instance, if you like books, you should be able to say what kind of books you enjoy reading. If you like sport, you should be able to name a few different types, and if you like music, you should be able to mention some local or international kinds of music. You can personalize the following lists by highlighting all the words that are especially relevant to your own tastes.

| **[moosikí]** | **Μουσική** | **Music** |
|---|---|---|
| [rok] | ροκ | _____ |
| [blooz] | μπλουζ | _____ |
| [laiká] | λαϊκά | *pop* |
| [tzaz] | τζαζ | _____ |
| [rebétika] | ρεμπέτικα | *Greek blues* |

| **[érga]** | **Έργα** | **Films** |
|---|---|---|
| [komoTHíes] | κωμωδίες | _____ |
| [THramatiká] | δραματικά | _____ |
| [thríler] | θρίλερ | *thriller* |
| [astinomiká] | αστυνομικά | *crime* |
| [epistimonikís fantasías] | επιστημονικής φαντασίας | *science fiction* |

| **[vivlía]** | **Βιβλία** | **Books** |
|---|---|---|
| [mithistorímata] | μυθιστορήματα | *novels* |
| [noovéles] | νουβέλες | _____ |
| [astinomiká] | αστυνομικά | *crime* |
| [istoríes agápis] | ιστορίες αγάπης | *love* _____ |
| [peripéties] | περιπέτειες | *adventure stories/thrillers* |

| **[spor]** | **Σπορ** | **Sports** |
|---|---|---|
| [poTHósfero] | ποδόσφαιρο | *football* |
| [ténis] | τένις | *tennis* |
| [vólei] | βόλεϋ | _____ |
| [ping pong] | πίνγκ πονγκ | *table tennis* |
| [básket] | μπάσκετ | _____ |

Most words here were given in plural. The table below has sorted out most of them according to gender. A few nouns with special endings were left out on purpose. Try to fill in the blanks.

| Masculine | Feminine | Neuter |
|---|---|---|
| | **-α ⟶ -ες** | **-ο ⟶ -α** |
| | κωμωδία – κωμωδίες,<br>_______ – νουβέλες,<br>_______ – ιστορίες,<br>_______ – περιπέτειες, | έργο – έργα,<br>_______ – δραματικά,<br>_______ – αστυνομικά,<br>_______ – βιβλία, |

**2 What types of movies do you like to watch? Give the equivalent in Greek:**

Crime drama

_______________

Science Fiction

_______________

Romance

_______________

Comedy

_______________

**3** 09.02 **Here are some questions and answers you might use when talking about hobbies. Complete the missing English words and then listen and try to imitate the speakers.**

| | | |
|---|---|---|
| [soo arési i moosikí]? | Σου αρέσει η μουσική; | *Do you like _____?* |
| [sarési to sinemá]? | Σ' αρέσει το σινεμά; | *Do you like the _____?* |
| [soo arésoon ta spor]? | Σου αρέσουν τα σπορ; | *Do you like _____?* |
| [ti hóbi éhis/éhete]? | Τι χόμπι έχεις/έχετε; | *What hobby do _____ have?* |
| [marési polí/lígho] | Μ' αρέσει πολύ/λίγο. | *I like it _____/a little bit.* |
| [Then marésoon ta spor] | Δεν μ' αρέσουν τα σπορ. | *I don't like sports.* |
| [Then kano ghimnastikí] | Δεν κάνω γυμναστική. | *I don't work out.* |
| [écho polá hóbi] | Έχω πολλά χόμπι. | *I _____ many hobbies.* |
| [marési na vlépo poTHósfero] | Μ' αρέσει να βλέπω ποδόσφαιρο. | *I like to watch _____.* |

# Conversation 1 What do you do in your free time?

## NEW WORDS AND EXPRESSIONS 1

09.03 **Listen to the words and expressions that are used in the next conversation. Note their meanings.**

| | | |
|---|---|---|
| [eléfthero] [hróno] | ελεύθερο χρόνο | *free time* |
| [marési] [nakoó-o] | μ' αρέσει ν' ακούω | *I like to listen to.* |
| [moosikí] | μουσική | *music* |
| [kiríos] | κυρίως | *mainly* |
| [laiká] | λαϊκά | *popular music* |
| [eléftheres óres] | ελεύθερες ώρες | *free time* (lit. *free hours*) |
| [tileórasi] | τηλεόραση | *television* |
| [raTHiófono] | ραδιόφωνο | *radio* |

09.04 *Angelos asks John about his free time.*

**1 What does John like to do?**

| | | |
|---|---|---|
| **Angelos** | [John], [ti kánis] [ton eléfthero hróno soo]? | *John, what do you do in your free time?* |
| **John** | [marési nakoó-o moosikí]. | *I like to listen to music.* |
| **Angelos** | [ti moosikí sarési]? | *What kind of music do you like?* |
| **John** | [kiríos laiká] [alá ke rok]. [esí pos pernás] [tis eléftheres óres soo]? | *Mainly pop but rock too. How do you spend your free time?* |
| **Angelos** | [vlépo tileórasi] [i akoó-o raTHiófono]. | *I watch TV or listen to the radio.* |
| **John** | [polí oréa]. | *Very nice.* |
| **Άγγελος** | John, τι κάνεις τον ελεύθερο χρόνο σου; | |
| **John** | μ' αρέσει ν' ακούω μουσική. | |
| **Άγγελος** | Τι μουσική σ' αρέσει; | |
| **John** | Κυρίως λαϊκά, αλλά και ροκ. Εσύ, πώς περνάς τις ελεύθερες ώρες σου; | |
| **Άγγελος** | Βλέπω τηλεόραση ή ακούω ραδιόφωνο. | |
| **John** | Πολύ ωραία. | |

**2 Now read the conversation and answer the following questions.**

**a** What kind of music does John like?

**b** What does Angelos do in his free time?

**3 Listen again and pay special attention to the words which run together. This time you can practice speaking the part of John.**

# Language discovery 1

**1 There are three expressions in the conversation which are used in a contracted form. Find these expressions using their English translations as a guide and try to guess which letter or letters are missing in each case.**

**a** I like **b** you like **c** to listen to

**2 What are the two ways of asking someone what they do in their free time?**

## 1 CONTRACTED FORMS

You have already seen that Greek uses many contracted forms. This unit includes the following contracted forms:

| Contracted form | Full form | English |
|---|---|---|
| [marési] **μ' αρέσει** | [moo] + [arési] **μου αρέσει** | *I like* (sing) |
| [marésoon] **μ' αρέσουν** | [moo] + [arésoon] **μου αρέσουν** | *I like* (pl) |
| [sarési] **σ' αρέσει** | [soo] + [arési] **σου αρέσει** | *you like* |
| [nakoó-o] **ν' ακούω** | [na] + [akoó-o] **να ακούω** | *to listen to* |

You can use either form. Simply remember that the contracted forms are more common.

## 2 QUESTION WORDS

In exercise 2, two different question words were used: [pos] **πώς** *how?* and [ti] **τι** *what?* Let's review some question words which you saw in previous units. If you cover the English translation, how many of these questions can you understand?

| | | |
|---|---|---|
| Unit 1: | **Πώς σε λένε; Γιατί είσαι εδώ;** | *What's your name? Why are you here?* |
| Unit 2: | **Από ποια πόλη; Από πού είσαι;** | *From which city? Where are you from?* |
| Unit 3: | **Πού μένεις; Ποιον / Ποια ξέρεις;** | *Where do you live? Who (male/female) do you know?* |
| Unit 4: | **Πόσα δωμάτια έχει;** | *How many rooms does it have?* |
| Unit 5: | **Πόσο χρονών είναι; Γιατί φεύγετε;** | *How old is he? Why are you leaving?* |
| Unit 6: | **Τι θέλεις; Τι θέλετε;** | *What do you want* (sing/pl)*?* |
| Unit 8: | **Τι ώρα είναι; Γιατί, τι θέλεις;** | *What time is it? Why, what do you want?* |

Question words are usually not declined. There are two exceptions, namely **πόσ-ος/-η/-ο** and **ποι-ος/-α/-ο**. For these two question words your attention should be geared towards gender (m/f/n), singular or plural, and case (nom./gen./acc.).

Grammatically speaking, these two words actually function as adjectives. Their full declination can be found in the grammar section at the back of the book. Check out the examples below and be aware of their different forms in context.

**πόσ-ος/-η/-ο Πόση ζάχαρη θες**; *How much sugar do you want?* **Πόσα βιβλία έχεις;** *How many books do you have?* **Πόσες ώρες κάνει το ταξίδι**; *How many hours does the trip take?*

**ποι-ος/-α/-ο Ποιος είναι αυτός**; *Who is this?* **Ποιον καφέ προτιμάς;** *Which (kind of) coffee do you prefer?* **Ξέρεις ποιες γυναίκες μιλούν ελληνικά εδώ;** *Do you know which women speak Greek here?*

### 3 TWO VERB PARTICLES

Past units briefly introduced two verb particles, namely [tha] **θα** *will/would* and [na] **να** *to*. Here are the examples from the previous units:

Unit 5: **Θέλω να σας ξαναδώ.** *I want to see you again.*

Unit 6: **Τι θα πάρετε παρακαλώ;** *What are you going to have* (lit. *will* you take) please? **Τι θα πιείτε;** What are you going to drink (lit. *will* you drink)?

Unit 7: **Έλα να σου δείξω το σπίτι.** Come and I'll (lit. *to*) show you the house.

These two verb particles are needed when you want to express intentions, decisions, wishes, and/or (dis)likes. Which verb stem will follow one of these two particles depends on what is actually meant with each particular message. Below are some similar examples which deliver two completely different messages. Read the examples carefully.

| Verb stem 1 | Verb stem 2 |
|---|---|
| **Repeated action(s) without time constraints** | **One single action with time constraints** |
| **1 Θέλω να τρώω πάντα πίτσα.** *I want to be always eating pizza (any time I have the chance to eat pizza).* **2 Σου αρέσει να βλέπεις τηλεόραση**; *Do you like watching TV (any time you have the chance to watch)?* **3 Δεν θα μιλάω με τη Μαρία συχνά.** *I'm not going to speak with Maria often (From now on, I plan not to speak with Maria often).* **4 Θα πηγαίνω πολλές βόλτες στην Αθήνα.** *I'll be taking many walks (when I am) in Athens (I'm planning to take many walks in Athens).* | **5 Θέλω να φάω μια πίτσα τώρα.** *I want to eat a pizza now (only one pizza, right now, and that's it).* **6 Θέλεις να δεις τηλεόραση σήμερα**; *Do you* want to watch *TV today (only today, in one given time)?* **7 Δεν θα μιλήσω στον Άρη το Σάββατο**. *I won't speak to Aris on Saturday (only one discussion at one given time and that's it).* **8 Θα πάω μια βόλτα στις 8:00**. *I'm going to go for a walk at 8 o'clock (only one walk at a specific time and that's it).* |

# Conversation 2 Do you have a hobby?

## NEW WORDS AND EXPRESSIONS 2

**09.05 Listen to the words and expressions that are used in the next conversation. Note their meanings.**

| | | |
|---|---|---|
| [enTHiaféron] | ενδιαφέρον | *interesting* |
| [troháTHin] | τροχάδην | *running* |
| [polés forés] | πολλές φορές | *often* (lit. *many times*) |
| [théatro] | θέατρο | *theater* |
| [vóltes] | βόλτες | *walks, strolls; car rides* |
| [káthome spíti] | κάθομαι σπίτι | *I stay at home* (lit. *I sit home*) |
| [THiavázo] | διαβάζω | *I read; I study* |
| [vivlía] | βιβλία | *books* |
| [mithistorímata] | μυθιστορήματα | *novels* |

**09.06** *Now Mary asks Elpida about her hobbies.*

**1 What does Mary like to do?**

| | | |
|---|---|---|
| **Mary** | [elpíTHa], [éhis hóbi]? | *Elpida, do you have a hobby?* |
| **Elpida** | [ne] [marésoon polí ta spor]. | *Yes, I like sports a lot.* |
| **Mary** | [enTHiaféron]. [ti spor]? | *Interesting. What sports?* |
| **Elpida** | [marési to troháTHin] [to básket] [ke to ténis]. [polés forés páo sto théatro] [i sto sinemá]. [esí]? [ti hóbi éhis]? | *I like running, basketball and tennis. I often go to the theater or the cinema. How about you? What are your hobbies?* |
| **Mary** | [marési na piyéno vóltes] [i na káthome spíti] [ke na THiavázo]. | *I like to go for a walk or stay at home and read.* |
| **Elpida** | [ti vivlía siníthos THiavázis]? | *What kind of books do you usually read?* |
| **Mary** | [kiríos mithistorímata] [alá ke] [vivlía thríler]. | *Mainly novels but also thrillers.* |

**Mary** Ελπίδα, έχεις χόμπι;

**Ελπίδα** Ναι, μ' αρέσουν πολύ τα σπορ.

| | |
|---|---|
| **Mary** | Ενδιαφέρον. Τι σπορ; |
| **Ελπίδα** | Μ'αρέσει το τροχάδην, το μπάσκετ και το τένις. Πολλές φορές πάω στο θέατρο ή στο σινεμά. Εσύ; Τι χόμπι έχεις; |
| **Mary** | Μ'αρέσει να πηγαίνω βόλτες ή να κάθομαι σπίτι και να διαβάζω. |
| **Ελπίδα** | Τι βιβλία συνήθως διαβάζεις; |
| **Mary** | Κυρίως μυθιστορήματα αλλά και βιβλία θρίλερ. |

**2 Now read the conversation and answer the following questions.**

- **a** What kind of sports does Elpida like?
- **b** What does Mary do in her free time?

**3 Listen again and pay special attention to the words which run together. This time you should practice speaking the part of Elpida.**

# Language discovery 2

**1 You will already know that there are many words in English of Greek origin, but have you also begun to notice just how many English loan words there are in Greek? Read the conversation again and complete the table with the Greek words for the following, including the article where relevant.**

| Words of Greek origin | Words of English origin |
|---|---|
| theater __________ | thriller __________ |
| book __________ | sports __________ |
| myth __________ | basketball __________ |
| story __________ | tennis __________ |
| interesting __________ | hobby __________ |

**2 There are also five words in the plural form. Look at the English translations and find the corresponding Greek words in the conversation. Note down the singular and plural forms of these words. Does anything catch your attention?**

- **a** books
- **b** novels
- **c** sports
- **d** hobbies
- **e** walks

### 1 LOAN WORDS

How easy did you find exercise 1? By now you should be aware of the number of Greek words found in English and vice versa. New technologies have given several words to the Greek language, such as *computer*, *internet*, *tablet*, etc. Of course many other Greek words, such as *theater*, *philosophy*, *athletics* and so on are found in several other languages, including English. Test yourself by covering the following English translations and guessing the meaning of each word.

***Words of Greek origin***

| | | |
|---|---|---|
| [moosikí] | **η μουσική** | *music* |
| [théatro] | **το θέατρο** | *theater* |
| [raTHiófono] | **το ραδιόφωνο** | *radio* |
| [istoría] | **η ιστορία** | *history/story* |

***Words of English origin***

| | | |
|---|---|---|
| *rock* | [rok] | **το ροκ** |
| *hobby* | [hóbi] | **το χόμπι** |
| *sports* | [spor] | **το σπορ** |
| *basketball* | [básket] | **το μπάσκετ** |
| *tennis* | [ténis] | **το τένις** |

Of course, some words are not so obvious at first glance. In Conversation 2 the meaning of the word [vivlía] **βιβλία** is perhaps not so clear until you think of words like *bibliography* and *bibliophile*, then it becomes apparent that [vivlía] **βιβλία** and *books* are closely related.

## 2 THE SINGULAR AND PLURAL FORMS OF NOUNS

Past units, especially Unit 7, went over certain rules regarding the singular and plural form of nouns. This section discusses two new points. First, there are some nouns which will add an extra syllable in their plural form. And second, there are also some nouns, mostly loan words from other languages, which have no declination and have only one form in all cases and in both singular and plural. Most loan words are actually neuter in Greek. The tables below illustrate these two new aspects.

**Nouns with extra syllable in plural formations**

| Masculine | Feminine | Neuter |
|---|---|---|
| καφές / καφέδες coffee(s), παππούς / παππούδες grandfather(s), καναπές / καναπέδες sofa(s) | μαμά / μαμάδες mom(s), αλεπού / αλεπούδες fox(es) | θέμα / θέματα theme(s), χρώμα / χρώματα color(s), μυθιστόρημα / μυθιστορήματα novel(s) |

**Nouns without change in plural formations**

| Masculine | Feminine | Neuter |
|---|---|---|
| ο σωφέρ / οι σωφέρ driver(s) | η ντισκοτέκ / οι ντισκοτέκ disco(s) | το χόμπι / τα χόμπι hobby / hobbies |

**3 THE VERB** *TO SIT*

The verb [káthome] **κάθομαι**, which means *to sit* or *to stay*, depending on the context, belongs to a new group of verbs with special endings which you have not met before. The main ending of these verbs is **-μαι** (instead of **-ω** which signals most other Greek verbs). The verb [íme] **είμαι** *to be*, which you saw in Unit 1, has certain similarities that you can draw upon. Study the verb:

| Verb group 5 | Verbs ending in-ομαι | |
|---|---|---|
| [káthome] | **κάθομαι** | *I sit/stay* |
| [káthese] | **κάθεσαι** | *you sit/stay* (sing/infml) |
| [káthete] | **κάθεται** | *he/she/it sits/stays* |
| [kathómaste] | **καθόμαστε** | *we sit/stay* |
| [kathósaste/kátheste] | **καθόσαστε/κάθεστε** | *you sit/stay* (pl/fml) |
| [káthonde] | **κάθονται** | *they sit/stay* |

There are two more verbs which are conjugated exactly like the verb **κάθομαι**. These verbs are [ergházome] **εργάζομαι** *to work/to be employed* from Unit 3 and [sikónome] **σηκώνομαι** *to get up* from Unit 8.

# Practice

**1** 09.07 **Dimitris, Nikos and Maria are asked the questions [ti kánis ton eléfthero hróno soo]? and [pos pernás tis eléftheres óres soo]? Listen to the audio and tick the activities they enjoy. Now say how often you do these activities.**

| Activities | Dimitris | Nikos | Maria |
|---|---|---|---|
| **1** smoke a cigarette | | | |
| **2** stay at home | | | |
| **3** read a newspaper | | | |

| 4 play football | | | |
|---|---|---|---|
| 5 drink coffee | | | |
| 6 listen to music | | | |
| 7 watch television | | | |

**LANGUAGE TIP**

| | | |
|---|---|---|
| [kapnízo] | **καπνίζω** | *I smoke* |
| [tsigáro] | **τσιγάρο** | *cigarette* |
| [efimeríTHa] | **εφημερίδα** | *newspaper* |
| [pézo] | **παίζω** | *I play* |

**2 Match each of the activities in the previous exercise with one of the following phrases. For more of a challenge, cover the transliteration column and work only with the Greek script!**

| | | |
|---|---|---|
| **a** | [THiavázo efimeríTHa]. | Διαβάζω εφημερίδα. |
| **b** | [pézo poTHósfero]. | Παίζω ποδόσφαιρο. |
| **c** | [akoó-o raTHiófono]. | Ακούω ραδιόφωνο. |
| **d** | [kapnízo tsigáro]. | Καπνίζω τσιγάρο. |
| **e** | [vlépo tileórasi]. | Βλέπω τηλεόραση. |
| **f** | [káthome spíti]. | Κάθομαι σπίτι. |
| **g** | [píno kafé]. | Πίνω καφέ. |

**3 Learn now the second stem of these verbs. We believe you shouldn't have any problems finding the correct pairs.**

| Verb stem 1 | Verb stem 2 |
|---|---|
| **a** [THiavázo] διαβάζω | **1** [THo] δω |
| **b** [pézo] παίζω | **2** [pio/p-yo] πιω |
| **c** [akoó-o] ακούω | **3** [THiaváso] διαβάσω |
| **d** [kapnízo] καπνίζω | **4** [kathíso] καθήσω |
| **e** [vlépo] βλέπω | **5** [pékso] παίξω |
| **f** [káthome] κάθομαι | **6** [kapníso] καπνίσω |
| **g** [píno] πίνω | **7** [akoóso] ακούσω |

**4 Match a–e with 1–5 to make complete sentences. Note that in some cases more than one option is possible and so you should give all possible answers in each case.**

| | | | |
|---|---|---|---|
| a | [sheTHón poté THen vlépo tileórasi ótan] ... | 1 | ... [káthome spíti]. |
| b | [pánda kapnízo tsigára ótan] ... | 2 | ... [éhi poTHósfero]. |
| c | [polés forés THiavázo vivlía ótan] ... | 3 | ... [íme megálos]. |
| d | [spánia pézo poTHósfero ótan] ... | 4 | ... [THen kséro ti álo na káno]. |
| e | [merikés forés akoó-o raTHiófono ótan] ... | 5 | ... [píno kafé]. |

**5 The verbs are missing in these sentences. Can you fill them in? The English verbs in the box might help you a little, if you translate them first!**

listen watch read
like drink prefer

**a** [o níkos poté THen] _____ [tileórasi].
**b** [i maría ke o THimítris pánda] _____ [raTHiófono].
**c** _____ [ta laiká ke to rok].
**d** [emís stin eláTHa] _____ [polá vivlía].
**e** [eghó THistihós] _______________ [polá tsighára]
**f** _______________ [kafé ke óhi tsái]

**6 Now translate each sentence in the previous exercise into English.**

**7 09.08 Listen to the audio and tick the types of music Angelos, Despina and Arianna like.**

| | Άγγελος | Δέσποινα | Αριάννα |
|---|---|---|---|
| [laiká]<br>[elafrolaiká]<br>[rebétika]<br>[tzaz]<br>[rok]<br>[blooz] | | | |

**8** 09.09 **Listen again to Conversation 2 and complete each sentence by choosing one word from the box. Then try to write the conversation in Greek script.**

[forés] [piyéno] [siníthos] [marésoon] [THiavázo] [enTHiaféron] [thríler] [troháTHin]

| | |
|---|---|
| **Mary** | [elpíTHa], [éhis hóbi]? |
| **Elpida** | [ne] **a** _____ [polí ta spor]. |
| **Mary** | **b** _____ [ti spor]? |
| **Elpida** | [marési to] **c** _____ [to básket] [ke to ténis]. [polés] **d** _____ [páo sto théatro] [i sto sinemá].[esí]? [ti hóbi éhis]? |
| **Mary** | [marési na] **e** _____ [vóltes] [i na káthome spíti] [ke na] **f** _____. |
| **Elpida** | [ti vivlía] **g** _____ [THiavázis]? |
| **Mary** | [kiríos mithistorímata] [alá ke] [vivlía] **h** _____. |

# Test yourself

1 Name three different kinds of music (not including jazz, rock or blues!).

2 Name three different kinds of books.

3 Name three different kinds of films.

4 Ask someone how they spend their free time.

5 How do you spend your free time? Give three answers.

6 In Conversation 2 you were introduced to the new words **[tréksimo], [vóltes], [enTHiaféron], [siníthos]** and **[kiríos]**. Can you write them in Greek script and then translate them into English?

7 Can you give the opposites of the following words: [poté], [spánia], [marési], [komoTHíes]?

## SELF CHECK

| | I CAN... |
|---|---|
| • | ... talk about my free time. |
| • | ... ask others about their hobbies. |
| • | ... name different kinds of Greek music and different types of books and films. |
| • | ... use some loanwords in Greek. |

# 10

**In this unit you will learn how to:**

» ask for things in different amounts and quantities.
» ask how much something costs.
» say the names of different fruit, vegetables and herbs.
» describe different moods you are in.
» count from 1,000 to 10,000.

# Στη λαϊκή αγορά

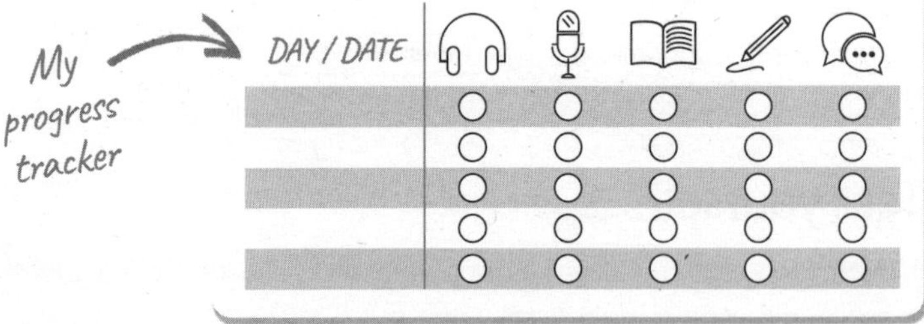


## At the fruit and vegetable market

Visitors to Greece will probably come across a [laikí agorá] **λαϊκή αγορά** *fruit and vegetable market* one way or another. Many local farmers sell their produce in different neighborhoods every day. You can also go directly to the [kendrikí laikí agorá] **κεντρική λαϊκή αγορά** *central market*, which is open five or six days a week in many cities. You will also find a [psaragorá] **ψαραγορά** *fish market* in many places, especially those close to the sea.

Greece produces several types of fruit, including [stafília] **σταφύλια** *grapes*, [karpoózia] **καρπούζια** *watermelons*, [portokália] **πορτοκάλια** *oranges* and [míla] **μήλα** *apples*. It also produces many different vegetables, such as [patátes] **πατάτες** *potatoes*, [domátes] **ντομάτες** *tomatoes* and [karóta] **καρότα** *carrots*. Some fish native to Greece are [barboónia] **μπαρμπούνια** *red mullets*, [tsipoóres] **τσιπούρες** *breams*, [lavrákia] **λαυράκια** *basses* and [péstrofes] **πέστροφες** *trouts*. Don't miss the opportunity to ask for local products wherever you are – many of them have a seal awarded by the National Food Association which testifies to their good quality. Look for products with the words **ΠΟΠ (Προϊόντα με Ονομασία Προέλευσης)** *Produce with Designation of Origin* or **ΠΓΕ (Προϊόντα με Γεωγραφική Ένδειξη)** *Produce with Geographical Indication.*

---

**The words for the different types of fruit, vegetables and fish in the text are in the plural. Can you work out what the singular forms are?**

---

## Vocabulary builder

**ΦΡΟΥΤΑ, ΛΑΧΑΝΙΚΑ ΚΑΙ ΜΥΡΩΔΙΚΑ** *FRUIT, VEGETABLES AND HERBS*

**1** 10.01 **Look at the words and complete the missing English expressions. Then listen and try to imitate the pronunciation of the speakers.**

| **[froóta]** | **Φρούτα** | **Fruit** |
|---|---|---|
| [o ananás] | ο ανανάς | ________ |
| [i banána] | η μπανάνα | *banana* |
| [i fráoola] | η φράουλα | *strawberry* |
| [to stafíli] | το σταφύλι | *grape* |
| [to pepóni] | το πεπόνι | *melon* |
| **[lahaniká]** | **Λαχανικά** | **Vegetables** |
| [i patáta] | η πατάτα | ________ |
| [i domáta] | η ντομάτα | ________ |
| [to karóto] | το καρότο | ________ |
| [to kolokitháki] | το κολοκυθάκι | *courgette* |
| **[miroTHiká]** | **Μυρωδικά** | **Herbs** |
| [o ánithos] | ο άνιθος | *dill* |
| [o maindanós] | ο μαϊντανός | *parsley* |
| [to aláti] | το αλάτι | ________ |
| [to pipéri] | το πιπέρι | ________ |

**2** 10.02 **The following are useful questions and answers that will help you if you go grocery shopping in Greece. Read the phrases and complete the missing English expressions. Then listen and repeat after the speakers.**

| | | |
|---|---|---|
| [póso thélete]? | Πόσο θέλετε; | *How much do you want?* |
| [pósa thélete]? | Πόσα θέλετε; | *How many _____?* |
| [pósa kilá]? | Πόσα κιλά; | *How _____ kilos?* |
| [póso káni]? | Πόσο κάνει; | *How _____ is it?* |
| [póso kánoon]? | Πόσο κάνουν; | *How much _____?* |
| [éna kiló]. | Ένα κιλό. | *One kilo.* |
| [THío kilá parakaló]. | Δύο κιλά παρακαλώ. | *Two kilos please.* |
| [misó kiló féta THoTHónis]. | Μισό κιλό φέτα Δωδώνης. | *Half a _____ of Dodonis feta.* |
| [triakósia ghramária parakaló]. | Τριακόσια γραμμάρια παρακαλώ. | *Three hundred _____ please.* |
| [kánoon tría evró akrivós]. | Κάνουν τρία ευρώ ακριβώς. | *They are three euros exactly.* |
| [káni THío evró ke íkosi leptá]. | Κάνει δύο ευρώ και είκοσι λεπτά. | *It's two _____ and 20 cents.* |

**3** 10.03 **Read the following Greek words and for each one choose the correct English equivalent from the box. Then listen and compare your answers. Listen again and repeat after the speakers.**

supermarket hypermarket mini market/greengrocer weekly fruit and vegetable market/grocery story fruit and vegetable shop

**a** [pandopolío] παντοπωλείο
**b** [manáviko] μανάβικο
**c** [oporopandopolío] οπωροπαντοπωλείο
**d** [laikí agorá] λαϊκή αγορά
**e** [super market] σούπερ μάρκετ
**f** [iperaghorá] υπεραγορά
**g** [bakáliko] μπακάλικο

# Conversation 1 Are you coming with me?

## NEW WORDS AND EXPRESSIONS 1

**10.04 Listen to the words and expressions that are used in the next conversation. Note their meanings.**

| | | |
|---|---|---|
| [koorazméni] | κουρασμένη | *tired* |
| [yiatí rotás]? | γιατί ρωτάς; | *Why do you ask?* |
| [prépi na páo] | πρέπει να πάω | *I have to go.* |
| [agorá] | αγορά | *market* |
| [laikí agorá] | λαϊκή αγορά | *fruit and vegetable market* |
| [yia lígo] | για λίγο | *for a little while* |
| [érhese]? | Έρχεσαι; | *Are you coming?* |
| [iTHéa] | ιδέα | *idea* |
| [me ta póTHia] | με τα πόδια | *on foot* (lit. *with the feet*) |
| [meriká] | μερικά | *some* |

Here is a list of the verbs above with both stems: [rotáo/rotó – rotíso] **ρωτάω/ρωτώ – ρωτήσω** *to ask*, [pighéno (páo) – páo] **πηγαίνω/πάω – πάω** *to go*, [érhome – értho] **έρχομαι – έρθω** *to come*.

**10.05** *Elpida has to go to the local fruit and vegetable market. She asks Mary to join her.*

**1 Listen to the conversation a couple of times. Will Mary go with Elpida?**

| | | |
|---|---|---|
| **Elpida** | Mary, [íse koorazméni]? | Mary, are you tired? |
| **Mary** | [óhi], [yiatí rotás]? | No, why do you ask? |
| **Elpida** | [prépi na páo] [stin laikí agorá] [yia lígo]. [érhese mazí moo]? | I have to go to the fruit and vegetable market for a little while. Are you coming with me? |
| **Mary** | [oréa iTHéa]. [poo íne]? | Good idea. Where is it? |
| **Elpida** | [íne kondá]. [boroóme na páme] [me ta póTHia]. [thélo na agoráso] [meriká froóta] [ke lahaniká] | It's close by. We can go on foot. I want to buy some fruit and vegetables. |
| **Mary** | [éla] [páme] | OK! Let's go! (lit. *Come on! [Let] us go!*) |

| | |
|---|---|
| **Ελπίδα** | Mary, είσαι κουρασμένη; |
| **Mary** | Όχι, γιατί ρωτάς; |
| **Ελπίδα** | Πρέπει να πάω στη λαϊκή αγορά για λίγο. Έρχεσαι μαζί μου; |
| **Mary** | Ωραία ιδέα. Πού είναι; |
| **Ελπίδα** | Είναι κοντά. Μπορούμε να πάμε με τα πόδια. Θέλω να αγοράσω μερικά φρούτα και λαχανικά. |
| **Mary** | Έλα. Πάμε. |

**2 Now read the conversation and answer the questions.**

**a** Is the fruit and vegetable market far away?

**b** How will they get there?

**3 Listen again and pay special attention to the words which run together. Practice speaking the part of Elpida.**

# Language discovery 1

**1 The conversation has three expressions that contain the particle να. Look at their English translations and find the corresponding Greek phrase in each case. Can you see when this particle is used?**

**a** I want to buy.

**b** We can go.

**c** I have to go.

**2 It is useful to be able to say where people, objects or places are. Look at the following pairs of adverbs. Can you match them with their Greek counterparts?**

**a** near/far — **1** εδώ/εκεί

**b** above/below — **2** κοντά/μακριά

**c** here/there — **3** πάνω/κάτω

**3 Elpida asks Mary if she is tired. If you look up the word for *tired* in a dictionary, you will find the following three forms. Decide which of the three is masculine, which is feminine and which is neuter.**

**a** κουρασμέν-ος

**b** κουρασμέν-η

**c** κουρασμέν-ο

## 1 CONNECTING TWO VERBS

Unit 9 has already introduced two verb particles, [tha] **θα** *will/would* and [na] **να** *to*. The word [na] **να** is used to connect two verbs, hence it is also sometimes called a 'connector'. Connectors are sometimes omitted in English; for instance in the sentences *I like buying fruit* and *I must go there* the two verbs *like + buy* and *must + go* can coexist in the same sentence quite happily. In Greek, on the other hand, it is necessary to use [na] **να** to connect the two verbs:

| | | |
|---|---|---|
| [marési na agorázo froóta]. | **Μ' αρέσει να αγοράζω φρούτα.** | *I like buying fruit.* |
| [prépi na páo ekí]. | **Πρέπει να πάω εκεί.** | *I must go there.* |

There is no exception to this rule. An additional thing to bear in mind is that after [na] **να**, a different form of the verb is often used. You don't need to know more about this for the time being – just learn each verb on a case-by-case basis as you go along.

## 2 ADVERBS OF PLACE

In past units you learned some adverbs of time and frequency. If you got the answers to exercise 2 correct, you will have matched the following:

- **a** *near/far*: **κοντά/μακριά**
- **b** *above/below*: **πάνω/κάτω**
- **c** *here/there*: **εδώ/εκεί**

Here are some more pairs of adverbs you will find useful when you want to indicate where something or someone is located. Try to learn them in pairs if you can.

| | |
|---|---|
| **μπροστά από/πίσω από** | *in front of/behind* |
| **μέσα σε/έξω από** | *inside/outside* |
| **δίπλα σε/γύρω από** | *next to/around* |

**LANGUAGE TIP**

Note that these words are all adverbs in Greek but in English *in front of*, *behind* and *next to* are all prepositions. *Inside*, *outside* and *around* can be either adverbs or prepositions.

## 3 ADJECTIVES DESCRIBING MOODS

You may have worked out by now that learning Greek adjectives can be challenging.

**4 Look at the pictures showing the different moods. Can you give the correct gender and the English translation in each case?**

a 

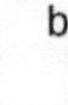

b 

c 

d 

e 

f 

g 

h 

**a** [eftihizméni] ευτυχισμένη
**b** [thimoménos] θυμωμένος
**c** [lipiméni] λυπημένη
**d** [ékplikti] έκπληκτη
**e** [pinazménos] πεινασμένος
**f** [THipsazménos] διψασμένος
**g** [taragméni] ταραγμένη
**h** [koorazméni] κουρασμένη

The two adjectives [pinazménos] **πεινασμένος** *hungry* and [THipsazménos] **διψασμένος** *thirsty* are not used very frequently. The verbs [pináo] **πεινάω** *be hungry* and [THipsáo] **διψάω** *be thirsty* are normally used instead. You should remember that you met the questions [pináte] **πεινάτε;** *are you hungry?* and [THipsáte] **διψάτε;** *are you thirsty?* in Unit 6.

# Conversation 2 At the fruit and vegetable market

## NEW WORDS AND EXPRESSIONS 2

**10.06 Listen to the words and expressions that are used in the next conversation. Note their meanings.**

| | | |
|---|---|---|
| [kózmos] | κόσμος | *people* (here: *crowded place*) |
| [poloós] | πολλούς | *many* |
| [anthrópoos] | ανθρώπους | *people* |
| [pánda] | πάντα | *always* |
| [ipárhoon] | υπάρχουν | *there are* |
| [míla] | μήλα | *apples* |
| [portokália] | πορτοκάλια | *oranges* |
| [banánes] | μπανάνες | *bananas* |
| [na pároome] | να πάρουμε | *to get/to buy* (lit. *to take*) |

| | | |
|---|---|---|
| [karpoózia] | καρπούζια | *watermelons* |
| [epohí] | εποχή | *season* |
| [fisiká] | φυσικά | *naturally* |
| [pio] | πιο | *more, further* |
| [fréska] | φρέσκα | *fresh* |
| [maroóli] | μαρούλι | *lettuce* |
| [agoória] | αγγούρια | *cucumbers* |

**10.07** *Elpida and Mary are walking in a noisy, crowded market among stalls with fresh fruit and vegetables.*

**1 Listen to the conversation a couple of times. Is the market always busy?**

| | | |
|---|---|---|
| **Mary** | [po-po kózmos]! [polis kózmos]! | *Wow! It's crowded! Very crowded!* |
| **Elpida** | [ne], [pánda éhi poloós anthrópoos eTHó]. [na]! [eTHó ipárhoon] [oréa míla] [portokália ke banánes]. [ti sarési na pároome]? | *Yes, there are always a lot of people. Here! There are some nice apples, oranges and bananas. What would you like us to get?* |
| **Mary** | [na pároome míla]. [ipárhoon karpoózia] [aftí tin epohí]? | *Let's get some apples. Are there any watermelons at this time of the year?* |
| **Elpida** | [ne, fisiká]. [lígo pio káto]. [eTHó éhi] [kalá ke fréska] [lahaniká]. [thélo nagoráso] [éna maroóli], [THío agoória] [kéna kilo domátes]. | *Yes, of course. A little bit further down. Here are some nice fresh vegetables. I want to buy one lettuce, two cucumbers and one kilo of tomatoes.* |

**Mary** Πω-πω κόσμος! Πολύς κόσμος!

**Ελπίδα** Ναι, πάντα έχει πολλούς ανθρώπους εδώ. Νά! Εδώ υπάρχουν ωραία μήλα, πορτοκάλια και μπανάνες. Τι σ' αρέσει να πάρουμε;

**Mary** Να πάρουμε μήλα. Υπάρχουν καρπούζια αυτή την εποχή;

**Ελπίδα** Ναι, φυσικά. Λίγο πιο κάτω. Εδώ έχει καλά και φρέσκα λαχανικά. Θέλω ν' αγοράσω ένα μαρούλι, δύο αγγούρια κι ένα κιλό ντομάτες.

**2 Now read the conversation and answer the questions.**

**a** What would Mary like to get?

**b** What vegetables does Elpida want?

**3 Listen again and pay special attention to the words which run together. Practice speaking the part of Elpida.**

# Language discovery 2

**1 The conversation has three expressions that use the particle [na] να. Look at their English translations and find the corresponding Greek phrase in each case.**

**a** I'd like to get.

**b** What would you like us to get?

**c** Let's get some apples.

**2 The conversation has a fourth να but this time the α has a stress mark – vά. What does vά mean?**

**3 There are three instances of an adjective describing a noun in this conversation. Look at their English translations and find the corresponding Greek phrase in each case. Can you work out the rule of thumb with regard to the endings of the adjectives?**

**a** nice apples **b** fresh vegetables **c** many people

### 1 OMITTING ONE OF TWO VERBS

As you have seen in this unit, the particle [na] **να** is necessary when two verbs are connected in one sentence. Here are some important verbal constructions that use this particle:

| | | |
|---|---|---|
| [prépi na] | **πρέπει να** | *must/have to/is necessary to* |
| [boró na] | **μπορώ να** | *can/be able to* |
| [borí na] | **μπορεί να** | *may/is possible to* |
| [thélo na] | **θέλω να** | *want to/would like to* |
| [marési na] | **μ' αρέσει να** | *like to* |

In this second conversation, you may have noticed a sentence with the particle [na] **να** where the first verb was omitted: [na pároome míla]. **Να πάρουμε μήλα.** This is idiomatic and you will encounter it in everyday language. In English, it is always necessary to use both verbs. Look at the following examples and their translations:

| | |
|---|---|
| **Να πάρουμε μήλα.** | *Let's get some apples.* |
| **Να πάρουμε μήλα;** | *Shall we get some apples?* |
| **Να ακούσουμε μουσική.** | *Let's listen to some music.* |
| **Να ακούσουμε μουσική;** | *Shall we listen to some music?* |

## 2 WORDS WITH OR WITHOUT A STRESS MARK

As exercise 2 will have shown you, there are a few words in Greek where the stress mark will signal a difference in either pronunciation or meaning or both! Here are a few examples, beginning with the one you have already seen:

**να/νά**: the first is the particle *to* and the second the word *here* or *there* when you show someone something.

**η/ή**: the first is the article *the* and the second the word *or*. The second word is pronounced differently, with a longer sound than the first.

**που/πού**: the first is the relative pronoun *where*, *who* or *which* and the second the question word *where?*

**μια/μία**: the first word means *a*, *an* and the second is the number *one*. The pronunciations of the two words are different: [miá] / [mía].

As a rule of thumb, the words above with a stress mark are pronounced for longer.

## 3 THE NUMBERS 1,000–10,000

10.08 **Now practice the numbers 1,000 to 10,000. If you prefer, you can say the numbers first and then listen and compare your pronunciation.**

| | | |
|---|---|---|
| [hílji], [hílies], [hília] | **χίλιοι** (m), **χίλιες** (f), **χίλια** (n) | *1,000* |
| [THío hiliáTHes] | **δύο χιλιάδες** | *2,000* |
| [tris hiliáTHes] | **τρεις χιλιάδες** | *3,000* |
| [téseris hiliáTHes] | **τέσσερις χιλιάδες** | *4,000* |
| [pénde hiliáTHes] | **πέντε χιλιάδες** | *5,000* |
| [éksi hiliáTHes] | **έξι χιλιάδες** | *6,000* |
| [eptá hiliáTHes] | **επτά χιλιάδες** | *7,000* |
| [októ hiliáTHes] | **οκτώ χιλιάδες** | *8,000* |
| [eniá hiliáTHes] | **εννιά χιλιάδες** | *9,000* |
| [THéka hiliáTHes] | **δέκα χιλιάδες** | *10,000* |

**GREEK MONEY**

The currency used in Greece is the euro. The word for *euro* is [evró] **ευρώ** (note the stress on the second syllable) and it does not change in the plural. Some examples:

| | | |
|---|---|---|
| [éna evró] | **ένα ευρώ** | *one euro* |
| [THéka evró] | **δέκα ευρώ** | *ten euros* |
| [hília evró] | **χίλια ευρώ** | *1,000 euros* |
| [pénde hiliádes evró] | **πέντε χιλιάδες ευρώ** | *5,000 euros* |

## 4 YES AND NO

The words [ne] **ναι** *yes* and [óhi] **όχι** *no* will come in useful in most situations. You might also encounter some other ways of answering affirmatively: [fisiká] **φυσικά** *naturally*, [vévea] **βέβαια** *of course/sure*, [amé] **αμέ** *yeah*.

Bear in mind that non-verbal ways of saying *yes* and *no* are probably different from those you are familiar with. Greek people express *yes* by tilting their head downwards and keeping it down. A non-verbal *no* is expressed by tilting the head backwards and looking up, with eyebrows raised. To answer *no*, it is sometimes sufficient to raise the eyebrows alone. The best way for you to understand these non-verbal nuances is of course to notice when Greek speakers use them in their conversations.

## 5 THE ADJECTIVE MUCH / MANY

Unit 7 introduced some important points for you to know about adjectives. A quick summary: **1** The main adjective form is always introduced in its 3 genders, i.e. **καλός, καλή, καλό** *good*. This also happens when you look up a Greek adjective in a dictionary. **2** A Greek adjective is declined and that means it does not only have 3 genders, but it also has a singular or plural and different cases, i.e. nom./gen./acc. **3** The adjective ending is also important in order to sort them into different groups. The two endings **-ος, -η, -ο** i.e. **καλός, καλή, καλό** *good* and **-ος, -α, -ο** i.e. **ωραίος, ωραία, ωραίο** *beautiful/nice* were found in previous units.

In this unit you'll look at an irregular adjective, not only in its various forms but also with its unique spelling, namely **πολύς, πολλή, πολύ** *much / many*. The table below will give you a better overview of this adjective and some exercises later will give you the opportunity to practice.

Singular

| | Masculine | Feminine | Neuter |
|---|---|---|---|
| (nom.) | [polís] πολύς | [polí] πολλή | [polí] πολύ |
| (gen.) | [poloó] πολλού | [polís] πολλής | [poloó] πολλού |
| (acc.) | [polí] πολύ | [polí] πολλή | [polí] πολύ |

Plural

| | Masculine | Feminine | Neuter |
|---|---|---|---|
| (nom.) | [polí] πολλοί | [polés] πολλές | [polá] πολλά |
| (gen.) | [polón] πολλών | [polón] πολλών | [polón] πολλών |
| (acc.) | [poloós] πολλούς | [polés] πολλές | [polá] πολλά |

You have probably noticed that the pronunciation [polí] is exactly the same for all three words, i.e. **πολύ, πολλή** or **πολλοί**. And it should not be confused with the word [póli] **πόλη** *city*. This is another reason to pay special attention to the stressed syllable of each word.

# Practice

**1 There are some fruits, herbs and vegetables mixed up in the box. Can you separate them into three groups?**

[banána] [kolokitháki] [fráoola] [roTHákino] [agoóri] [domáta] [stafíli] [mílo] [karóto] [ánithos] [maindanós] [karpoózi]

| ΦΡΟΥΤΑ | ΛΑΧΑΝΙΚΑ | ΜΥΡΩΔΙΚΑ |
|---|---|---|
| | | |

**2 Remember that the various forms for the definite article (the word *the*) can be challenging in Greek. Go back to the previous exercise and add both the singular and plural form of the definite article to each word. The first ones have been done for you.**

[i banána] – [i banánes] [to kolokitháki] – [ta kolokithákia]

**3 Can you now write out all the words in the previous exercise in Greek script? Give it a try and see how familiar you have now become with the Greek alphabet. The first ones have been done for you.**

η μπανάνα – οι μπανάνες το κολοκυθάκι – τα κολοκυθάκια

**4 Look at the picture. Can you name the fruit and vegetables? The new vocabulary you need has been provided. Give the appropriate singular or plural form as needed. The first ones have been done for you.**

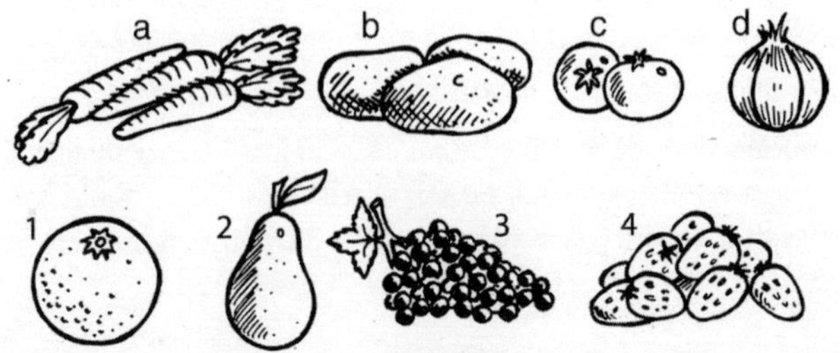


| | | |
|---|---|---|
| [to skórTHo] | **το σκόρδο** | *garlic* |
| [to ahláTHi] | **το αχλάδι** | *pear* |

**a** [ta karóta] **1** [to portokáli]
**b** ____________ **2** ____________
**c** ____________ **3** ____________
**d** ____________ **4** ____________

**5 The shopkeeper has told you how much you need to pay for the things you have just bought. Write the transliteration and/or Greek script for each amount.**

**a** 50€ ____________ **d** 12€ ____________
**b** 17€ ____________ **e** 34€ ____________
**c** 100€ ____________ **f** 70€ ____________

**6 Match each figure with the correct words.**

**a** 1650 **1** οχτώ χιλιάδες τριακόσια
**b** 2500 **2** πέντε χιλιάδες εφτακόσια πενήντα
**c** 4100 **3** δύο χιλιάδες πεντακόσια
**d** 5750 **4** έξι χιλιάδες εννιακόσια
**e** 6900 **5** χίλια εξακόσια πενήντα
**f** 8300 **6** τέσσερις χιλιάδες εκατό

**7** **Use the phrases in the box to help you translate the following sentences. Then write the sentences in Greek script.**

| [prépi na] [thélo na] [boró na] [marési na] [borí na] |
|---|

**a** I like going for walks with you.
**b** I want to go to the fruit and vegetable market.
**c** I must see you.
**d** I can eat a pizza now.
**e** Perhaps her name is Helen.

**8** **Look at the people in the picture and work out what mood they are in. Then choose the correct word from the right-hand column. Work with the transliteration or, for more of a challenge, the Greek script.**

**a** _____ 
**b** _____ 
**c** _____ 
**d** _____ 
**e** _____ 
**f** _____ 

**1** [lipiméni] λυπημένη
**2** [thimoménos] θυμωμένος
**3** [eftihizméni] ευτυχισμένη
**4** [pinazménos] πεινασμένος
**5** [THipsazménos] διψασμένος
**6** [koorazméni] κουρασμένη

**9** **Which is the correct form of the challenging adjective πολύς/πολλή/πολύ?**

**a** Υπάρχει _______________ κόσμος εδώ.
**b** Υπάρχουν _______________ άνθρωποι από την Αγγλία.
**c** Ξέρω _______________ ανθρώπους από την Αθήνα.
**d** Δεν ξέρω _______________ γυναίκες από το Λονδίνο.
**e** Ο _______________ καφές δεν κάνει καλό!
**f** _______________ παιδιά παίζουν ποδόσφαιρο.

**10** 10.09 **Listen again to Conversation 2 and complete each sentence by choosing one word from the box. Note that one answer is used twice!**

| [kiló] [fisiká] [epohí] [agoória] [lahaniká] [káto] [portokália] [ipárhoon] |
|---|

| | |
|---|---|
| **Mary** | [po-po kózmos]! [polís kózmos]! |
| **Elpida** | [ne], [pánda éhi poloós anthrópoos eTHó]. [na]! [eTHó] **a** ________ [oréa míla] **b** ________ [ke banánes]. [ti sarési na pároome]? |
| **Mary** | [na pároome míla]. **c** ________[karpoózia] [aftí tin] **d** ________? |
| **Elpida** | [ne] **e** ________[lígo pio] **f** ________ [eTHó éhi] [kalá ke fréska ] **g** ________ [thélo nagoráso] [éna maroóli], [THío] **h** ________ [kéna] **i** ________ [domátes]. |

**11 The above conversation uses two useful expressions, namely *there is* and *there are*. Fill in the correct form of these two expressions in the examples below. Then translate the phrases into English.**

**a** ________________ μπανάνες τώρα;

**b** Όχι. Δεν ________________ καλές ντομάτες αυτή την εποχή.

**c** ________________ λαχανικά πιο κάτω;

**d** Φυσικά ________________ καλός καφές εδώ.

**e** Πω, πω! ________________ πολύς κόσμος εδώ!

**f** ________________ καρπούζια αυτή την εποχή;

## Test yourself

1 Name four different fruits that you like.

2 Name four of your favorite vegetables or herbs.

3 Tell a friend about your moods. Name at least four.

4 How do you say the following numbers in Greek?

| | | | |
|---|---|---|---|
| **a** | 450 | **e** | 5,000 |
| **b** | 670 | **f** | 7,400 |
| **c** | 1,200 | **g** | 9,500 |
| **d** | 3,900 | **h** | 10,000 |

5 Name three different places where you might buy food.

6 Ask for half a kilo of apples and one kilo of oranges.

7 Can you ask for the price of something? State both possible ways.

### SELF CHECK

| | **I CAN...** |
|---|---|
| • | ... ask for things in different amounts and quantities. |
| • | ... ask how much something costs. |
| • | ... say the names of different fruit, vegetables and herbs. |
| • | ... describe different moods I am in. |
| • | ... count from 1,000 to 10,000. |

# Revision test 3

**1 Some people tell you when they do certain activities. Match each clock with the correct phrase.** *(12 points)*

**a** [THoolévo apó tis októ méhri tis téseris].
**b** [i maría íne sto spíti apó tis eniámisí méhri tis éksi].
**c** [THen tró-o poté apó tis THoTHekámisi méhri tis eniá].
**d** [íme sti THooliá apó tis eftá méhri tis téseris].
**e** [THen marési na THoolévo apó tis eniá méhri tis pénde].
**f** [o yiórgos vlépi tileórasi apó tis THéka ke misí méhri tis eptámisi].

**2 Now translate each phrase from exercise 1 into English.** *(12 points)*

**a** ______________________________
**b** ______________________________
**c** ______________________________
**d** ______________________________
**e** ______________________________
**f** ______________________________

**3 Match the phrases with the illustrations.** *(12 points)*

**a** [i maría íne stin koozína ke mayirévi].
**b** [o yiánis íne ékso apó to spíti].
**c** [i mitéra moo vlépi polí tileórasi].
**d** [o patéras moo pánda THiavázi efimeríTHa].
**e** [o kóstas akoó-i moosikí óli tin iméra].
**f** [i eléni íne sto grafío apó tis eniá méhri ti mía].

**4 Now translate each phrase from Activity 3 into English.** *(12 points)*

**a** ______
**b** ______
**c** ______
**d** ______
**e** ______
**f** ______

**5 Can you match each action to the phrase?** *(10 points)*

**a** [káno dooz]
**b** [tró-o proinó]
**c** [páo yia ípno]
**d** [ksipnáo stis eptá]
**e** [THiavázo sto kreváti]
**f** [páo sti THooliá]
**g** [févgo apó ti THooliá]
**h** [sikónome apó to kreváti]
**i** [etimázome yia THooliá*]
**j** [etimázome yia ípno]

**1** I go to sleep
**2** I eat breakfast
**3** I read in bed
**4** I go to work
**5** I get ready for bed
**6** I get out of bed
**7** I get ready for work
**8** I take a shower
**9** I wake up at seven
**10** I leave work

* [etimázome] **Ετοιμάζομαι** *to get ready/to get prepared* is a new verb in the examples above. It belongs to verb group 5 and it is conjugated exactly like [káthome] **κάθομαι** *to sit* found in Unit 9.

6 **Now write the ten phrases in exercise 5 in Greek script.** *(10 points)*

7 **Now describe your daily routine in Greek.** *(24 points)*

8 **What is the correct form of the adjective πολύς/πολλή/πολύ in the following examples? (4 points)**

**a** Υπάρχουν ________________ άνθρωποι στην ταβέρνα σήμερα.
**b** Έχει ________________ ζάχαρη ο καφές μου! Δεν μου αρέσει!
**c** Συμφωνώ με ________________ παιδιά.
**d** Δεν ξέρω ________________ Έλληνες.

9 **Which is the correct verb-stem of the following phrases? (4 points)**

**a** Δε θέλω να ________________ (τρώω / φάω) τώρα.
**b** Μ'αρέσει να ________________ (πίνω / πιω) καφέ κάθε πρωί.
**c** Πρέπει να ________________ (φεύγω / φύγω) σε λίγο.
**d** Δε μ'αρέσει να ________________ (ξυπνάω / ξυπνήσω) στις 7:00 το πρωί.
**e** Τώρα θέλω να ________________ (διαβάζω / διαβάσω) ένα βιβλίο στο κρεβάτι.

**TOTAL: 100 POINTS**

Have you scored more than 60 points? Well done! If not, it might be a good idea to revise the last four units again. There was a lot of new vocabulary and it is OK if you have already forgotten some words. Don't forget to make some word lists, for example a list of vocabulary related to your daily routine.

Congratulations! You have now completed the last exercise in this book. We hope that your journey through *Beginners' Greek* was an entertaining one and that you learned many things about this language and rich culture along the way. We also hope that you are going to continue this journey, either by revising some past units or moving on to *Teach Yourself Complete Greek*. No matter what you do, we'd like to wish you **Καλό ταξίδι!**

# Grammar summary

This grammar summary is intended mainly to act as a reference guide to the language used in the course. It is by no means a complete grammar, although some elements in this section do not appear in the course and are included for learners who wish to progress a little further.

You can skim through this section before you start Unit 1 and you can always refer back whenever you meet a new grammatical point in a unit and compare it with the notes here. Grammatical explanations in the units are somewhat short with some examples for practical application. Here the approach is different and more organized and systematic in terms of grouping grammatical points together.

The most important grammatical groups outlined in this section are: **Articles**, **Nouns**, **Adjectives**, **Adverbs**, **Pronouns**, **Prepositions** and **Verbs**. In most instances you will find tables to which the different groups belong, along with a few examples and direct references back to units.

## 1 Articles

The words *a*, *an* and *the* are called **articles** in English. *A* and *an* are called **indefinite articles** and *the* is called the **definite article**. All articles usually come before a noun or an adjective. Greek articles have a lot more than three forms! This is because the nouns they define are divided into three genders: masculine (m), feminine (f) and neuter (n). The Greek words for *a*, *an* and *the* are therefore different for each gender. In addition, each noun group has further forms in the singular and plural, so the articles have to agree with these, too.

Greek also has different endings for nouns and their articles (and adjectives – see below) when nouns are used in different ways within a sentence – for example, if they are the subject or the object of the sentence. These different forms of nouns are called **cases**. There are three main cases: nominative (nom), used when the word is the subject of the sentence; genitive (gen), used to show possession, i.e., that something belongs to someone; and accusative (acc), used when the word is the object of the sentence. English grammar has lost virtually all examples of case. The English word *who* is one of the few that can illustrate the idea of case. It is *who* in the nominative case, *whose* in the genitive case and *whom* in the accusative case. The following tables show the different forms of Greek articles.

### INDEFINITE ARTICLE *A/AN*

| | Masculine | Feminine | Neuter |
|---|---|---|---|
| nom | **ένας** [énas] | **μία** [mía]/**μια** [m-ya] | **ένα** [éna] |
| gen | **ενός** [enós] | **μίας** [mías] | **ενός** [enós] |
| acc | **έναν** [énan] | **μία** [mía] | **ένα** [éna] |

### DEFINITE ARTICLE *THE*

| | Singular | | | Plural | | |
|---|---|---|---|---|---|---|
| | Masculine | Feminine | Neuter | Masculine | Feminine | Neuter |
| nom | **ο** [o] | **η** [i] | **το** [to] | **οι** [i] | **οι** [i] | **τα** [ta] |
| gen | **του** [too] | **της** [tis] | **του** [too] | **των** [ton] | **των** [ton] | **των** [ton] |
| acc | **τον** [ton] | **τη(ν)** [ti(n)] | **το** [to] | **τους** [toos] | **τις** [tis] | **τα** [ta] |

Articles are often used with the preposition [se] **σε** *at*, *to*, *in*, *on*, creating compound definite articles in the genitive and accusative cases only.

| Singular | | | Plural | | |
|---|---|---|---|---|---|
| Masculine | Feminine | Neuter | Masculine | Feminine | Neuter |
| στου | στης | στου | στων | στων | στων |
| στον | στην | στο | στους | στις | στα |

# 2 Nouns

The names of people and things are called **nouns**. As already stated, Greek nouns are divided into three genders, and each noun has a singular and plural form, and changes according to the role it plays in the sentence (its case) – nominative, genitive, accusative. When you look up nouns in a dictionary you will find them in the nominative singular form. You can usually tell their gender by their endings. Check the table below showing the main noun groups and provide some examples for each. All examples below are taken from past units in this course book.

| Masculine | Feminine | Neuter |
|---|---|---|
| **-ας, -ες, -ης, -ος, -ους** | **-α, -η** | **-ι, -ο, -μα** |
| [niptíras] νιπτήρας *washbasin*, [kafés] καφές *coffee*, [kathréftis] καθρέφτης *mirror*, [ánthropos] άνθρωπος *man / person*, [papoós] παππούς *grandfather* | [istoría] ιστορία *story / history*, [moosikí] μουσική *music* | [spíti] σπίτι *house*, [vivlío] βιβλίο *book*, [hróma] χρώμα *colour*, [hóbi] χόμπι *hobby* |

Many nouns usually have the same number of syllables in both singular and plural numbers. That was the case of all three nouns declined above. There are also some nouns which have one extra syllable in their plural formation. Some examples here include: **καφές / καφέδες** *coffee(s)*, **παππούς / παππούδες** *grandfather(s)*, **μαμά / μαμάδες** *mom(s)*, **χρώμα / χρώματα** *color(s)*. Another point regarding Greek nouns is that most loan words (words stemming from other languages) are usually neuter. These words usually have one form, not only in singular and plural number, but also in all three different cases. Some examples here include: **χόμπι** *hobby*, **σπορ** *sport*, **μπάσκετ** *basketball*.

# 3 Adjectives

**Adjectives** are words which describe people or things. They give more information about the noun they describe. Note: *a car* (noun), *a **big** car* (adjective-noun), *a **big red** car* (adjective-adjective-noun). The endings of adjectives change according to the noun they describe, i.e. masculine, feminine or neuter endings, singular or plural number and different cases, i.e. nominative, genitive, accusative. Most adjectives usually have the ending **-ος**, **-η**, **-ο** as in **μεγάλος** / **μεγάλη** / **μεγάλο** *big* or **-ος**, **-α**, **-ο** as in **ωραίος** / **ωραία** / **ωραίο** *nice*. These two adjective groups, along with an irregular adjective, namely **πολύς** / **πολλή** / **πολύ**, were introduced in past units of this course book. Below is a full declination of **μεγάλος** / **μεγάλη** / **μεγάλο**, and Unit 10 has the full declination of **πολύς** / **πολλή** / **πολύ**. All Greek adjectives will be written out in all three genders in singular number and nominative case in every dictionary.

SINGULAR

| | Masculine | Feminine | Neuter |
|---|---|---|---|
| nom | **μεγάλος** [megálos] | **μεγάλη** [megáli] | **μεγάλο** [megálo] |
| gen | **μεγάλου** [megáloo] | **μεγάλης** [megális] | **μεγάλου** [megáloo] |
| acc | **μεγάλο** [megálo] | **μεγάλη** [megáli] | **μεγάλο** [megálo] |

PLURAL

| | Masculine | Feminine | Neuter |
|---|---|---|---|
| nom | **μεγάλοι** [megáli] | **μεγάλες** [megáles] | **μεγάλα** [megála] |
| gen | **μεγάλων** [megálon] | **μεγάλων** [megálon] | **μεγάλων** [megálon] |
| acc | **μεγάλους** [megáloos] | **μεγάλες** [megáles] | **μεγάλα** [megála] |

# 4 Adverbs

**Adverbs** are words which usually describe the way things happen. Unlike adjectives, which give more information about the nouns they describe, adverbs give more information about the verbs they describe. Many Greek adverbs end in **-α** [-a] or **-ως** [-os], similar to the ending *-ly* of many English adverbs. Some examples include: **γρήγορα** [grígora] *quickly*, **καλά** [kalá] *well, nicely*, **βέβαια** [vévea] *of course, surely*.

Many Greek adverbs are formed from their corresponding adjectives. Notice the changes below: [grígoros] **γρήγορος** *fast, quick*, [grígora] **γρήγορα** *quickly*, [kalós] **καλός** *good, nice*, [kalá] **καλά** *nicely*, [véveos] **βέβαιος** *certain, sure*, [vévea] **βέβαια** *surely*. Unlike adjectives, adverbs have only one form. There is an exception regarding a few adverbs which have two almost similar forms which are interchangeable in use. Some examples are [vévea] **βέβαια** and [vevéos] **βεβαίως** *of course, surely* and [spánia] **σπάνια** and [spaníos] **σπανίως** *rarely*. The adverbs ending in **-α** are usually used in everyday, informal speech and the adverbs ending in **-ως** are usually found in formal speech. Unit 8 has a small list of time adverbs.

# 5 Pronouns

Words such as *I*, *you*, *he* or *my*, *your*, *his* or *myself*, *yourself*, *himself* or *me*, *you*, *him*, etc. are pronouns. Pronouns are grouped into several sub-categories: personal, reflexive, demonstrative, possessive, relative, interrogative and indefinite pronouns.

## PERSONAL PRONOUNS

| | Nominative | | Genitive | | Accusative | |
|---|---|---|---|---|---|---|
| | strong | weak | strong | weak | strong | weak |
| *I* | **εγώ** [egó] | – | **εμένα** [eména] | **μου** [moo] | **εμένα** [eména] | **με** [me] |
| *you* (sing/ infml) | **εσύ** [esí] | – | **εσένα** [eséna] | **σου** [soo] | **εσένα** [eséna] | **σε** [se] |
| *he* | **αυτός** [aftós] | | **αυτού** [aftoó] | **του** [too] | **αυτόν** [aftón] | **τον** [ton] |
| *she* | **αυτή** [aftí] | | **αυτής** [aftís] | **της** [tis] | **αυτή(ν)** [aftí(n)] | **τη(ν)** [ti(n)] |
| *it* | **αυτό** [aftó] | | **αυτού** [aftoó] | **του** [too] | **αυτό** [aftó] | **το** [to] |
| *we* | **εμείς** [emís] | – | **εμάς** [emás] | **μας** [mas] | **εμάς** [emás] | **μας** [mas] |
| *you* (pl/ fml) | **εσείς** [esís] | – | **εσάς** [esás] | **σας** [sas] | **εσάς** [esás] | **σας** [sas] |
| *they* | **αυτοί** [aftí]<br>**αυτές** [aftés]<br>**αυτά** [aftá] | | **αυτών** [aftón]<br>**αυτές** [aftés]<br>**αυτά** [aftá] | **τους** [toos]<br>**τις/τες** [tis/tes]<br>**τα** [ta] | **αυτούς** [aftoós] | **τους** [toos] |

Most Greek verbs like [ého] **έχω** *I have* take the nominative form of the personal pronoun, which is not absolutely necessary as it is in English, because the ending of the verb itself shows who is the subject.

That means that conjugated verbs often stand alone, without the need of a personal pronoun to help distinguish between them, for example, *I have, you have, we have, or they have* in English. Instead, in Greek, these are four completely different verb forms, i.e. **έχω**, **έχεις / έχετε** (singular / plural), **έχουμε**, **έχουν(ε)** and there is no misunderstanding when one of these forms is used. This is not the case with a few other verbs which are not conjugated, for example, **μου αρέσει** or **με λένε**, then the personal pronouns, especially in genitive or accusative case, come and help. All three verbs above do not need the strong form of personal pronouns but it is not a mistake to use them, especially when emphasis or clarification is needed. Check the examples below:

| Verbs without the strong form of personal pronouns | Verbs with the strong form of personal pronouns |
|---|---|
| 1 **Έχω ένα μεγάλο σπίτι.**<br>*I have a big house.* | 1 **Εγώ έχω ένα μεγάλο σπίτι.**<br>*I have a big house.* |
| 2 **Μου αρέσει το κολύμπι.**<br>*I like swimming.* | 2 **Εμένα μου αρέσει το κολύμπι.**<br>*I like swimming.* |
| 3 **Με λένε Άρη.**<br>*My name's Aris.* | 3 **Εμένα με λένε Άρη.**<br>*My name's Aris.* |

Perhaps the words run together faster in the examples without the strong forms, whereas a brief stop might be detected in the examples with the strong form but this small difference is not easily distinguished. The translation though, similar at one level, might be seen differently at another level and here is a small help: Έχω ένα μεγάλο σπίτι. *I have a big house.* (it is just pure information) whereas Εγώ έχω ένα μεγάλο σπίτι. *I have a big house.* (here apart from the information alone, it might also distinguish the ownership between *I* and *not my sister or not my friend!*) Specific context and language melody might help you with this point further.

## DEMONSTRATIVE PRONOUNS

| | Masculine | Feminine | Neuter |
|---|---|---|---|
| *this* | **αυτός** [aftós] | **αυτή** [aftí] | **αυτό** [aftó] |
| *these* | **αυτοί** [aftí] | **αυτές** [aftés] | **αυτά** [aftá] |
| *that* | **εκείνος** [ekínos] | **εκείνη** [ekíni] | **εκείνο** [ekíno] |
| *those* | **εκείνοι** [ekíni] | **εκείνες** [ekínes] | **εκείνα** [ekína] |
| *such a* | **τέτοιος** [tétios] | **τέτοια** [tétia] | **τέτοιο** [tétio] |
| *such* (pl) | **τέτοιοι** [tétyi] | **τέτοιες** [téties] | **τέτοια** [tétia] |
| *so much* | **τόσος** [tósos] | **τόση** [tósi] | **τόσο** [tóso] |
| *so many* | **τόσοι** [tósi] | **τόσες** [tóses] | **τόσα** [tósa] |

Note that the different forms in the singular and plural for **αυτός**, **εκείνος** and **τόσος** are identical to the adjective **μεγάλος**, **-η**, **-ο** as shown in the previous paragraph in this section.

Note too that the demonstrative pronouns **αυτός** and **εκείνος** need the corresponding article for the noun in use, e.g. [aftós o ándras] **αυτός ο άντρας** *this man*, [ekíni i yinéka] **εκείνη η γυναίκα** *that woman*, [aftá ta peTHiá] **αυτά τα παιδιά** *these children*. Demonstrative pronouns were not introduced in this book.

## POSSESSIVE PRONOUNS

| | | |
|---|---|---|
| *my* | **μου** | [moo] |
| *your* (sing/infml) | **σου** | [soo] |
| *his* | **του** | [too] |
| *her* | **της** | [tis] |
| *its* | **του** | [too] |
| *our* | **μας** | [mas] |
| *your* (pl/fml) | **σας** | [sas] |
| *their* | **τους** | [toos] |

Possessive pronouns have only one form in Greek. They always come after the noun they modify, whereas in English they come before the noun. In Greek, the noun is accompanied by its corresponding article, e.g. [to spíti moo]

**το σπίτι μου** *my house*, [ta spítia mas] **τα σπίτια μας** *our houses*, [o fílos tis] **ο φίλος της** *her friend*, [i fíli toos] **οι φίλοι τους** *their friends*.

These words are called possessive pronouns in Greek grammar and possessive adjectives in English grammar!

## RELATIVE PRONOUNS

Relative pronouns are single words, declined or not declined, which help to connect two sentences together. Some examples here include:

| | |
|---|---|
| 1 **Αυτή είναι η μαμά του Νίκου <u>που</u> μιλάει Αγγλικά.**<br>*This is Niko's mom <u>who</u> speaks English.* | 3 **Μπορείς να φας <u>ό,τι</u> θέλεις και να πιεις <u>όσο</u> θες.**<br>*You can eat <u>whatever</u> you want and you can drink <u>as much as</u> you want.* |
| 2 **Πάρε με τηλέφωνο <u>όποτε</u> θες.**<br>*Call me <u>whenever</u> you want.* | 4 **Δε θέλω να κάνω αυτό <u>όπως</u> το κάνει ο φίλος μου.**<br>*I don't want to do that <u>the way</u> (<u>lit. as</u>) my friend does that.* |

## INTERROGATIVE PRONOUNS

Most interrogative pronouns are single words. Some examples include:

*what?* **τι;** [ti]?
*where?* **πού;** [poo]?
*how?* **πώς;** [pos]?
*why?* **γιατί;** [yiatí]?

There are also some interrogative pronouns which are used with certain prepositions. Some examples here are:

*With what?* **Με τι;** [me ti]
*Where from?* **Από πού;** [apó poo]
*Since when?* **Από πότε;** [apó póte]
*Until when?* **Μέχρι πότε;** [méchri póte]

There are also two interrogative pronouns which are declined, namely **ποι-ος/-α/-ο** *who* and **πόσ-ος/-η/-ο** *how much / how many*. The table below gives you a better overview:

### ΠΟΙ-ΟΣ/-Α/-Ο *WHO/WHICH*

| | Singular | | | Plural | | |
|---|---|---|---|---|---|---|
| | Masculine | Feminine | Neuter | Masculine | Feminine | Neuter |
| **Nom.** | ποιος | ποια | ποιο | ποιοι | ποιες | ποια |
| **Gen.** | ποιου | ποιας | ποιου | ποιων | ποιων | ποιων |
| **Acc.** | ποιον | ποια | ποιο | ποιους | ποιες | ποια |

ΠΟΣ-ΟΣ/-Η/-Ο *HOW MUCH/MANY*

| | Singular | | | Plural | | |
|---|---|---|---|---|---|---|
| | Masculine | Feminine | Neuter | Masculine | Feminine | Neuter |
| **Nom.** | πόσος | πόση | πόσο | πόσοι | πόσες | πόσα |
| **Gen.** | πόσου | πόσης | πόσου | πόσων | πόσων | πόσων |
| **Acc.** | πόσο | πόση | πόσο | πόσους | πόσες | πόσα |

### INDEFINITE PRONOUNS

*all, everything* **όλ-ος/-η/-ο** [ólos/óli/ólo]
*something, anything?* **κάτι** [káti]
*nothing, anything?* **τίποτα** [típota]
*every, each* **κάθε** [káthe]

| | Masculine | Feminine | Neuter |
|---|---|---|---|
| *everyone/everything* (m/f/n) | **καθένας** [kathénas] | **καθεμία** [kathemía] | **καθένα** [kathéna] |
| *everybody* (m/f/n) (pl) | **όλοι** [óli] | **όλες** [óles] | **όλα** [óla] |
| *some* (pl) | **μερικοί** [merikí] | **μερικές** [merikés] | **μερικά** [meriká] |
| *someone, something* (m/f/n) | **κάποιος** [kápios] | **κάποια** [kápia] | **κάποιο** [kápio] |

# 6 Prepositions

**Prepositions** in English are such words as *between, from, in, by, for, with*, etc. All corresponding Greek prepositions have only one form. Greek prepositions will sometimes be followed by a noun in the genitive or more often in the accusative case. Some frequent prepositions are:

### GENITIVE

**εναντίον** [enandíon] *against*
**μεταξύ** [metaxí] *between*
**υπέρ** [ipér] *in favor, for*

### ACCUSATIVE

**από** [apó] *from*
**για** [yia] *for, to, over*
**με** [me] *with, by*
**χωρίς** [horís] *without*
**μετά** [metá] *after*

| | | |
|---|---|---|
| **μέχρι** | [méhri] | *until* |
| **πριν** | [prin] | *before* |
| **προς** | [pros] | *towards* |
| **σε** | [se] | *to, in, on, at* (place) |

This last preposition [se] **σε** is a little bit tricky, firstly in terms of its translation, meaning *at, to, in, on etc.*, but also in terms of its actual use. It can be used as a single word, for example [se lígho] **σε λίγο** *in a little while* or [se mía méra] **σε μία μέρα** *in one day*. It is also used as a compound word, whenever found with articles together, for example [stin athína] **στην Αθήνα** *in/towards Athens* or [stoos THelfoós] **στους Δελφούς** *to/towards Delphi* or [stis marías] **στης Μαρίας** *at/by/to Marias (place/restaurant/flat, etc.)*.

| | | |
|---|---|---|
| **στις** | [stis] | *at* (time) |

There are also some two-word prepositions. All of them are followed by nouns in the accusative.

ACCUSATIVE

| | | |
|---|---|---|
| **πάνω από** | [páno apó] | *over, above* |
| **κάτω από** | [káto apó] | *underneath, below* |
| **μπροστά από** | [brostá apó] | *in front of* |
| **πίσω από** | [píso apó] | *behind* |
| **κοντά σε** | [kondá se] | *close to* |
| **δίπλα σε** | [THípla se] | *next to* |
| **γύρω από** | [yíro apó] | *around from* |
| **μέσα σε** | [mésa se] | *inside* |
| **έξω από** | [ékso apó] | *outside, out of* |

The book has introduced only a few prepositions, including [se] **σε**, from the three lists above.

# 7 Verbs

### *7.1 WHAT IS A VERB?*

Words that indicate action, being, or feeling are called verbs. [káno] **Κάνω** *I do*, [miláo] **μιλάω** *I speak* or [méno] **μένω** *I live* are three examples from the several verbs this course includes.

## *7.2 THE MAIN VERB FORM*

Remember that a dictionary will list these three verbs, and all others, using the *I* form of the verb. This is the main form used for reference to Greek verbs (as the infinitive form in English – *to do, to speak, to live*, etc. – does not exist in Greek) as well as for the *I* form in the present tense simple or continuous. That is to say that most Greek verbs have three major functions at the same time, namely, either as infinitive form, or as a first-person singular in simple present, or also as a first-person singular in present continuous. Then if we take the verb **κάνω** as an example, its three functions can serve first as *to do/to make*, then as *I do/I make*, but also as *I am doing/I am making.*

## *7.3 VERB TENSES*

Verb tenses refer to different points in time, such as the present, the future, and the past. This course relies mostly on present tense, touches on the future and past tenses, and introduces some imperatives and some verb forms after the particles [na] **να** or [tha] **θα** in Unit 9.

## *7.4 VERBS AND PERSONAL PRONOUNS*

Also, remember that personal pronouns, words like *I, he, they*, etc. in English, are not necessary in Greek because of the change in the verb ending. So, **κάνω** can be seen as **κάν-** (the verb stem which remains unchanged) and **-ω** (the verb ending which tells you whether *I, he* or *they*, etc. is performing the action). There are two verb endings in Greek for the *I* form: **-ω** [-o] and **μαι** [-me], e.g. [periméno] **περιμένω** *to wait / I wait / I am waiting* and [káthome] **κάθομαι** *to sit / I sit / I am sitting.*

## *7.5 TWO VERB STEMS*

Most verbs have two stems. Stem 1 is the main verb form discussed above with its three functions and it can be used, with or without a verb particle, to build many verb tenses. Stem 2 is a complimentary verb form and it cannot be used alone without preceded by a verb particle (see below). Both stems are important for learners of Greek because they are needed to build all different tenses for past, present, and future. This book has introduced verbs mainly in the present tense, simple or continuous. Nevertheless, the notion of these two verb stems was given in the last few units of the book starting with Unit 6. It was also pointed out that some stems are easily detected and some not and therefore a table was introduced for a better overview of this point.

| Verbs with two exactly the same verb stems | Verbs with two different stems but almost similar | Verbs with two completely different verb stems |
|---|---|---|
| έχω – έχω *to have*, κάνω – κάνω *to do*, ξέρω – ξέρω *to know* ... | φέρνω – φέρω *to bring*, πίνω – πιω *to drink*, γράφω – γράψω *to write* ... | βλέπω – δω *to see*, παίρνω – πάρω *to take*, εργάζομαι – εργαστώ *to work* ... |

The above grouping is an arbitrary decision which we believe will help you grasp this matter easier and faster. Good to also know here is that most Greek verbs are part of the second grouping above. The decision which verb stem is needed was introduced in Unit 9 and the table below tries to help further with this notion. Although the examples taken were almost similar in wording, they actually serve two completely different messages. Read the examples carefully and try to understand the important function of these verb stems.

| Verb stem 1<br>Repeated action(s) without time constrains | Verb stem 2<br>One single action with time constrains |
|---|---|
| **1 Θέλω να τρώω πάντα πίτσα.** *I want to be always eating pizza (any time I have the chance to eat pizza).* **2 Σου αρέσει να βλέπεις τηλεόραση;** *Do you like watching TV (any time you have the chance to watch)?* **3 Δεν θα μιλάω με τη Μαρία συχνά.** *I'm not going to speak with Maria often (From now on, I plan not to speak with Maria often).* **4 Θα πηγαίνω πολλές βόλτες στην Αθήνα.** *I'll be taking many walks (when I am) in Athens (I'm planning to take many walks in Athens).* | **5 Θέλω να φάω μια πίτσα τώρα.** *I want to eat a pizza now (only one pizza, right now, and that's it).* **6 Θέλεις να δεις τηλεόραση σήμερα;** *Do you want to watch TV today (only today, in one given time)?* **7 Δεν θα μιλήσω στον Άρη το Σάββατο.** *I won't speak to Aris on Saturday (only one discussion at one given time and that's it).* **8 Θα πάω μια βόλτα στις 8:00.** *I'm going to go for a walk at 8:00 o'clock (only one walk at a specific time and that's it).* |

### *7.6 TWO VERB PARTICLES*

The book introduced two verb particles, namely [tha] **θα** *will/shall/would* and **να** [na] *to*. Greek has more than those two particles but we leave intentionally out the rest of those particles. Both particles here, when used, always precede the verb which can follow either in stem 1 or 2. Which verb stem will be used depends on and is decided upon the meaning of the message the speaker is trying to express. As a rule of thumb, stem 1 will be used to express the notion of '*a repeated action(s) without time constrains*' whereas stem 2 will be used to express the notion of '*a single action within time constrains*'. Please go over the 8 examples given in 7.5 above and make sure this point is clear enough for you to use it from theory into practice.

## *7.7 VERB GROUPS*

The book has sorted out all Greek verbs in 8 groups. Verb groups 1, 2, 3, and 4 include all verbs, also called active verbs, ending in **-ω** (regardless **-ω**, **-άω/ώ**, **-ώ**, or special **-ω** verbs). Verb groups 5, 6, 7, and 8 include all verbs, also called passive verbs, ending in **-μαι** (regardless **-ομαι**, **-ιέμαι**, **-ούμαι** or special **-μαι** verbs). This arbitrary naming as verb group 1-8 is clear and easier compared to what most other grammar books name as verb group A, B1, B2, A/B, Γ1, Γ2, Γ3, and Γ4! Verb groups are sorted out below according to their verb endings and each verb group has a '*standard-regular*' verb conjugation. Verb group 4 and 8 respectively do pose a small challenge as they include '*special-irregular*' verbs not conforming to the other 6 verb groups. The book introduced all verb groups except verb group 6 and 7.

### Greek verbs ending in -ω, -άω/ώ, -ώ, or special -ω conjugations

| Verb group 1<br>Ending in -ω | Verb group 2<br>Ending in -άω/ώ | Verb group 3<br>Ending in -ώ | Verb group 4<br>Special -ω verbs |
|---|---|---|---|
| θέλω<br>θέλεις<br>θέλει<br>θέλουμε<br>θέλετε<br>θέλουν(ε) | διψάω-διψώ<br>διψάς<br>διψάει-διψά<br>διψάμε<br>διψάτε<br>διψούν(ε) - διψάνε | παρακαλώ<br>παρακαλείς<br>παρακαλεί<br>παρακαλούμε<br>παρακαλείτε<br>παρακαλούν(ε) | πάω<br>πας<br>πάει<br>πάμε<br>πάτε<br>πάνε |
| *(to want)* | *(to be thirsty)* | *(to please)* | *(to go)* |

### Verbs ending in -ομαι, -ιέμαι, -ούμαι, or special -μαι conjugations

| Verb group 5<br>Ending in -ομαι | Verb group 6<br>Ending in -ιέμαι | Verb group 7<br>Ending in -ούμαι | Verb group 8<br>Special -μαι verbs |
|---|---|---|---|
| κάθομαι<br>κάθεσαι<br>κάθεται<br>καθόμαστε<br>καθόσατε/κάθεστε<br>κάθονται | βαριέμαι<br>βαριέσαι<br>βαριέται<br>βαριόμαστε<br>βαριόσαστε/βαριέστε<br>βαριούνται | καλούμαι<br>καλείσαι<br>καλείται<br>καλούμεθα<br>καλείστε<br>καλούντε | είμαι<br>είσαι<br>είναι<br>είμαστε<br>είσαστε/είστε<br>είναι |
| *(to sit)* | *(to be bored)* | *(to be called)* | *(to be)* |

### *7.8 SPECIAL VERBS*

There are a few verbs which do not have a full conjugation and/or do not appear in all possible verb tenses, i.e. past, present, or future. The book has already introduced some special verbs without any specific notification but we can go ahead and list them for you here: [prépi] **πρέπει** *have to, has to, must*, [íme] **είμαι** *to be*, [écho] **έχω** *to have*, [ipárchi] **υπάρχει** *there is*, and [ipárchoon] **υπάρχουν** *there are*. It will go beyond the scope of this grammar section for us to try to provide here more information. Nevertheless, these five special verbs are important for you to check and make sure you understand how to use them.

### *7.9 IMPERATIVE FORMS*

The imperative is a form of the verb you can use to request, tell or order someone to do something, e.g. *Come here!, Stop!, Don't speak!, Turn left!, Go now!*. This form is very frequent and important in everyday language. Remember that since Greek has two *you* forms (informal/singular and formal/plural), you need to learn two individual words for the imperatives.

| (sing/infml) | (pl/fml) | |
|---|---|---|
| **πήγαινε** [píyene]! | **πηγαίνετε** [piyénete]! | *Go!* |
| **στρίψε** [strípse]! | **στρίψτε** [strípste]! | *Turn!* |
| **βγες** [vyes]! | **βγείτε** [vyíte]! | *Get off! Get out!* |
| **συνέχισε** [sinéhise]! | **συνεχίστε** [sinehíste]! | *Continue!* |
| **σταμάτα** [stamáta]! | **σταματήστε** [stamatíste]! | *Stop!* |
| **περπάτησε** [perpátise]! | **περπατήστε** [perpatíste]! | *Walk!* |
| **οδήγησε** [oTHíyise]! | **οδηγήστε** [oTHiyíste]! | *Drive!* |

# English–Greek glossary

(Note: m = masculine, f = feminine, n = neuter; vg = verb group)

All verbs are written with their corresponding verb group, i.e. (vg1) for verb group 1 all the way to (vg8) for verb group 8.

*a.m.* **[pi-mi]** π.μ.

(written this way but [pro mesimvrías] **προ μεσημβρίας** when spoken)

| | | |
|---|---|---|
| *a/an/one* | **[énas], [mía-mya], [éna]** | ένας, μία-μια, ένα |
| *about/approximately* | **[perípoo]** | περίπου |
| *across/opposite* | **[apénandi]** | απέναντι |
| *adventure story/thriller* | **[peripétia]** | περιπέτεια (f) |
| *afterwards, later* | **[metá]** | μετά |
| *again* | **[páli]** | πάλι |
| *agree* | **[simfonó]** | συμφωνώ |
| *airplane* | **[aeropláno]** | αεροπλάνο (n) |
| *airport* | **[aeroTHrómio]** | αεροδρόμιο (n) |
| *almost* | **[sheTHón]** | σχεδόν |
| *along/together* | **[mazí]** | μαζί |
| *always* | **[pánda]** | πάντα |
| *America* | **[amerikí]** | Αμερική (f) |
| *and* | **[ke]** | και |
| *angry* | **[thimoménos, -i, -o]** | θυμωμένος, -η -ο |
| *another* | **[álos, -i, -o]** | άλλος, -η, -ο |
| *apartment building* | **[polikatikía]** | πολυκατοικία (f) |
| *apartment/flat* | **[THiamérizma]** | διαμέρισμα (n) |
| *appetizer, starter* | **[orektikó]** | ορεκτικό (n) |
| *April* | **[aprílios]** | Απρίλιος (m) |
| *architect* | **[arhitéktonas]** | αρχιτέκτονας (m/f) |
| *area* | **[hóros]** | χώρος (m) |
| *armchair* | **[poliTHróna]** | πολυθρόνα (f) |
| *around, about* | **[yíro], [perípoo]** | γύρω, περίπου |
| *arrive* | **[ftháno]** | φθάνω (vg1) |
| *as* | **[ópos]** | όπως |
| *Athens* | **[athína]** | Αθήνα (f) |

| | | |
|---|---|---|
| *August* | **[ávgoostos]** | Αύγουστος (m) |
| *Australia* | **[afstralía]** | Αυστραλία (f) |
| *autumn/fall* | **[fthinóporo]** | φθινόπωρο (n) |
| *availability* | **[THiathesimótita]** | διαθεσιμότητα (f) |
| | | |
| *baby* | **[moró]** | μωρό (n) |
| *baby boy* | **[bébis]** | μπέμπης (m) |
| *baby girl* | **[béba]** | μπέμπα (f) |
| *balcony/porch* | **[balkóni]** | μπαλκόνι (n) |
| *banana* | **[banána]** | μπανάνα (f) |
| *bank* | **[trápeza]** | τράπεζα (f) |
| *basement* | **[ipóyio]** | υπόγειο (n) |
| *basketball* | **[básket]** | μπάσκετ (n) |
| *bass* (fish) | **[lavráki]** | λαβράκι (n) |
| *bathroom* | **[bánio]** | μπάνιο (n) |
| *bathroom, toilet* | **[tooaléta]** | τουαλέτα (f) |
| *be* | **[íme]** | είμαι (vg8) |
| *be able* | **[boró]** | μπορώ (vg3) |
| *be glad/happy/pleased* | **[hérome]** | χαίρομαι (vg5) |
| *be interested* | **[enTHiaférome]** | ενδιαφέρομαι (vg5) |
| *beach* | **[plaz, paralía]** | πλαζ, παραλία (f) |
| *bean* | **[fasóli]** | φασόλι (n) |
| *beautiful, nice* | **[oréos, -a, -o]** | ωραίος, -α, -ο |
| *because* | **[yatí/THyóti]** | γιατί/διότι |
| *bed* | **[kreváti]** | κρεβάτι (n) |
| *bedroom* | **[krevatokámara], [ipnoTHomátio]** | κρεβατοκάμαρα (f), υπνοδωμάτιο (n) |
| *beef* | **[mosharísios, -a, -o]** | μοσχαρίσιος, -α, -ο |
| *beefsteak* | **[mosharísia brizóla]** | μοσχαρίσια μπριζόλα (f) |
| *beer* | **[bíra]** | μπύρα (f) |
| *behind* | **[píso]** | πίσω |
| *beige* | **[bez]** | μπεζ |
| *bell* | **[kooTHoóni]** | κουδούνι (n) |
| *Berlin* | **[verolíno]** | Βερολίνο (n) |
| *between* | **[metaksí]** | μεταξύ |
| *beverage, drink* | **[potó]** | ποτό (n) |
| *big, large* | **[megálos, -i, -o]** | μεγάλος, -η, -ο |

| | | |
|---|---|---|
| *bill* | **[logariazmós]** | λογαριασμός (m) |
| *black* | **[mávros, -i, -o]** | μαύρος, -η, -ο |
| *block* | **[tetrágono]** | τετράγωνο (n) |
| *blue* | **[ble]** | μπλε |
| *blues* (music) | **[blooz]** | μπλουζ (n) |
| *boat* | **[várka]** | βάρκα (f) |
| *book* | **[vivlío]** | βιβλίο (n) |
| *bookshop* | **[vivliopolío]** | βιβλιοπωλείο (n) |
| *booklet* | **[filáTHio]** | φυλλάδιο (n) |
| *bottle* | **[bookáli]** | μπουκάλι (n) |
| *bottled* (mineral) *water* | **[emfialoméno neró]** | εμφιαλωμένο νερό (n) |
| *boy* | **[agóri]** | αγόρι (n) |
| *bravo* | **[brávo]** | μπράβο |
| *bread* | **[psomí]** | ψωμί (n) |
| *breakfast* | **[proinó]** | πρωινό (n) |
| *bream or gilthead* | **[tsipoora]** | τσιπούρα (f) |
| *bridge* | **[yéfira]** | γέφυρα (f) |
| *brother* | **[aTHelfós]** | αδελφός (m) |
| *brown* | **[kafé]** | καφέ |
| *bus* | **[leoforío]** | λεωφορείο (n) |
| *bus station* | **[stathmós leoforíon]** | σταθμός λεωφορείων (m) |
| *bus stop* | **[stási leoforíon]** | στάση λεωφορείων (f) |
| *busy* | **[apasholiménos, -i, -o]** | απασχολημένος, -η, -ο |
| *but* | **[alá], [ma]** | αλλά, μα |
| *butcher's shop* | **[kreopolíon]** | κρεοπωλείο (n) |
| *butter* | **[voótiro]** | βούτυρο (n) |
| *café* | **[kafetéria]** | καφετέρια (f) |
| *can* | **[boró]** | μπορώ (vg3) |
| *can/tin* | **[kootí]** | κουτί (n) |
| *car* | **[aftokínito]** | αυτοκίνητο (n) |
| *car park* | **[párkin]** | πάρκιν (n) |
| *card* | **[kárta]** | κάρτα (f) |
| *carrot* | **[karóto]** | καρότο (n) |
| *cash desk* | **[tamío]** | ταμείο (n) |
| *celery* | **[sélino]** | σέλινο (n) |
| *central* | **[kendrikós, -í, -ó]** | κεντρικός, -ή, -ό |

| | | |
|---|---|---|
| *centre* | **[kéndro]** | κέντρο (n) |
| *century* | **[eónas]** | αιώνας (m) |
| *cereal* | **[dimitriaká]** | δημητριακά (n/pl) |
| *chair* | **[karékla]** | καρέκλα (f) |
| *changing room* | **[THokimastírio]** | δοκιμαστήριο (n) |
| *cheap* | **[fthinós, -í, -ó]** | φθηνός, -ή, -ό |
| *checked* | **[karó]** | καρώ (m/f/n) |
| *check* | **[epitayí]** | επιταγή (f) |
| *child* | **[peTHí]** | παιδί (n) |
| *church* | **[eklisía]** | εκκλησία (f) |
| *cigarette* | **[tsigáro]** | τσιγάρο (n) |
| *cinema* | **[sinemá]** | σινεμά (n) |
| *close to* | **[kondá]** | κοντά |
| *closed* | **[klistós, -í, -ó]** | κλειστός, -ή, -ό |
| *closet/wardrobe* | **[doolápa]** | ντουλάπα (f) |
| *Coca Cola* | **[kóka kóla]** | κόκα κόλα (f) |
| *coffee* | **[kafés]** | καφές (m) |
| *coffee house* | **[kafenío]** | καφενείο (n) |
| *coffee* (medium sweet) | **[métrios]** | μέτριος (m) |
| *coffee* (sweet) | **[glikós]** | γλυκός (m) |
| *coffee* (without sugar) | **[skétos]** | σκέτος (m) |
| *comedy* | **[komoTHía]** | κωμωδία (f) |
| *company* | **[etería]** | εταιρ(ε)ία (f) |
| *computer* | **[kompioóter]** | κομπιούτερ (n) |
| *conservatory* | **[thermokípio]** | θερμοκήπιο (n) |
| *contrast, antithesis* | **[antíthesi]** | αντίθεση (f) |
| *cook* | **[mayirévo]** | μαγειρεύω (vg1) |
| *cooked foods* | **[mayireftá]** | μαγειρευτά (n/pl) |
| *corner* | **[gonía]** | γωνία (f) |
| *counter* | **[pángos]** | πάγκος (m) |
| *country* | **[hóra]** | χώρα (f) |
| *courgette, zucchini* | **[kolokitháki]** | κολοκυθάκι (n) |
| *cousin* | **[(e)ksaTHélfi], [(e)ksáTHelfos]** | (ε)ξαδέλφη (f), (ε)ξάδελφος (m) |
| *credit card* | **[pistotikí kárta]** | πιστωτική κάρτα (f) |
| *crème caramel* | **[krem karamelé]** | κρεμ καραμελέ (n) |
| *croissant* | **[krooasán]** | κρουασάν (n) |
| *cucumber* | **[agoóri]** | αγγούρι (n) |
| *cup* | **[flitzáni]** | φλυτζάνι (n) |

| | | |
|---|---|---|
| *currency* | **[nómizma]** | νόμισμα (n) |
| *customs* | **[telonío]** | τελωνείο (n) |
| *cutlet* | **[brizóla]** | μπριζόλα (f) |
| | | |
| *dark* | **[skoóros, -a, -o]** | σκούρος, -α, -ο |
| *date* | **[imerominía]** | ημερομηνία (f) |
| *daughter* | **[kóri]** | κόρη (f) |
| *day* | **[(i)méra]** | (η)μέρα (f) |
| *December* | **[THekémvrios]** | Δεκέμβριος (m) |
| *deposit, down payment* | **[prokatavolí]** | προκαταβολή (f) |
| *dessert* | **[glikó]** | γλυκό (n) |
| *dialogue* | **[THiálogos]** | διάλογος (m) |
| *difficult* | **[THískolos, -i, -o]** | δύσκολος, -η, -ο |
| *dill* | **[ánithos]** | άνιθος (m) |
| *dining room* | **[trapezaría]** | τραπεζαρία (f) |
| *dinner* | **[vraTHinó]** | βραδινό (n) |
| *disagree* | **[THiafonó]** | διαφωνώ (vg3) |
| *dislike* | **[antipathó]** | αντιπαθώ |
| *doctor* | **[yiatrós]** | γιατρός (m/f) |
| *door* | **[pórta]** | πόρτα (f) |
| *double room* | **[THíklino]** | δίκλινο (n) |
| *down* | **[káto]** | κάτω |
| *dress* | **[fórema]** | φόρεμα (n) |
| *drink* | **[píno]** | πίνω (vg1) |
| | | |
| *early* | **[norís]** | νωρίς |
| *easy* | **[éfkolos, -i, -o]** | εύκολος, -η, -ο |
| *eat* | **[tró-o]** | τρώω (vg4) |
| *eight* | **[októ]/[ohtó]** | οκτώ/οχτώ |
| *eight hundred* | **[oktakósia]/[ohtakósia]** | οκτακόσια/οχτακόσια |
| *eighteen* | **[THekaoktó]** | δεκαοκτώ |
| *eighty* | **[ogTHónda]** | ογδόντα |
| *eleven* | **[éndeka]** | έντεκα |
| *England* | **[anglía]** | Αγγλία (f) |
| *English* (language) | **[angliká]** | Αγγλικά (n/pl) |
| *entrance* | **[ísoTHos]** | είσοδος (f) |
| *envelope* | **[fákelos]** | φάκελος (m) |
| *Euro* | **[evró]** | ευρώ (n) |

| | | |
|---|---|---|
| *evening* | **[vráTHi]** | βράδυ (n) |
| *every* | **[káthe]** | κάθε |
| *everything/all* | **[óla]** | όλα |
| *everywhere* | **[pandoó]** | παντού |
| *exactly* | **[akrivós]** | ακριβώς |
| *excuse me, pardon me* | **[signómi], [me sinhoríte]** | συγνώμη, με συγχωρείτε (pl/fml) |
| *exit* | **[éksoTHos]** | έξοδος (f) |
| | | |
| *fall* (verb) | **[péfto]** | πέφτω (vg1) |
| *family* | **[ikoyénia]** | οικογένεια (f) |
| *father* | **[patéras]** | πατέρας (m) |
| *February* | **[fevrooários]** | Φεβρουάριος (m) |
| *ferryboat* | **[feribót]** | φεριμπότ (n) |
| *fifteen* | **[THekapénde]** | δεκαπέντε |
| *fifth* | **[pémptos, -i, -o]** | πέμπτος, -η, -ο |
| *fifty* | **[penínda]** | πενήντα |
| *film* | **[érgo] [film] [tenía]** | έργο (n), φιλμ (n), ταινία (f) |
| *finally* | **[teliká]** | τελικά |
| *finish* | **[telióno]** | τελειώνω (vg1) |
| *first* | **[prótos, -i, -o]** | πρώτος, -η, -ο |
| *fish* | **[psári]** | ψάρι (n) |
| *fish restaurant* | **[psarotavérna]** | ψαροταβέρνα (f) |
| *five* | **[pénde]** | πέντε |
| *five hundred* | **[pendakósia]** | πεντακόσια |
| *flat, apartment* | **[THiamérizma]** | διαμέρισμα (n) |
| *flight* | **[ptísi]** | πτήση (f) |
| *floor* | **[órofos]** | όροφος (m) |
| *flying dolphin, hydrofoil* | **[iptámeno THelfíni]** | ιπτάμενο δελφίνι (n) |
| *food* | **[fayitó]** | φαγητό (n) |
| *food cooked in oil* | **[laTHerá]** | λαδερά (n/pl) |
| *foot* | **[póTHi]** | πόδι (n) |
| *football* | **[poTHósfero]** | ποδόσφαιρο (n) |
| *for* | **[yia]** | για |
| *fork* | **[piroóni]** | πιρούνι (n) |
| *fortnight* | **[THekapenthímero]** | δεκαπενθήμερο (n) |
| *forty* | **[saránda]** | σαράντα |
| *four* | **[téseris, -is, -a]** | τέσσερις, -ις, -α |

| | | |
|---|---|---|
| *four hundred* | **[tetrakósia]** | τετρακόσια |
| *fourteen* | **[THekatéseris, -is, -a]** | δεκατέσσερις, -ις, -α |
| *fourth* | **[tétartos, -i, -o]** | τέταρτος, -η, -ο |
| *France* | **[galía]** | Γαλλία (f) |
| *free* | **[eléftheros, -i, -o]** | ελεύθερος, -η, -ο |
| *French* (language) | **[galiká]** | γαλλικά (n/pl) |
| *friend* | **[fílos] [fíli]** | φίλος (m), φίλη (f) |
| *from* | **[apó]** | από |
| *front* | **[brostá]** | μπροστά |
| *fruit* | **[froóto]** | φρούτο (n) |
| *fruit and vegetable market* | **[laikí agorá]** | λαϊκή αγορά (f) |
| | | |
| *garage* | **[garáz]** | γκαράζ (n) |
| *garlic* | **[skórTHo]** | σκόρδο (n) |
| *German* (language) | **[yermaniká]** | Γερμανικά (n/pl) |
| *Germany* | **[yermanía]** | Γερμανία (f) |
| *get up* | **[sikónome]** | σηκώνομαι (vg5) |
| *girl* | **[korítsi]** | κορίτσι (n) |
| *glass* | **[potíri]** | ποτήρι (n) |
| *go* | **[páo]** | πάω (vg4) |
| *go for a walk* | **[páo vólta]** | πάω βόλτα |
| *good evening* | **[kalispéra]** | καλησπέρα |
| *good morning* | **[kaliméra]** | καλημέρα |
| *goodnight* | **[kaliníhta]** | καληνύχτα |
| *grandchild* | **[egóni]** | εγγόνι (n) |
| *granddaughter* | **[egoní]** | εγγονή (f) |
| *grandfather* | **[papoós]** | παππούς (m) |
| *grandmother* | **[yiayiá]** | γιαγιά (f) |
| *grandson* | **[egonós]** | εγγονός (m) |
| *grape* | **[stafíli]** | σταφύλι (n) |
| *Greece* | **[eláTHa]** | Ελλάδα (f) |
| *Greek* (language) | **[eliniká]** | Ελληνικά (n/pl) |
| *green* | **[prásinos, -i, -o]** | πράσινος, -η, -ο |
| *grilled foods* | **[psitá]** | ψητά (n/pl) |
| *ground floor* | **[isóyio]** | ισόγειο (n) |
| | | |
| *hairdresser's* | **[komotírio]** | κομμωτήριο (n) |
| *half* | **[misós, -í, -ó]** | μισός, -ή, -ό |

| | | |
|---|---|---|
| *hallway* | **[hol]** | χωλ (n) |
| *hand* | **[héri]** | χέρι (n) |
| *hand basin* | **[niptíras]** | νιπτήρας (m) |
| *happy* | **[eftihizménos, -i, -o]** | ευτυχισμένος, -η, -ο |
| *have* | **[ého]** | έχω (vg1) |
| *he* | **[aftós]** | αυτός |
| *heating* | **[thérmansi]** | θέρμανση (f) |
| *hello / goodbye* | **[hérete]** | χαίρετε (pl/fml) |
| *hello / goodbye* | **[yiásas]** | γεια σας (pl/fml) |
| *hello / see you* | **[yiásoo]** | γεια σου (sing/infml) |
| *her* | **[tis]** | της |
| *herb* | **[aromatikó fitó]** | αρωματικό φυτό (n) |
| *here* | **[eTHó]** | εδώ |
| *here you are!* | **[oríste]** | ορίστε |
| *hi* | **[yia]** | γεια |
| *his* | **[too]** | του |
| *hobby* | **[hóbi]** | χόμπι (n) |
| *homemade* | **[spitikós, -í, -ó]** | σπιτικός, -ή, -ό |
| *hospital* | **[nosokomío]** | νοσοκομείο (n) |
| *hotel* | **[ksenoTHohío]** | ξενοδοχείο (n) |
| *house/home* | **[spíti]** | σπίτι (n) |
| *how/what* | **[pos]** | πώς |
| *hungry* | **[pinazménos, -i, -o]** | πεινασμένος, -η, -ο |
| *husband/wife, spouse* | **[sízigos]** | σύζυγος (m/f) |
| | | |
| *I* | **[egó]** | εγώ |
| *iced coffee/frappé* | **[frapés/frapé]** | φραπές (m)/φραπέ (n) |
| *idea* | **[iTHéa]** | ιδέα (f) |
| *immediately* | **[amésos]** | αμέσως |
| *in* | **[se]** | σε |
| *information* (piece of) | **[pliroforía]** | πληροφορία (f) |
| *instant coffee* | **[nes kafé]** | νες καφέ (n) |
| *interested (I'm)* | **[enTHiaférome]** | ενδιαφέρομαι (vg5) |
| *interest* | **[enTHiaféron]** | ενδιαφέρον (n) |
| *introduce* | **[sistíno]** | συστήνω (vg1) |
| *Ireland* | **[irlanTHía]** | Ιρλανδία (f) |
| *island music* | **[nisiótika]** | νησιώτικα (n/pl) |
| *it* | **[aftó]** | αυτό |
| *Italian* (language) | **[italiká]** | Ιταλικά (n/pl) |

*Italy* **[italía]** Ιταλία (f)
*its* **[too]** του

*January* **[ianooários]** Ιανουάριος (m)
*jazz music* **[tzaz]** τζαζ (f)
*job/work* **[THooliá]** δουλειά (f)
*juice* **[himós]** χυμός (m)
*July* **[ioólios]** Ιούλιος (m)
*June* **[ioónios]** Ιούνιος (m)

*key* **[kliTHí]** κλειδί (n)
*kilo* **[kiló]** κιλό (n)
*kiosk* **[períptero]** περίπτερο (n)
*kitchen* **[koozína]** κουζίνα (f)
*knife* **[mahéri]** μαχαίρι (n)
*know* **[kséro]** ξέρω (vg1)

*lamb* **[arnáki]** αρνάκι (n)
*late* **[argá]** αργά
*lawn/grass* **[grasíTHi]** γρασίδι (n)
*learn* **[mathéno]** μαθαίνω (vg1)
*leave* **[févgo]** φεύγω (vg1)
*left* **[aristerá]** αριστερά
*lemonade* **[lemonáTHa]** λεμονάδα (f)
*letter* **[gráma]** γράμμα (n)
*lettuce* **[maroóli]** μαρούλι (n)
*lift/elevator* **[asansér]** ασανσέρ (n)
*light* (color), *open* **[aniktós, -í, -ó]** ανοικτός, -ή, -ό
*like* (sing) **[marési/moo arési]** μ' αρέσει/μου αρέσει (vg4)
*like* (pl) **[marésoon/ moo arésoon]** μ' αρέσουν/μου αρέσουν (vg4)
*likely, probably* **[pithanós, -í, -ó]** πιθανός, -ή, -ό
*little* **[lígos, -i, -o]** λίγος, -η, -ο
*live* **[méno]** μένω (vg1)
*living room* **[salóni]** σαλόνι (f)
*London* **[lonTHíno]** Λονδίνο (n)
*love* **[agápi]** αγάπη (f)
*love story* **[istoría agápis]** ιστορία αγάπης (f)

| | | |
|---|---|---|
| *lucky* | **[tiherós, -í, -ó]** | τυχερός, -ή, -ό |
| *luggage* | **[aposkeví]** | αποσκευή (f) |
| *lunch* | **[mesimerianó]** | μεσημεριανό (n) |
| *lyre* | **[líra]** | λύρα (f) |
| | | |
| *Madrid* | **[maTHríti]** | Μαδρίτη (f) |
| *mainly* | **[kiríos]** | κυρίως |
| *man/husband* | **[ándras]** | άνδρας (m) |
| *map* | **[hártis]** | χάρτης (m) |
| *March* | **[mártios]** | Μάρτιος (m) |
| *market* | **[agorá]** | αγορά (f) |
| *marmalade/jam* | **[marmeláTHa]** | μαρμελάδα (f) |
| *May* | **[máios]** | Μάιος (m) |
| *may/can be/is possible to* | **[borí (na)]** | μπορεί (να) (vg4) |
| *me* (after a preposition) | **[(e)ména]** | (ε)μένα |
| *me* (before a verb) | **[moo]** | μου |
| *medium, middle* | **[meséos, -a, -o]** | μεσαίος, -α, -ο |
| *melon* | **[pepóni]** | πεπόνι (n) |
| *mezzanine* (floor) | **[imiórofos]** | ημιόροφος (m) |
| *midday/afternoon* | **[mesiméri]** | μεσημέρι (n) |
| *milk* | **[gála]** | γάλα (n) |
| *minute* | **[leptó]** | λεπτό (n) |
| *mirror* | **[kathréftis]** | καθρέφτης (m) |
| *Miss* | **[THespiníTHa]** | δεσποινίδα (f) |
| *moment* | **[stigmí]** | στιγμή (f) |
| *month* | **[mínas]** | μήνας (m) |
| *more* | **[pio]** | πιο |
| *more* | **[perisóteros, -i, -o]** | περισσότερος, -η, -ο |
| *morning* | **[proí]** | πρωί (n) |
| *mother* | **[mitéra]** | μητέρα (f) |
| *motorcycle* | **[motosikléta]** | μοτοσυκλέτα (f) |
| *mountain* | **[voonó]** | βουνό (n) |
| *Mr/Sir* | **[kírios]** | κύριος (m) |
| *Mrs/Madam* | **[kiría]** | κυρία (f) |
| *much/very* | **[polís, polí, polí]** | πολύς, πολλή, πολύ |
| *museum* | **[moosío]** | μουσείο (n) |
| *mushroom* | **[manitári]** | μανιτάρι (n) |
| *music* | **[moosikí]** | μουσική (f) |
| *musician* | **[moosikós]** | μουσικός (m/f) |

| | | |
|---|---|---|
| *must/have to* | **[prépi (na)]** | πρέπει (να) (vg4) |
| *my* | **[moo]** | μου |
| | | |
| *name* | **[ónoma]** | όνομα (n) |
| *My name's* | **[me léne]** | με λένε (vg4) |
| *national* | **[ethnikós, -í, -ó]** | εθνικός, -ή, -ό |
| *naturally* | **[fisiká]** | φυσικά |
| *nought/zero* | **[miTHén]** | μηδέν (n) |
| *near, close to* | **[kondá]** | κοντά |
| *need* | **[hriázome]** | χρειάζομαι (vg5) |
| *neighborhood* | **[yitoniá]** | γειτονιά (f) |
| *never* | **[poté]** | ποτέ |
| *New York* | **[néa iórki]** | Νέα Υόρκη (f) |
| *newspaper* | **[efimeríTHa]** | εφημερίδα (f) |
| *next to* | **[THípla]** | δίπλα |
| *nice, beautiful* | **[oréos, -a, -o], [ómorfos, -i, -o]** | ωραίος, -α, -ο, όμορφος, -η, -ο |
| *nine* | **[enéa]/[eniá]** | εννέα/εννιά |
| *nine hundred* | **[eniakósia]** | ενιακόσια |
| *nineteen* | **[THekaeniá]** | δεκαεννιά |
| *ninety* | **[enenínda]** | ενενήντα |
| *no* | **[óhi]** | όχι |
| *not* | **[THen]** | δεν |
| *nothing* | **[típota]** | τίποτα |
| *novel* | **[noovéla], [mithistórima]** | νουβέλα (f), μυθιστόρημα (n) |
| *November* | **[noémvrios]** | Νοέμβριος (m) |
| *now* | **[tóra]** | τώρα |
| *number, size* (of clothes) | **[noómero]** | νούμερο (n) |
| *nurse* | **[nosokóma], [nosokómos]** | νοσοκόμα (f), νοσοκόμος (m) |
| | | |
| *October* | **[októvrios]** | Οκτώβριος (m) |
| *of course, naturally* | **[vévea]** | βέβαια |
| *often* | **[sihná]** | συχνά |
| *oh* | **[ah]** | αχ |
| *OK, all right* | **[kalá], [endáksi]** | καλά, εντάξει |
| *one* | **[énas], [mía/mya], [éna]** | ένας, μία/μια, ένα |
| *one hundred* | **[ekató]** | εκατό |

| | | |
|---|---|---|
| *one thousand* | **[hílies], [hílji], [hília]** | χίλιες (f), χίλιοι (m) χίλια (n) |
| *one-family house* | **[monokatikía]** | μονοκατοικία (f) |
| *orange* (color) | **[portokalí]** | πορτοκαλί |
| *orange* (fruit) | **[portokáli]** | πορτοκάλι (n) |
| *orangeade* | **[portokaláTHa]** | πορτοκαλάδα (f) |
| *our* | **[mas]** | μας |
| *out, outside* | **[ékso]** | έξω |
| *oven* | **[foórnos]** | φούρνος (m) |
| *over* | **[péra]** | πέρα |
| | | |
| *p.m.* | **[mi-mi]** | μ.μ. |

(written as such, but as **[metá mesimvrías]** μετά μεσημβρίας when spoken)

| | | |
|---|---|---|
| *pair* | **[zevgári]** | ζευγάρι (n) |
| *Paris* | **[parísi]** | Παρίσι (n) |
| *parsley* | **[maindanós]** | μαϊντανός (m) |
| *passport* | **[THiavatírio]** | διαβατήριο (n) |
| *peach* | **[roTHákino]** | ροδάκινο (n) |
| *pear* | **[ahláTHi]** | αχλάδι (n) |
| *penthouse/top floor flat* | **[retiré]** | ρετιρέ (n) |
| *petrol/gas* | **[venzíni]** | βενζίνη (f) |
| *petrol/gas station* | **[pratírio venzínis]** | πρατήριο βενζίνης (n) |
| *pharmacy* | **[farmakío]** | φαρμακείο (n) |
| *phrase* | **[ékfrasi]** | έκφραση (f) |
| *pianist* | **[pianístria], [pianístas]** | πιανίστρια (f), πιανίστας (m) |
| *pineapple* | **[ananás]** | ανανάς (m) |
| *pink* | **[roz]** | ροζ |
| *plate* | **[piáto]** | πιάτο (n) |
| *play* | **[pézo]** | παίζω (vg1) |
| *please/you're welcome* | **[parakaló]** | παρακαλώ (vg3) |
| *police* | **[astinomía]** | αστυνομία (f) |
| *pop music* | **[laiká]** | λαϊκά (n/pl) |
| *pork* | **[hirinó]** | χοιρινό (n) |
| *portion* | **[meríTHa]** | μερίδα (f) |
| *post office* | **[tahiTHromío]** | ταχυδρομείο (n) |
| *potato* | **[patáta]** | πατάτα (f) |
| *pound* (sterling) | **[líra aglías]** | λίρα Αγγλίας (f) |
| *practical* | **[praktikós, -í, -ó]** | πρακτικός, ή, -ό |

| | | |
|---|---|---|
| *prefer* | **[protim-áo/-ó]** | προτιμ-άω/-ώ (vg2) |
| *prepare* | **[etimázo]** | ετοιμάζω (vg1) |
| *price* | **[timí]** | τιμή (f) |
| *private* | **[iTHiotikós], [-í], [-ó]** | ιδιωτικός, -ή, -ό |
| *problem* | **[próvlima]** | πρόβλημα (n) |
| *prospectus* | **[prospéktoos/filáTHio]** | προσπέκτους (n)/ φυλλάδιο (n) |
| *purple* | **[mov]** | μωβ |
| | | |
| *question* | **[erótisi]** | ερώτηση (f) |
| | | |
| *radio* | **[raTHiófono]** | ραδιόφωνο (n) |
| *rain* | **[vrohí]** | βροχή (f) |
| *rarely* | **[spánia]** | σπάνια |
| *read* | **[THiavázo]** | διαβάζω (vg1) |
| *realize, see* | **[vlépo]** | βλέπω (vg1) |
| *reception* | **[ipoTHohí]** | υποδοχή (f) |
| *red* | **[kókinos, -i, -o]** | κόκκινος, -η, -ο |
| *red mullet* | **[barboóni]** | μπαρμπούνι (n) |
| *remember* | **[thimáme]** | θυμάμαι (vg8) |
| *reservation* | **[krátisi]** | κράτηση (f) |
| *residence* | **[katikía]** | κατοικία (f) |
| *restaurant* | **[estiatório]** | εστιατόριο (n) |
| *return* | **[epistréfo]** | επιστρέφω (vg1) |
| *return/round trip* | **[me epistrofí]** | με επιστροφή |
| *right* (direction) | **[THeksiá]** | δεξιά |
| *right* (justice) | **[THíkio]** | δίκιο (n) |
| *river* | **[potamós]** | ποταμός (m) |
| *rock music* | **[rok]** | ροκ (f/n) |
| *Rome* | **[rómi]** | Ρώμη (f) |
| *room* | **[THomátio]** | δωμάτιο (n) |
| *round* (in shape) | **[strongilós, -í, -ó]** | στρογγυλός/-ή/-ό |
| *running* | **[tréksimo]** | τρέξιμο (n) |
| | | |
| *sad* | **[lipiménos, -i, -o]** | λυπημένος, -η, -ο |
| *salad* | **[saláta]** | σαλάτα (f) |
| *sale/discount* | **[ékptosi]** | έκπτωση (f) |
| *same* | **[íTHios, -a, -o]** | ίδιος, -α, -ο |
| *Saturday* | **[sávato]** | Σάββατο (n) |

| | | |
|---|---|---|
| *saucer* | **[piatáki]** | πιατάκι (n) |
| *school* | **[sholío]** | σχολείο (n) |
| *science fiction* | **[epistimonikí fantasía]** | επιστημονική φαντασία (f) |
| *Scotland* | **[skotía]** | Σκωτία (f) |
| *sea* | **[thálasa]** | θάλασσα (f) |
| *season* | **[epohí]** | εποχή (f) |
| *second* (adjective) | **[THéfteros, -i, -o]** | δεύτερος, η-, -ο |
| *second* (with time) | **[THefterólepto]** | δευτερόλεπτο (n) |
| *see* | **[vlépo]** | βλέπω (vg1) |
| *see again* | **[ksanavlépo]** | ξαναβλέπω (vg1) |
| *September* | **[septémvrios]** | Σεπτέμβριος (m) |
| *server* | **[servitóros]/ [servitóra]** | σερβιτόρος (m)/ σερβιτόρα (f) |
| *sesame bagel* | **[kooloóri]** | κουλούρι (n) |
| *seven* | **[eptá]/[eftá]** | επτά/εφτά |
| *seven hundred* | **[eptakósia]/ [eftakósia]** | επτακόσια/ εφτακόσια |
| *seventeen* | **[THekaeftá]** | δεκαεφτά |
| *seventy* | **[evTHomínda]** | εβδομήντα |
| *shampoo* | **[sabooán]** | σαμπουάν (n) |
| *she* | **[aftí]** | αυτή |
| *ship* | **[plío]** | πλοίο (n) |
| *shirt* | **[pookámiso]** | πουκάμισο (n) |
| *shoe* | **[papoótsi]** | παπούτσι (n) |
| *shoe lace* | **[korTHóni]** | κορδόνι (n) |
| *shop window* | **[vitrína]** | βιτρίνα (f) |
| *shower* | **[dooz]** | ντους (n) |
| *side* | **[plevrá]** | πλευρά (f) |
| *single room* | **[monóklino]** | μονόκλινο (n) |
| *sister* | **[aTHelfí]** | αδελφή (f) |
| *sit* | **[káthome]** | κάθομαι (vg5) |
| *sitting room* | **[kathistikó]** | καθιστικό (n) |
| *six* | **[éksi]** | έξι |
| *six hundred* | **[eksakósia]** | εξακόσια |
| *sixteen* | **[THekaéksi]** | δεκαέξι |
| *sixty* | **[eksínda]** | εξήντα |
| *size* | **[mégethos]** | μέγεθος (n) |
| *sky blue* | **[galázios, -a, -o]** | γαλάζιος, -α, -ο |

| | | |
|---|---|---|
| *sleep* | **[kimáme]** | κοιμάμαι (vg8) |
| *slip-ons* (loafers) | **[mokasinía]** | μοκασίνια (n) |
| *slipper* | **[pandófla]** | παντόφλα (f) |
| *small* | **[mikrós, -í, -ó]** | μικρός, -ή, -ό |
| *smoke* | **[kapnízo]** | καπνίζω (vg1) |
| *smoking* | **[kápnizma]** | κάπνισμα (n) |
| *so* | **[étsi], [tósos, -i, -o]** | έτσι, τόσος, -η, -ο |
| *soap* | **[sapoóni]** | σαπούνι (n) |
| *soda water* | **[sóTHa]** | σόδα (f) |
| *sofa* | **[kanapés]** | καναπές (m) |
| *soft* | **[malakós, -iá, -ó]** | μαλακός, -ιά, -ό |
| *soft pop* | **[elafrolaiká]** | ελαφρολαϊκά (n/pl) |
| *son* | **[yios]** | γιος (m) |
| *sorry* | **[signómi]** | συγνώμη/ συγγνώμη (f) |
| *(to be) sorry* | **[lipáme]** | λυπάμαι (vg8) |
| *soup spoon* | **[kootáli]** | κουτάλι (n) |
| *space, area* | **[hóros]** | χώρος (m) |
| *Spain* | **[ispanía]** | Ισπανία (f) |
| *Spanish* (language) | **[ispaniká]** | Ισπανικά (n/pl) |
| *speak* | **[mil-áo/-ó]** | μιλ-άω/-ώ (vg2) |
| *sport* | **[spor]** | σπορ (n) |
| *spring* | **[águiksi]** | άνοιξη (f) |
| *stamp* | **[gramatósimo]** | γραμματόσημο (n) |
| *stay* (verb) | **[káthome]** | κάθομαι (vg5) |
| *stay* | **[THiamoní], [paramoní]** | διαμονή (f), παραμονή (f) |
| *still/yet* | **[akóma/akómi]** | ακόμα/ακόμη |
| *stool* | **[skambó]** | σκαμπό (n) |
| *story/history* | **[istoría]** | ιστορία (f) |
| *straight* | **[efthía]** | ευθεία |
| *straight ahead* | **[efthía brostá], [ísia]** | ευθεία μπροστά, ίσια |
| *strawberry* | **[fráoola]** | φράουλα (f) |
| *striped* | **[riyé]** | ριγέ (m/f/n) |
| *studio/bedsit* | **[garsoniéra]** | γκαρσονιέρα (f) |
| *study* (verb) | **[THiavázo]** | διαβάζω (vg1) |
| *stuffed vegetables* | **[yemistá]** | γεμιστά (n/pl) |
| *suitcase* | **[valítsa]** | βαλίτσα (f) |

| | | |
|---|---|---|
| *summer* | **[kalokéri]** | καλοκαίρι (n) |
| *Sunday* | **[kiriakí]** | Κυριακή (f) |
| *supermarket* | **[soópermarket]** | σούπερμαρκετ (n) |
| *Sure!* | **[amé]**! | αμέ! |
| *surprised* | **[ékpliktos, -i, -o]** | έκπληκτος, -η, -ο |
| *sweet* | **[glikós, -iá, ó]** | γλυκός, -ιά, -ό |
| *swimming* | **[bánio] [kolíbi]** | μπάνιο (n), κολύμπι (n) |
| *Sydney* | **[síTHnei]** | Σίδνεϋ (n) |
| *table* | **[trapézi]** | τραπέζι (n) |
| *table tennis* | **[ping pong]** | πίνγκ πονγκ (n) |
| *take* | **[pérno]** | παίρνω (vg1) |
| *taxi* | **[taksí]** | ταξί (n) |
| *tea* | **[tsái]** | τσάι (n) |
| *teaspoon* | **[kootaláki]** | κουταλάκι (n) |
| *teacher* | **[THaskála], [THáskalos]** | δασκάλα (f), δάσκαλος (m) |
| *television* | **[tileórasi]** | τηλεόραση (f) |
| *ten* | **[THéka]** | δέκα |
| *tennis* | **[ténis]** | τένις (n) |
| *thanks* (lit. I thank) | **[efharistó]** | ευχαριστώ (vg3) |
| *thanks* (lit. we thank) | **[efharistoóme]** | ευχαριστούμε |
| *that / who* | **[poo]** | που |
| *the* | **[o], [i], [to]** | ο, η, το |
| *theater* | **[théatro]** | θέατρο (n) |
| *their* | **[toos]** | τους |
| *them* | **[aftoós], [aftés], [aftá]** | αυτούς (m), αυτές (f), αυτά (n) |
| *then, afterwards* | **[metá]** | μετά |
| *then/after that/later* | **[épita]** | έπειτα |
| *there* | **[ekí]** | εκεί |
| *Thessaloniki* | **[thesaloníki]** | Θεσσαλονίκη (f) |
| *they* (only females) | **[aftés]** | αυτές |
| *they* (only males) | **[aftí]** | αυτοί |
| *they* (only things) | **[aftá]** | αυτά |
| *think* | **[nomízo]** | νομίζω (vg1) |
| *third* | **[trítos, -i, -o]** | τρίτος, -η, -ο |

| | | |
|---|---|---|
| *thirsty* | **[THipsazménos, -i, -o]** | διψασμένος, -η, -ο |
| *thirteen* | **[THekatrís, -ís, -ía]** | δεκατρείς, -είς, -ία |
| *thirty* | **[triánda]** | τριάντα |
| *though, although, but* | **[ómos]** | όμως |
| *three* | **[tris, tris, tría]** | τρεις, τρεις, τρία |
| *three hundred* | **[trakósia]** | τριακόσια |
| *thriller/horror* (film) | **[thríler]** | θρίλερ (n) |
| *ticket* | **[isitírio]** | εισιτήριο (n) |
| *time* | **[óra], [hrónos]** | ώρα (f), χρόνος (m) |
| *timetable* | **[pínakas THromoloyíon]** | πίνακας δρομολογίων (m) |
| *tired* | **[koorazménos, -i, -o]** | κουρασμένος, -η, -ο |
| *tiring* | **[koorastikós, -í, -ó]** | κουραστικός, -ή, -ό |
| *to* (used with verbs) | **[na]** | να |
| *to/ in/at the* | **[ston], [stin], [sto]** | στον, στη(ν), στο |
| *to, until* | **[méhri]** | μέχρι |
| *today* | **[símera]** | σήμερα |
| *toilet* | **[tooaléta]** | τουαλέτα (f) |
| *tomato* | **[domáta]** | ντομάτα (f) |
| *toothbrush* | **[oTHondóvoortsa]** | οδοντόβουρτσα (f) |
| *toothpaste* | **[oTHondópasta]** | οδοντόπαστα (f) |
| *towel* | **[petséta]** | πετσέτα (f) |
| *town/city* | **[póli]** | πόλη (f) |
| *train* | **[tréno]** | τρένο (n) |
| *train station* | **[stathmós trénon]** | σταθμός τρένων (m) |
| *travel agency* | **[taksiTHiotikó grafío]** | ταξιδιωτικό γραφείο (n) |
| *trip* | **[taksíTHi]** | ταξίδι (n) |
| *triple room* | **[tríklino THomátio]** | τρίκλινο δωμάτιο (n) |
| *trout* | **[péstrofa]** | πέστροφα (f) |
| *truth* | **[alíthia]** | αλήθεια (f) |
| *twelve* | **[THóTHeka]** | δώδεκα |
| *twenty* | **[íkosi]** | είκοσι |
| *two* | **[THío/THyo]** | δύο/δυο |
| *two hundred* | **[THiakósia]** | διακόσια |
| *underground* | **[metró]** | μετρό (n) |
| *understand* | **[katalavéno]** | καταλαβαίνω (vg1) |
| *unfortunately* | **[THistihós]** | δυστυχώς |
| *until* | **[méhri], [óspoo]** | μέχρι, ώσπου |

| | | |
|---|---|---|
| *up* | **[páno]** | πάνω |
| *upset* | **[taragménos, -i, -o]** | ταραγμένος, -η, -ο |
| *usually* | **[siníthos]** | συνήθως |
| | | |
| *vegetable* | **[lahanikó]** | λαχανικό (n) |
| *view* | **[théa]** | θέα (f) |
| *volleyball* | **[vólei]** | βόλεϊ (n) |
| | | |
| *WC* | **[vesé]** | WC (no Greek script) (n) |
| *wait* | **[periméno]** | περιμένω (vg1) |
| *wake up* | **[ksipn-áo/-ó]** | ξυπν-άω/-ώ (vg2) |
| *Wales* | **[oo-alía]** | Ουαλία (f) |
| *walk* | **[perpat-áo/-ó]** | περπατ-άω/-ώ (vg2) |
| *walk, stroll, car ride* | **[vólta]** | βόλτα (f) |
| *want* | **[thélo]** | θέλω (vg1) |
| *watch* | **[vlépo]** | βλέπω (vg1) |
| *water* | **[neró]** | νερό (n) |
| *we* | **[emís]** | εμείς |
| *weather* | **[kerós]** | καιρός (m) |
| *week* | **[evTHomáTHa]** | εβδομάδα (f) |
| *weekend* | **[savatokíriako]** | Σαββατοκύριακο (n) |
| *well* (e.g. I'm well) | **[kalá]** | καλά |
| *well* (e.g. Well, what?) | **[lipón]** | λοιπόν |
| *what/how* | **[ti]** | τι |
| *when* (question word) | **[póte]** | πότε |
| *when* (time adverb) | **[ótan]** | όταν |
| *where* | **[poo]** | πού |
| *white* | **[áspros, -i, -o]** | άσπρος, -η, -ο |
| *white wine* | **[áspro krasí]** | άσπρο κρασί (n) |
| *why* | **[yiatí]** | γιατί |
| *window* | **[paráthiro]** | παράθυρο (n) |
| *wine* | **[krasí]** | κρασί (n) |
| *winter* | **[himónas]** | χειμώνας (m) |
| *woman/wife* | **[yinéka]** | γυναίκα (f) |
| *word* | **[léksi]** | λέξη (f) |
| *work* (verb) | **[THoolévo]** | δουλεύω (vg1) |
| *work* (noun) | **[THooliá]** | δουλειά (f) |
| *world* | **[kózmos]** | κόσμος (m) |

| | | |
|---|---|---|
| *write* | **[gráfo]** | γράφω (vg1) |
| *writer* | **[sigraféas]** | συγγραφέας (m/f) |
| | | |
| *yard* | **[avlí]** | αυλή (f) |
| *year* | **[hrónos]** | χρόνος (m) |
| *yellow* | **[kítrinos, -i, -o]** | κίτρινος, -η, -ο |
| *yes* | **[ne]** | ναι |
| *Yes, sure! Of course!* | **[málista]** | μάλιστα |
| *you* (pl/fml) | **[esís]** | εσείς |
| *you* (pl/fml) (e.g. to you) | **[sas]** | σας |
| *you* (sing/infml) | **[esí]** | εσύ |
| *you're welcome* | **[parakaló]** | παρακαλώ |
| *your* (pl/fml) | **[sas]** | σας |
| *your* (sing/infml) | **[soo]** | σου |

# Answer key

## UNIT 1
## Greetings, introductions and wishes

**1** γεια, γεια σου, γεια σας
**2** Με λένε ... / Είμαι ο/η ...

### Vocabulary builder

**Greetings:** goodbye, good night; **Wishes:** Welcome!, thanks

### Conversation 1

**1** [ti kánis]? Τι κάνεις;
**2 a** Fine, just fine. **b** Fine. **c** He's waiting for two friends from London.

### Language discovery 1

**1 a** είμαι, **b** είσαι, **c** περιμένω.
**2** Άγγελος is used when you speak about this person. Άγγελε is used when you speak directly to that person.

### Conversation 2

**1** Καλώς ορίσατε στην Ελλάδα!
**2 a** (I) thank you and (we) thank you. **b** Από means *from* and Πώς *How?*

### Language discovery 2

**a** ο John, **b** η Mary, **c** στην Ελλάδα

### Practice

**1 a** [kaliméra], **b** [kalispéra], **c** [kaliníhta]
**2 a** 3, **b** 5, **c** 1, **d** 2, **e** 4
**3 a** 1, **b** 3, **c** 2, **d** 4
**4 a** [sto], **b** [to], **c** [tin], **d** [stin]
**5 a** [i], **b** [o], **c** [o], **d** [o], **e** [i], **f** [i]
**6 a** [sas], **b** [o], **c** [i], **d** [polí], **e** [stin], **f** [se], **g** [me]

**7**

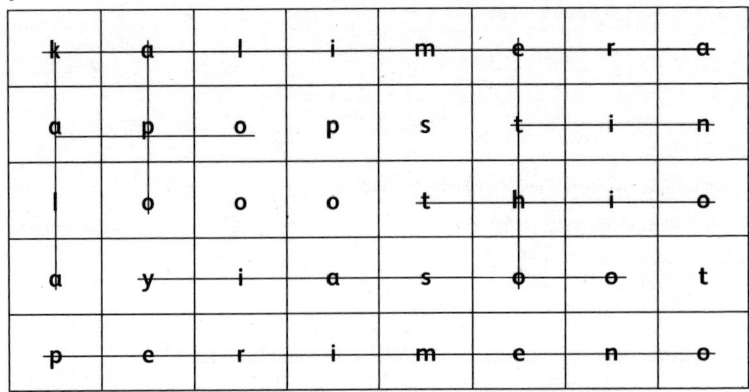

| k | a | l | i | m | e | r | a |
|---|---|---|---|---|---|---|---|
| a | p | o | p | s | t | i | n |
| l | o | o | o | t | h | i | o |
| a | y | i | a | s | o | o | t |
| p | e | r | i | m | e | n | o |

**8 a** [kalimera] καλημέρα, **b** [apo] από, **c** [stin] στην, **d** [thio] δύο, **e** [yiasoo] γεια σου, **f** [perimeno] περιμένω, **g** [kala] καλά, **h** [apo] από, **i** [etho] εδώ
**9 a** No
**10** Κωτσόβολος, Ράδιο Αθήναι Νέο / ΝΕΟ. **ράδιο** *radio*, **Αθήναι** *Athens*, **νέο** *new*

### Test yourself

**1 a** [yiásoo], **b** [ti kánis]?, **c** [ti kánis eTHó sto aeroTHrómio]?, **d** [efharistó], **e** [yiásas], **f** [kaliméra] – [kaliníhta], **g** [héro polí]
**2 b** 1, **d** 2, **a** 3, **c** 4
**3 a** [kalimera] καλημέρα good morning, **b** [apo] από from, **c** [stin] στην in (the), **d** [thio] δύο two, **e** [yiasoo] γεια σου hello/goodbye, **f** [perimeno] περιμένω I am waiting/I wait, **g** [kala] καλά good/fine, **h** [apo] από from, **i** [etho] εδώ here

## UNIT 2

### Greece

[athína] Αθήνα, [ólimbos] Όλυμπος, [kríti] Κρήτη

### Vocabulary builder

Είμαι από το Μάντσεστερ. *I'm from Manchester*, Είμαι από το Μπρίστολ. *I'm from Bristol*, Είμαι από το Κάρντιφ. *I'm from Cardiff*.

### Conversation 1

**1** [elinikά] Ελληνικά, [anglikά] Αγγλικά, [ghermanikά] Γερμανικά
**2 a** English and a little bit of Greek, **b** Greek, English and a little bit of German.

## Language discovery 1

**1 a** Εσύ, **b** Εγώ
**2 a** [elinikά] Ελληνικά, **b** [anglikά] Αγγλικά, **c** [ghermanikά] Γερμανικά. All three languages end in -κά.

## Conversation 2

**1** John comes from Australia and Mary is from the US.
**2 a** Anna comes from the island of Poros. **b** She lives in Athens now.

## Language discovery 2

**1** The three articles are: το for neuter, την for feminine and τον for masculine. All Greek nouns are one of three genders.
**2 a** [esí] εσύ, **b** [esís] εσείς, **c** [eghó] εγώ, **d** [eghó] εγώ
**3 ναι** *yes* and **όχι** *no*

## Language discovery 3

**1 ο Καναδάς** *Canada*, **το Βέλγιο** *Belgium*
**2 το παιδί** *child*
**3** Most Greek adverbs do have a flexible word order and they can be placed either at the beginning, in the middle, or even at the end of a sentence.

## Practice

**1 a** [eláTHa] Ελλάδα/[elinikά] ελληνικά, **b** [ispanía] Ισπανία/[ispanikά] ισπανικά, **c** [italía] Ιταλία/[italikά] ιταλικά, **d** [galía] Γαλλία/[galikά] γαλλικά, **e** [anglía] Αγγλία/[anglikά] αγγλικά.
**2 a** 4, **b** 2, **c** 3, **d** 1
**3 a** [íne apó tin thesaloníki]. Είναι από τη Θεσσαλονίκη. He/she is from Thessaloniki. **b** [alá tóra méno stin pátra]. Αλλά τώρα μένω στην Πάτρα. But now I live in Patras. **c** [miláo italikά ke líga ispanikά]. Μιλάω Ιταλικά και λίγα Ισπανικά. I speak Italian and a little Spanish. **d** [i athína íne stin eláTHa]. Η Αθήνα είναι στην Ελλάδα. Athens is in Greece. **e** [ke to parísi sti galía]. Και το Παρίσι στη Γαλλία. And Paris in France.
**4 a** Athens, **b** Thessaloniki, **c** Patras, **d** Heraklion, **e** Larisa, **f** Volos
**5 a** 2, **b** 3, **c** 2, **d** 2, **e** 1, **f** 2
**6 a** [apó], **b** [óhi], **c** [egó], **d** [esí], **e** [óhi], **f** [alá]
**7** You hear a dialogue mentioning the [pális] Πάλλης Pallis company.

## Test yourself

**1** [apó poo íse]? or [apó poo íste]?
**2** [poo ménis tóra]? or [poo ménete tóra]?

**3** [íme apó to Cardiff] [alá tóra méno sto Manchester].
**4** [anglikά], [galikά], [ispanikά], [yermanikά], [elinikά], [italikά]
**5** [lonTHíno], [rómi], [athína]

## UNIT 3

### Employment in Greece

It means to work/be employed. The text included the following words: [erghasía] employment and [erghátis-erghátria] worker.

### The verb [ergházome]

**εργάζομαι** means *to work, I work, I am working.* Although there are two verbs with the same meaning, the difference between **δουλεύω** and **εργάζομαι** is that **δουλεύω** is used in everyday speech, informally, whereas **εργάζομαι** is used formally.

### Vocabulary builder

**1** musician, server (female), actress

### Conversation 1

**1** She is a teacher.
**2 a** He lives in London. **b** He's an architect. **c** She writes children's books. **d** No. She's a teacher.

### Language discovery 1

**1 a** αρχιτέκτονας, **b** συγγραφέας, **c** δασκάλα
**2 a** μένω, **b** δουλεύω, **c** γράφω, **d** είμαι
Have you answered **NAI** *YES* to all 8 statements? If yes, well done!

### Conversation 2

**1** Yes, she does.
**2 a** She knows Athens better. **b** [ne] [óchi]

### Language discovery 2

**1 a** ... ξέρεις ...;, **b** Πού μένεις;, **c** Μένεις ...
**2** The two words have a different sound for this double letter.

### Practice

**1 b** [esí], **c** [aftí]/[aftés]/[aftá], **d** [egó], **e** [aftós], **f** [aftí], **g** [emís], **h** [aftí]/[aftés]/[aftá]
**2 a** [THen miláme yermanikά]. **b** [THen kséro ton ángelo]. **c** [THen ksérete tin ána]. **d** [THen periméni tris fíloos]. **e** [THen ménoon sta yiánena]. **f** [THen íme apó tin amerikí]. **g** [THen íne apó tin italía].

**3 a** [esís ménete stin yermanía]? **b** [aftí íne apó tin afstralía]? **c** [kséris líga elinikά]? **d** [aftés periménoon THío fíloos]? **e** [esí milás anglikά]? **f** [esís THen miláte ispanikά]? **g** [esís íste apó tin anglía]?
**4 a** [yiatrós] γιατρός, **b** [THaskála] δασκάλα, **c** [nosokóma] νοσοκόμα, **d** [sigraféas] συγγραφέας, **e** [servitóros] σερβιτόρος, **f** [arhitéktonas] αρχιτέκτονας
**5 a** false, **b** true, **c** false, **d** true, **e** false, **f** true
**6** The man is [servitóros] σερβιτόρος and the woman [THaskála] δασκάλα.
**7 a** 4, **b** 5, **c** 1, **d** 2, **e** 3
**8 a** 2, **b** 1, **c** 2, **d** 3, **e** 2
**9 a** [íme servitóra. THen íme pianístria]. Είμαι σερβιτόρα. Δεν είμαι πιανίστρια. I'm a server. I'm not a pianist. **b** [THen íme sigraféas]. Δεν είμαι συγγραφέας. I'm not a writer. **c** [íste yiatrós]? [óhi], [íme moosikós]. Είστε γιατρός; Όχι, είμαι μουσικός. Are you a doctor? No, I'm a musician. **d** [méno kondá sti thesaloníki]. Μένω κοντά στη Θεσσαλονίκη. I live close to (near) Thessaloniki. **e** [THen ímaste apó tin anglía]. Δεν είμαστε από την Αγγλία. We are not from England.
**10 a** [kséris], **b** [óhi], **c** [móno], **d** [poo], **e** [kondá], **f** [ne]
**11 a** -ου, **b** -ει, **c** -γγ

## Test yourself

**1** [ti THooliá kánis]? [ti THooliá kánete]?
**2** [íme THáskalos / THaskála].
**3** He/she is a writer.
**4** I live in Manchester. I live close to Manchester.
**5** [íse] is informal, [íste] is more formal. The question means: Are you from England?
**6** what?, how/what?, where?, who/which/what?

## REVISION TEST 1

**1 a** [kaliméra], **b** [hérete], **c** [kalispéra], **d** [kaliníhta], **e** [kaliníhta]
**2** Γεια σου Νίκο! Χάρηκα! Ευχαριστώ. Χαίρομαι που είμαι εδώ. Όχι, είμαι από το Λίβερπουλ.
**3 a** Τι κάνεις εδώ; **b** Πώς είσαι; **c** Πώς σε λένε; **d** Μιλάς Ελληνικά; **e** Πού μένεις;
**4 a** 4, **b** 5, **c** 1, **d** 2, **f** 3
**5 a** [amerikí], **b** [yermanía], **c** [galía], **d** [italía], **e** [eláTHa], **1** [anglikά], **2** [yermanikά], **3** [galikά], **4** [italikά], **5** [elinikά]
**6 a** 2, **b** 1, **c** 2, **d** 3, **e** 3
**7 a** 2, **b** 3, **c** 1, **d** 2, **e** 1, **f** 1

**8 a** [sigraféas], **b** [servitóra], **c** [athína], **d** [kaliméra], **e** [yiatrós], **f** [amerikí], **g** [moosikós], **h** [patéras], **i** [THoolévo], **j** [kondá], **k** [pianístas], **l** [THáskalos]
**9 1** [yasoo maría] [hárika] (or [hérome poo se ghnorízo]) [pos se léne]? **2** [apó tin amerikí] [apó tin néa iórki] [ke esí]? **3** [ke eghó méno stin athína] [THoolévo se éna ghrafío] [ke esí]? [esí THoolévis]?

## UNIT 4

### A Greek home

**1** Μένω σε ένα σπίτι / διαμέρισμα.
**2** [xílo] ξύλο, [túvlo] τούβλο, [pétra] πέτρα, [métalo] μέταλλο
**3** *metal*, *metallic*, *metallurgy*, and *xylophone*

### Vocabulary builder

**3 a** Εγώ μένω σε μια πολυκατοικία. **b** Εγώ μένω σε ένα διαμέρισμα. **c** Εγώ μένω σε μια μονοκατοικία. **d** Εγώ μένω σε ένα σπίτι.

### Conversation 1

**1** Anna lives in a four-room apartment in a block of flats.
**2 a** κουζίνα, μπάνιο, χωλ, **b** megalomania, megaphone, megahertz and microcomputer, microbiology, microfilm

### Language discovery 1

**1 a** ένα χωλ, **b** ένα μπάνιο, **c** μία κουζίνα, **d** μία πολυκατοικία
**2 a** ένα, **b** μία, **c** τέσσερα

**LANGUAGE TIP**

The hidden Greek numbers are as follows: **δέκα** in *decathlon*, **τρία** in *triathlon*, **πέντε** in *pentagon*, **δύο/δυο** in *duet*, and **τρία** in *trigonometry*!

### Conversation 2

**1** There are five bedrooms. [ipnoTHomátia]
**2 a** It's a detached house. [monokatikía], **b** [salóni] [trapezaría] [bánio] [ipnoTHomátio]

### Language discovery 2

**1 a** [meghálo spíti], **b** [álo spíti], **c** [mikró hol], **d** [megálo salóni]
**2 a** [μπάνια], **b** [κτίρια], **c** [ξύλα], **d** [μέταλλα]
**3** The meaning will not change but the pronunciation will be slower and clearer.

## Practice

**1 a** 4, **b** 1, **c** 2, **d** 5, **e** 3

**2 a** [kondá] κοντά near – [makriá] μακριά far, **b** [spíti] σπίτι house – [THiamérizma] διαμέρισμα apartment/flat, **c** [salóni] σαλόνι living room – [kathistikó] καθιστικό sitting room, **d** [koozína] κουζίνα kitchen – [trapezaría] τραπεζαρία dining room, **e** [mikró] μικρό small – [megálo] μεγάλο big

**3 a** 4, **b** 2, **c** 1, **d** 5, **e** 3

**4** c, e, b, d, f, a

**5 a** [salóni], **b** [trapezaría], **c** [koozína], **d** [bánio], **e** [ipnoTHomátio], **f** [hol]

**6 a** [éna]/[miTHén]/[miTHén], **b** [éna] [éna] [THío], **c** [éna]/[tría]/[tésera], **d** [éna]/[éksi]/[éksi], **e** [éna]/[éksi]/[eniá], **f** [éna]/[eptá]/[éna], **g** [éna], [eniá], [eniá]

**7 a** [spíti], **b** [garsoniéra], **c** [salóni], **d** [koozína], **e** [bánio], **f** [retiré] vertical: saloni

**8 a** [spíti] σπίτι, **b** [garsoniéra] γκαρσονιέρα, **c** [salóni] σαλόνι, **d** [koozína] κουζίνα, **e** [bánio] μπάνιο, **f** [retiré] ρετιρέ, **g** vertical: [salóni] σαλόνι

**9 a** [sálo], **b** [pósa], **c** [megálo], **d** [mazí], **e** [pénde], **f** [polí]

**10** electricity: ηλεκτρισμού, programmes: προγράμματα [o THímos] ο δήμος / ο Δήμος stands for *municipality* or even *local community*. This word is also part of ancient Greek names, including Δημοσθένης in *Demosthenes*!

**11 a** οι φίλοι, **b** ο δάσκαλος, **c** οι τζαμαρίες, **d** η κουζίνα, **e** τα σπίτια, **f** το κτίριο

**12 a** μεγάλη κουζίνα, **b** άλλη δασκάλα, **c** μικρό σπίτι, **d** καλός γιατρός

**13 a Μία/Μια** δασκάλα γράφει βιβλία. **b** Μένω σε **μία/μια** μονοκατοικία. **c** Ξέρω έναν γιατρό. **d** Δουλεύω σε **μία/μια** ταβέρνα.

## Test yourself

**1 a** [bánio], [tooaléta], [vesé]

**b** [tzamaría], [trapezaría], [ipnoTHomátio], [koozína] **c** [retiré], [THiamérizma], [garsoniéra], [katikía]

**d** [méno se mía monokatikía sto lonTHíno]

**e** [mikró], [makriá], [polikatikía]

**f** [kathistikó], [tooaléta], [katikía]

**2** electricity: ηλεκτρισμού, programmes: προγράμματα [o TH.mos] ο δήμος / ο Δήμος stands for municipality or even local community. This word is also part of ancient Greek names, including Δημοσθένης in Demosthenes!

**3 a** οι φίλοι, **b** ο δάσκαλος, **c** οι τζαμαρίες, **d** η κουζίνα, **e** τα σπίτια, **f** το κτίριο

## UNIT 5

### Greek names

Αγάπη, Ελπίδα, Ζωή

### Vocabulary builder

mother, grandfather, grandchild, sister

### Conversation 1

**1** They have two children, a boy and a girl.
**2 a** Μισό λεπτό. **b** The son is five years old. **c** The daughter is three years old.

### Language discovery 1

**1 a** Έχεις οικογένεια; **b** πέντε χρονών **c** Μισό λεπτό. **d** Έχετε παιδιά; The underlined English words are not translated in Greek.
**2 a** ένα/μια-μία, **b** δύο, **c** τριών, **d** πέντε. When saying your age, you need a new form of the following numbers: 1 ενός, 3 τριών, 4 τεσσάρων. The rest of the numbers do not require a different form.
**3 a** σπίτι - σπίτια, **b** αγόρι – αγόρια, **c** κορίτσι - κορίτσια, **d** παιδί – παιδιά
**4 a** έχετε, **b** Έχουμε, **c** Έχεις, **d** Έχω, **e** έχει, **f** έχουν

### Conversation 2

**1** They have three children, two boys and one girl.
**2 a** [servitóros], **b** 12 [THóTHeka] and 7 [eftá], **c** 10 [THéka]

### Language discovery 2

**1 a** ο άντρας μου, **b** τα ονόματά τους. An article is necessary and the possessive adjective comes after the Greek noun. Word for word: the husband my and the names their
**2 a** His name is Yiorgos. **b** Your name is Yiorgos. **c** I want to see you again. **d** I want to see him again.
**3 a** εφτά, **b** δέκα, **c** δώδεκα The number 7 has two alternative forms: **εφτά** (*informally*) and **επτά** (*formally*)

### Practice

**1 a** 4, **b** 2, **c** 3, **d** 6, **e** 5, **f** 3
**2 a** 4, **b** 3, **c** 1, **d** 5, **e** 2
**3 a** 15, **b** 17, **c** 12, **d** 13, **e** 11, **f** 14

**4 a** 7849321, **b** 9904057
**5 a** [to THiamérizmá too], **b** [to spíti mas], **c** [o papoós toos], **d** [i mitéra tis], **e** [to THomátió moo], **f** [o ándras soo] or [o ándras sas] or [o sízigos soo] or [o sízigos sas]
**6**

| p | a | p | o | o | s | y |
|---|---|---|---|---|---|---|
| a | n | p | l | h | e | i |
| m | y | i | n | e | k | a |
| e | o | a | e | n | a | y |
| k | o | r | i | t | s | i |
| k | m | i | t | e | r | a |

**7** Across: παππούς, γυναίκα, ένα, κορίτσι, μητέρα, Down: πάμε, μου, ποια, έχω, και, γιαγιά
**8 a** [ándras], **b** [ton], **c** [peTHiá], **d** [korítsi], **e** [níkos], **f** [hronón], **g** [THóTHeka], **h** [THéka], **i** [eptá], **j** [yiatí]

### Test yourself

**1** [patéras], [mitéra], [peTHí], [papoós], [yiayiá], [yios], [kóri], [egonós], [egoní], [aTHelfós], [aTHelfí], [(e)ksáTHelfos], [(e)ksaTHélfi]
**2** 11 [éndeka], 12 [THóTHeka], 14 [THekatésera], 17 [THekaeptá] or [THekaeftá], 19 [THekaeniá] or [THekaenéa], 20 [íkosi]
**3** Any answer is possible here. Say it to a Greek speaker!
**4** [póso hronón íse/íste]?
**5** [pos to léne] [sta eliniká]?

## UNIT 6
### Ordering drinks

**1** καφές, καφενείο, καφετέρια
**2** σκέτο, μέτριο, γλυκό

### Vocabulary builder

**1** b, d, c, a
**2** a Greek coffee without sugar, an iced coffee with sugar, an orangeade, a lemonade, a medium Greek coffee, an iced coffee without sugar and without milk

**3** Hot beverages: Greek coffee, iced coffee, tea, hot chocolate, Refreshments: Orangeade, lemonade, (pineapple) juice, (small) water, (Alcoholic) drinks: Beer, glass of wine, bottle of retsina, small carafe of ouzo
**4 a** 1, **b** 1, **c** 2

### Conversation 1

**1** [kalós se vríkame] Καλώς σε βρήκαμε.
**2 a** Αντώνης, Γιωργία, **b** κύριε, κυρία, **c** First, it does have to do with the two verb stems which are **βλέπω** and **δω**. The word for *again* is hidden in [ksaná] **ξανά** as a prefix to these two verb forms.

### Language discovery 1

**1 d** Καλώς ορίσατε! The answers a and c are appropriate when you informally welcome a friend or relative. The answers b and d are used either formally when addressing one or more people or informally when addressing friends or relatives.
**2** The phrase is used by Mary, Andonis and Yioryía. Mary addresses the children, Andonis addresses John and Mary, and Yioryía addresses John and Mary.

### Conversation 2

**1** She is asking them if they want to eat or drink something, e.g. coffee or cola.
**2 a** Nice house, very nice and very big. **b** Mary would like an orangeade and John an iced coffee.

### Language discovery 2

**1 a** έλα-ελάτε, **b** κάθισε-καθίστε, **c** πάρε-πάρτε
**2 a** πεινάς-πεινάτε, **b** διψάς-διψάτε, **c** θέλεις-θέλετε. The first form is used when addressing a friend or relative and the second form when addressing one person formally or more people formally or informally.
**3 a** έναν καφέ, **b** μία κόκα κόλα, **c** μία πορτοκαλάδα, **d** ένα(ν) φραπέ. The choice of the article does not depend on the sound of the word that follows. It depends on the gender (masculine, feminine, neuter) of the noun.
**4 a** Θέλω έναν χυμό. **b** Έχω έναν καναπέ. **c** Ξέρω έναν γιατρό.

### Practice

**1 a** 1; **b** 2, **c** 4, **d** 6, **e** 3, **f** 5
**2 a** 4, **b** 5, **c** 1, **d** 3, **e** 2
**3** c, e, a, d, f, b

**4** [kondá soo]? [yiatí]? / [angliká]? [egó], [thélo na miláo] [eliniká]! / [yiatí óhi]? [kafé stin arhí]. [éna frapé] [yia ména].
**5 a** [eláte], **b** [kanapé], **c** [karékla], **d** [pináte], **e** [éna], **f** [mía], **g** [éhis], **h** [yia], **i** [ména]
**6 a** [thélo éna mikró bukáli neró], **b** [tha íthela éna meghálo bukáli neró], **c** [the íthela éna metalikó neró], **d** [thélo éna potíri neró]
**7 a** [énan skéto], **b** [Θα πάρω], **c** [Θα πάρω], **d** [μία λεμονάδα], **e** [kafé gia (ya) ména], **f** [Μου φέρνετε], **g** [σκέτο χωρίς γάλα]
**8 a** [έναν ελληνικό γλυκό], **b** [ένα(ν) φραπέ με γάλα χωρίς ζάχαρη], **c** [ένα μικρό μπουκάλι νερό], **d** [ένα καραφάκι ούζο], **e** [μία μπίρα], **f** [μία ζεστή σοκολάτα]
**9 Verb group 1:** θέλεις, θέλετε, **Verb group 2:** διψάς, διψάτε, **Verb group 3:** παρακαλείς, παρακαλείτε, **Verb group 4:** πας, πάτε
**10** Have you answered all statements with **NAI**? Congratulations!

### Test yourself

**1** [kafés], [portokaláTHa], [tsái], [himós], [lemonáTHa], [frapés], [gála]
**2** [éla ke kátse kondá moo]
**3** [éhete] [portokaláTHa i himó]?
**4** [kathíste] or [párte mía karékla]

### REVISION TEST 2

**1 b** [hol], **c** [koozína], **d** [salóni], **e** [ipnoTHomátio], **f** [trapezaría], **g** [bánio]
**2 1** b, **2** d, **3** e, **4** a, **5** c
**3 a** [tría], [pénde], **b** [eptá], [THéka], **c** [éndeka], [THóTHeka], [THekatésera], **d** [THekaéksi], [THekaeniá], [íkosi]
**4 1** c, **2** d, **3** e, **4** a, **5** b
**5** All five statements are false.
**6 a** 3, **b** 5, **c** 7, **d** 1, **e** 6, **f** 2, **g** 4
**7 a** This is my grandmother Artemis and my grandfather Odysseus. **b** My wife's name is Elpida. **c** We have two children. A boy and a girl. **d** Our son's name is Angelos and our daughter's name is Niovi. **e** We live in a big apartment building.
**8 a** Δουλεύει ο άντρας σου τώρα; **b** Πόσα παιδιά έχετε; **c** Έχεις μεγάλη οικογένεια; **d** Πώς λένε τη γυναίκα σου; **e** Μιλάς καθόλου ελληνικά;
**9** Ευχαριστώ. Μεγάλο και ωραίο σπίτι! / Καλή ιδέα. Έναν καφέ για μένα. / Ναι. Ένα φραπέ μέτριο χωρίς γάλα. Και λίγο νερό παρακαλώ. / Ένα ποτήρι νερό παρακαλώ. / Δεν καταλαβαίνω. Πώς είναι αυτό στα Αγγλικά;

## UNIT 7

### Greek hospitality

ευχαριστώ, παρακαλώ, φιλοξενία, άδικο, διαμονή, παραμονή

### Vocabulary builder

**1** Το παράθυρο, η βιβλιοθήκη, η πολυθρόνα, η μπρίζα, το κάδρο, η πόρτα
**2 a** Η κουρτίνα, **b** η τηλεόραση, **c** το τηλέφωνο, **d** το τραπεζάκι, **e** η πόρτα, **f** ο καναπές
**3** ο πάγκος, ο νεροχύτης, ο καθρέφτης, ο νιπτήρας, η καρέκλα, η ντουλάπα, η μπανιέρα, η πολυθρόνα, το τραπέζι, το κρεβάτι, το τραπεζάκι, το κάδρο
**4** refrigerator, machine, stove, microwave oven, coffee

### Conversation 1

**1** She shows her the bedroom.
**2 a** She saw an armchair and a big bed. **b** A big table can fit into the kitchen.

### Language discovery 1

**1 a** [polés], **b** [meghálo], **c** [oréa], **d** [meghálo], **e** [meghálo]
**2 a** Μπράβο, **b** μεγάλο, **c** υπνοδωμάτιο, **d** κουζίνα, **e** πολύ, **f** τραπέζι

### Conversation 2

**1** WC or guest bathroom
**2 a** She likes the round mirror a lot. **b** The bathroom is black and white.

### Language discovery 2

**1 a** [megháli], **b** [strongilós], **c** [mikró], **d** [praktikó], **a** μεγάλη αντίθεση, **b** στρογγυλός καθρέφτης, **c** μικρό WC, **d** πρακτικό WC
**2 a** [Έχεις δίκιο], **b** [Ναι, βέβαια], **c** [Συμφωνώ], **d** [Μου αρέσει πολύ], **a** [éghis THíkio], **b** [ne vévea], **c** [simfonó], **d** [moo arési polí]
**3 a** [Μου αρέσει πολύ], **b** [Μου αρέσουν τα χρώματα], **c** [Σου αρέσει; / Εσένα σου αρέσει;]

### Practice

**1 a** [ble] + [áspro], **b** [prásino] + [áspro] + [kókino], **c** [mávro] + [kókino] + [kítrino], **d** [kókino] + [áspro], **e** [ble] + [áspro] + [kókino], **f** [kókino] + [kítrino]
**2 a** [moo arésoon i kathréftes], **b** [moo arésoon i kanapéTHes], **c** [moo arésoon i karékles], **d** [moo arésoon i polithrónes], **e** [moo arésoon ta bánia], **f** [moo arésoon ta krevátia]

**3 a** 5, **b** 4, **c** 1, **d** 3, **e** 2
**4 a** [mikrós, mikrí, mikró], **b** [oréos, oréa, oréo], **c** [THíkeos, THíkea, THíkeo], **d** [ligos, lígi, lígo], **e** [áshimos, áshimi, áshimo], **f** [polís, polí, polí], **g** [áTHikos, áTHiki, áTHiko] **h** [megálo], **i** [tetrágono]
**5** e, b, d, a, f, c
**6 a** [praktikó], **b** [vévea], **c** [lootró], **d** [arésoon], **e** [kathréftis], **f** [áspro], **g** [alá], **h** [THíkio]
**7 a** false, **b** true, **c** true, **d** false, **e** true
**8 Mary:** I like Greece because it's small.
**Elpida:** I don't agree. It's not very small.
**Mary:** I disagree but ... I like the weather in Greece.
**Elpida:** Here I agree with you. You are right.
**Mary:** Of course, because I don't prefer the rain in London.
**Elpida:** You are not wrong.
**9** It is not Nikos' house.
**10** ο κήπος, η κουζίνα, η τραπεζαρία, το σαλόνι, το υπνοδωμάτιο, το μπάνιο. The three words not of Greek origin are all neuter: το χωλ, το γκαράζ, το βε-σε.

### Test yourself

**1** [áspro], [mávro], [mov], [ble], [prásino], [kítrino], [portokalí], [kókino]
**2** [antipathó], [THiafonó], [ého áTHiko]
**3** [moo arési] or [moo arésoon], [simfonó], [ého THíkio]
**4** [antipathó], [THen marési]
**5** [karékla], [trapézi], [kanapés], [polithróna], [kreváti]
**6** [strongilós], [mikrós], [áspros]
**7** [tetrágonos], [megálos], [mávros]
**8** [fúrnos], [kafetiéra], [vrastíras], plindírio rúhon]

## UNIT 8
## Breakfast, lunch and dinner

κουλούρι, τυρόπιτα, τοστ, σπανακόπιτα

### Vocabulary builder

**1** I don't like ...., hobby, day, I don't have ...., sport
**2** Man: T, F, T, F, T, T Woman: F, F, F, F, T, T
**3** The phrases correspond to the cartoons: e, a, k, j, n, d, m, c, h, b, g, i, f, l

### Conversation 1

**1** She usually gets up at 7 o'clock.

**2 a** Έπειτα πάω για ψώνια. **b** She's not too happy about it. The word δυστυχώς helps us understand that.

### Language discovery 1

**1 a** τελικά, **b** έπειτα, **c** συνήθως, **d** νωρίς, **e** ακριβώς
**2 a** Τι ώρα είναι; **b** Είναι μία ακριβώς. **c** Συνήθως σηκώνομαι στις επτά.

### Conversation 2

**1** Mary usually gets up at 7:30.
**2 a** She works from 10 a.m. to 4 p.m. **b** Around 7 p.m. at home or 8 p.m. when going out.

### Language discovery 2

**1 a** Γύρω στις επτά στο σπίτι. **b** από τις δέκα μέχρι τις τέσσερις, **c** Ξυπνάω στις επτάμιση
**2 a** Επιστρέφω σπίτι, **b** Δουλεύω συνήθως, **c** Πάω στη δουλειά, **d** Παίρνω το τρένο, **e** Κάνω ένα ντους, **f** Τρώω πρωινό
**3 a** [epistréfo/epistrépso] επιστρέφω / επιστρέψω, **b** [THoolévo/THoolépso] δουλεύω / δουλέψω, **c** [pighéno (páo)/páo] πηγαίνω (πάω) / πάω, **d** [pérno/páro] παίρνω / πάρω, **e** [káno/káno] κάνω / κάνω, **f** [tró-o/fáo] τρώω / φάω

### Practice

**1** b, i, g, e, a, j, h, k, c, f, l, d
**2 a** I arrive at work at 8 o'clock. **b** I get up early. **c** I return home late. **d** I go to bed late. **e** I go to work. **f** I have dinner at 9 o'clock. **g** I don't have (lit. eat) breakfast, only coffee. **h** I have lunch at work. **i** I take a shower. **j** I have (lit. drink) a lot of coffee at work. **k** I finish work at 6 o'clock. **l** I watch some TV at 10 o'clock.
**3** There are no correct or incorrect answers in this exercise. Just remember that using a mix of different media will enhance your learning and speed up your tempo. Revision will always help you ensure that you have truly mastered a particular grammar or vocabulary point and it is recommended as your best double-check whenever you are learning alone.
**4 a** 3, **b** 5, **c** 1, **d** 6, **e** 2, **f** 4
**5 a** 8:05, **b** 8:30, **c** 10:30, **d** 1:45, **e** 11:45, **f** 7:05
**6 a** 2, **b** 2, **c** 4, **d** 3
**7 a** [óli], **b** [ksipnáo], **c** [tró-o], **d** [pérno], **e** [epistréfo], **f** [apó], **g** [méhri], **h** [tróte], **i** [yíro], **j** [ékso]

## Test yourself

**1 a** [ekató tésera], **b** [ekató ogTHónda tésera], **c** [THiakósia triánda éna], **d** [tetrakósia penínda éksi], **e** [oktakósia íkosi eptá], **f** [eniakósia penínda éna] **g** [hília]
**2 a** [eftá ke íkosi], **b** [októmisi], **c** [eniá], **d** [éndeka ke tétarto], **e** [miámisi], **f** [téseris ke THéka], **g** [éksi pará tétarto] **3 a** [sikónome], **b** [ftáno], **c** [telióno], **d** [epistréfo], **e** [pérno]
**4 a** [pánda sikónome stis eksímisi]. **b** [poté THen ftáno sti THooliá norís]. **c** [merikés forés telióno ti THooliá moo argá]. **d** [spánia tró-o ékso]. **e** [sheTHón pánda pérno to tréno].
**5** [tileórasi] [básket] [poTHósfero] [ghimnastikí]

## UNIT 9
## Hobbies and Greek music

television: τηλεόραση, gym: γυμναστική, computer: κομπιούτερ, traveling: ταξίδι

### Vocabulary builder

**1** rock, blues, jazz, comedies, drama, novels, love stories, volleyball, basketball
**2** Εγκληματικό δράμα *crime drama*, Ειδύλλιο *romance*, Επιστημονική φαντασία *science fiction*, Κωμωδία *comedy*.
**3** music, cinema, sports, you (sing/pl), a lot, have, football

### Conversation 1

**1** He likes to listen to music.
**2 a** John likes pop and rock music. **b** Angelos likes to watch TV or listen to the radio.

### Language discovery 1

**1 a** μ'αρέσει / μου αρέσει, **b** σ'αρέσει / σου αρέσει, **c** ν'ακούω / να ακούω
**2** τι κάνεις τον ελεύθερο χρόνο σου; or πώς περνάς τις ελεύθερες ώρες σου;

### Conversation 2

**1** Mary likes to do sports a lot.
**2 a** running, basketball and tennis, **b** Mary likes to go for a walk or stay home and read.

### Language discovery 2

**1** Words of Greek origin: το θέατρο, το βιβλίο, ο μύθος, η ιστορία, ενδιαφέρον, Words of English origin: το θρίλλερ, το σπορ, το μπάσκετ, το τέννις, το χόμπι / το χόμπυ
**2 a** βιβλίο/βιβλία, **b** μυθιστόρημα/μυθιστορήματα, **c** σπορ/σπορ, **d** χόμπι/χόμπι, **e** βόλτα/βόλτες. Loan words normally have only one form.

### Practice

**1** [THimítris] 1, 3, 6, 7, [níkos] 2, 3, 4, [maría] 1, 2, 5, 6
**2 a** 3, **b** 4, **c** 6, **d** 1, **e** 7, **f** 2, **g** 5
**3 a** 3, **b** 5, **c** 7, **d** 6, **e** 1, f 4, **g** 2
**4 a** 1, 2, 4, 5, **b** 1, 2, 4, 5, **c** 1, 2, 4, 5, **d** 3 **e** 1, 2, 4, 5
**5 a** [vlépi], **b** [akoón], **c** [moo arésoon] or [mas arésoon], **d** [THiavázoome], **e** [kapnízo] and **f** [protimás]
**6 a** Nick never watches TV. **b** Mary and James always listen to the radio. **c** I like pop and rock music. **d** We read many books in Greece. **e** Unfortunately, I smoke a lot of cigarettes. **f** Do you prefer the radio or the TV?
**7** [ángelos] 1, 2, 4, 6, [THéspina] 2, 3, 5, 6, [ariána] 1, 3, 4, 5
**8 a** [marésoon], **b** [enTHiaféron], **c** [troháTHin], **d** [forés], **e** [piyéno], **f** [THiavázo], **g** [siníthos], **h** [istorías] You can double check your efforts with the Greek script in Conversation 2.

### Test yourself

**1** [laiká], [elafrolaiká], [rebétika]
**2** [noovéles], [mithistorímata], [astinomiká], [istoríes agápis], [peripéties]
**3** [komoTHíes], [THramatiká], [thríler], [astinomiká]
**4** [ti kánis ton eléfthero hróno soo]? and [pos pernás tis eléftheres óres soo]?
**5** for example: [vlépo tileórasi], [káno vóltes], [páo théatro], etc.
**6** τρέξιμο running, βόλτες walks/rides, ενδιαφέρον interesting, συνήθως usually, κυρίως mainly
**7** [pánda], [sheTHón pánda], [sihénome] or [antipathó], [dramatiká]

## UNIT 10

### At the fruit and vegetable market

σταφύλι, καρπούζι, πορτοκάλι, μήλο, πατάτα, ντομάτα, καρότο, μπαρμπούνι, τσιπούρα, λαυράκι, πέστροφα

## Vocabulary builder

**1** pineapple, potato, tomato, carrot, salt, pepper
**2** do you want, many, much, are they, kilo, grams, euro
**3 a** fruit and vegetable shop, **b** greengrocer, **c** grocery store, **d** weekly fruit and vegetable market, **e** supermarket, **f** hypermarket, **g** mini market

## Conversation 1

**1** Mary will go with Elpida.
**2 a** No, it's close by. **b** They will go on foot.

## Language discovery 1

**1 a** Θέλω να αγοράσω, **b** Μπορούμε να πάμε, **c** Πρέπει να πάω. This particle is necessary when connecting two verbs.
**2 a** 2, **b** 3, **c** 1
**3 a** masculine, **b** feminine, **c** neuter
**4 a** happy, **b** angry, **c** sad, **d** surprised, **e** hungry, **f** thirsty, **g** upset, **h** tired.

## Conversation 2

**1** Yes, it's always busy.
**2 a** She would like to get some apples and perhaps a watermelon. **b** One lettuce, two cucumbers and one kilo of tomatoes.

## Language discovery 2

**1 a** Θέλω ν'αγοράσω, **b** Τι σ'αρέσει να πάρουμε; **c** Να πάρουμε μήλα.
**2** It means *Here you are! Here! There!* especially when you point out something.
**3 a** ωραία μήλα, **b** φρέσκα λαχανικά, **c** πολλούς ανθρώπους. As a rule of thumb, the ending of the adjective normally matches the ending of the noun it modifies.

## Practice

**1**

| Fruit | Vegetables | Herbs |
|---|---|---|
| banána<br>fráula<br>roTHákino<br>stafíli<br>mílo<br>karpoózi | kolokitháki<br>agoóri<br>domáta<br>karóto | ánithos<br>maindanós |

**2**

| i banana – i banánes<br>i fráula – i fráules<br>to roTHákino – ta roTHákina<br>to stafíli – ta stafília<br>to mílo – ta míla<br>to karpoózi – ta karpoózia | to kolokitháki – ta kolokithákia<br>to agoóri – ta agoória<br>i domáta – i domátes<br>to karóto – ta karóta | o ánithos – i ánithi<br>o maindanós – i maindaní |
|---|---|---|

**3**

| Η μπανάνα -οι μπανάνες<br>Η φράουλα – οι φράουλες<br>Το ροδάκινο – τα ροδάκινα<br>Το σταφύλι – τα σταφύλια<br>Το μήλο – τα μήλα<br>Το καρπούζι – τα καρπούζια | Το κολοκυθάκι – τα κολοκυθάκια<br>Το αγγούρι – τα αγγούρια<br>Η ντομάτα – οι ντομάτες<br>Το καρότο – τα καρότα | Ο άνιθος – οι άνιθοι<br>Ο μαϊντανός – οι μαϊντανοί |
|---|---|---|

**4 b** [i patátes], **c** [i domátes], **d** [to skórTHo], **2** [to ahláTHi], **3** [ta stafília], **4** [i fráooles]

**5 a** [penínda evró] πενήντα ευρώ, **b** [THekaeftá evró] δεκαεφτά ευρώ, **c** [ekató evró] εκατό ευρώ, **d** [THóTHeka evró] δώδεκα ευρώ, **e** [triánda tésera evró] τριάντα τέσσερα ευρώ, **f** [evTHomínda evró] εβδομήντα ευρώ

**6 a** 5, **b** 3, **c** 6, **d** 2, **e** 4, **f** 1

**7 a** [marési na piyéno vóltes mazí soo]. **b** [thélo na páo sti laikí agorá]. **c** [prépi na se THo]. **d** [boró na fáo mía/m-ya pítsa tóra]. **e** [borí na tin léne eléni].

Greek script: **a** Μ'αρέσει να πηγαίνω βόλτες μαζί σου. **b** Θέλω να πάω στην λαϊκή αγορά. **c** Πρέπει να σε δω. **d** Μπορώ να φάω μία/μια πίτσα τώρα. **e** Μπορεί να την λένε Ελένη.

**8 1** c, **2** b, **3** a, **4** d, **5** e, **6** f

**9 a** Υπάρχει **πολύς** κόσμος εδώ. **b** Υπάρχουν **πολλοί** άνθρωποι από την Αγγλία. **c** Ξέρω **πολλούς** ανθρώπους από την Αθήνα. **d** Δεν ξέρω **πολλές** γυναίκες από το Λονδίνο. **e** Ο **πολύς** καφές δεν κάνει καλό! **f Πολλά** παιδιά παίζουν ποδόσφαιρο.

**10 a** [ipárhoon], **b** [portokália], **c** [epohí], **d** [fisiká], **e** [káto], **f** [lahaniká], **g** [agoória], **h** [kiló]

**11 a Υπάρχουν** μπανάνες τώρα; **b** Όχι. Δεν **υπάρχουν** καλές ντομάτες αυτή την εποχή. **c Υπάρχουν** λαχανικά πιο κάτω; **d** Φυσικά **υπάρχει** καλός καφές εδώ. **e** Πω, πω! **Υπάρχει** πολύς κόσμος εδώ! **f Υπάρχουν** καρπούζια αυτή την εποχή;

**a** Are there (any) bananas now? **b** No. There are not (any) good tomatoes at this time. **c** Are there (any) vegetables further down? **d** Of course, there is good coffee here. **e** There are a lot of people here! (lit. There is much crowd here!) **f** Are there (any) watermelons at this time?

## Test yourself

**1** [ananás], [hoormás], [yiarmás], [banána], [fráoola], [agriófrapa] or [gréipfroot], [stafíli], [pepóni], [roTHákino], [portokáli], [karpoózi]
**2** [ánithos], [maintanós], [arakás] or [bizéli], [patáta], [domáta], [melitzána], [karóto], [sélino], [kolokitháki], [maroóli], [agoóri]
**3** [eftihizménos], [pinazménos], [thimoménos], [THipsazménos], [lipiménos], [taragménos], [ékpliktos], [koorazménos]; (the masculine ending [-os] changes to [-i] for the feminine form)
**4 a** [tetrakósia penínda], **b** [eksakósia evTHomínda], **c** [hília THiakósia], **d** [tris hiliáTHes eniakósia], **e** [pénde hiliáTHes], **f** [eptá hiliáTHes tetrakósia], **g** [eniá hiliáTHes pendakósia], **h** [THéka hiliáTHes]
**5** [bakáliko, manáviko, pandopolío]
**6** [misó kilo míla parakaló] and [éna kiló portokália parakaló]
**7** [póso káni]? and [póso kánun]?

## REVISION TEST 3

**1 a** 5, **b** 2, **c** 4, **d** 1, **e** 6, **f** 3
**2 a** I work from 8:00 to 4:00. **b** Mary is at home from 9:30 to 6:00. **c** I never eat from 12:30 to 9:00. **d** I am at work from 7:00 to 4:00. **e** I don't like to work from 9:00 to 5:00. **f** George watches TV from 10:30 to 7:30.
**3 a** 4, **b** 2, **c** 1, **d** 3, **e** 6, **f** 5
**4 a** Mary is in the kitchen and is cooking. **b** John is outside the house. **c** My mother watches TV a lot. **d** My father always reads the newspaper. **e** Kostas listens to music all day. **f** Helen is in the office from 9:00 to 1:00.
**5 a** 8, **b** 2, **c** 1, **d** 9, **e** 3, **f** 4, **g** 10, **h** 6, **i** 7, **j** 5
**6 a** Κάνω ντους. I take a shower. **b** Τρώω πρωινό. I have breakfast. **c** Πάω για ύπνο. I go to bed (lit. sleep). **d** Ξυπνάω στις 7:00. I wake up at 7:00. **e** Διαβάζω στο κρεβάτι. I read in bed. **f** Πάω στη δουλειά. I go to work. **g** Φεύγω από τη δουλειά. I leave work. **h** Σηκώνομαι από το κρεβάτι. I get out of bed. **i** Ετοιμάζομαι για δουλειά. I get ready for work. **j** Ετοιμάζομαι για ύπνο. I get ready for sleep.
**8 a** πολλοί, **b** πολλή, **c** πολλά, **d** πολλούς
**9 a** φάω, **b** πίνω, **c** φύγω, **d** ξυπνάω, **e** διαβάζω

# Can-do statements

| UNIT | CEFR level | ACTFL level | CAN-DO STATEMENTS |
|---|---|---|---|
| **UNIT 1** | **A1** | **Novice High** | I can make an introduction and use basic greeting and leave-taking expressions. I can introduce myself and others. I can ask and answer questions about personal details. |
| **UNIT 2** | **A1** | **Novice High** | I can produce simple questions and statements regarding where people come from and where they currently live. I can ask which languages people speak. |
| **UNIT 3** | **A1** | **Elementary** | I can ask and answer questions about where I live and can understand sentences and frequently used expressions. I can describe aspects of my environment, e.g. people, work, interests. |
| **UNIT 4** | **A1** | **Elementary** | I can handle numbers, quantities and costs, and can ask people for things. I can understand different types of accommodation. I can describe my own home. I can count from 0 to 10. |
| **UNIT 5** | **A1** | **Elementary** | I can understand sentences and frequently used expressions related to personal and family information. I can describe in simple terms aspects of my background. I can give and receive information about numbers from 11 to 100. |
| **UNIT 6** | **A1** | **Elementary** | I can find specific, predictable information in simple everyday material such as menus. I can locate specific information in lists and isolate the information required. I can understand short, simple texts containing the highest frequency vocabulary, including a portion of shared international vocabulary item. I can establish social contact: greetings and farewells, introductions, giving thanks. |

| | | | |
|---|---|---|---|
| **UNIT 7** | **A1** | **Elementary** | I can describe in simple terms aspects of my immediate environment. I can write about everyday aspects of my environment. I can explain what I like or dislike. I can agree or disagree. |
| **UNIT 8** | **A1** | **Elementary** | I can use a series of phrases and sentences to describe daily routines. I can give and receive information about numbers. I can indicate time. |
| **UNIT 9** | **A1** | **Elementary** | I can ask and answer questions about habits and routines. I can ask and answer questions about pastimes and past activities. |
| **UNIT 10** | **A1** | **Elementary** | I can deal with common aspects of everyday living such as shopping, and can make simple purchases by stating what is wanted and asking the price. |